THE

Heart

OF A

Great Nation

THE

Heart

OF A

Great Nation

TIMELESS WISDOM
FROM RONALD REAGAN

RONALD REAGAN

Foreword by Marco Rubio

EDITED BY ADAM KEIPER

SENTINEL

Sentinel
An imprint of Penguin Random House LLC
penguinrandomhouse.com

Foreword copyright © 2020 by Marco Rubio
Compilation and speech introductions copyright © 2020 by Penguin Random House LLC

Most Sentinel books are available at a discount when purchased in quantity for sales
promotions or corporate use. Special editions, which include personalized covers, excerpts, and
corporate imprints, can be created when purchased in large quantities. For more information,
please call (212) 572-2232 or e-mail specialmarkets@penguinrandomhouse.com. Your local
bookstore can also assist with discounted bulk purchases using the Penguin Random
House corporate Business-to-Business program. For assistance in locating a
participating retailer, e-mail B2B@penguinrandomhouse.com.

Library of Congress Cataloging-in-Publication Data
Names: Reagan, Ronald, author. | Keiper, Adam, editor. |
Rubio, Marco, 1971- writer of foreword.
Title: The heart of a great nation: timeless wisdom from Ronald Reagan /
Ronald Reagan; foreword by Senator Marco Rubio; edited by Adam Keiper.
Other titles: Speeches. Selections | Timeless wisdom from Ronald Reagan
Description: New York: Sentinel, [2020] | Includes index.
Identifiers: LCCN 2020028769 (print) | LCCN 2020028770 (ebook) |
ISBN 9780593329757 (trade paperback) | ISBN 9780593329764 (ebook)
Subjects: LCSH: Reagan, Ronald—Oratory. | United States—Politics and
government—1981-1989. | United States—Foreign relations—1981-1989. |
Speeches, addresses, etc., American.
Classification: LCC E838.5 .R432 2020 (print) | LCC E838.5 (ebook) |
DDC 973.927092—dc23
LC record available at https://lccn.loc.gov/2020028769
LC ebook record available at https://lccn.loc.gov/2020028770

Printed in the United States of America
1   3   5   7   9   10   8   6   4   2

Contents

Foreword

BY MARCO RUBIO

I was in fourth grade when Ronald Reagan took his first oath of office, and I was proud to live in his America. Reagan's America was a confident America. It was optimistic, generous, and kind. Despite the difficulties of the early 1980s, Reagan knew that American economic strength could be regained. He knew it wouldn't come from the heavy hand of government regulation, but rather from the sweat of the workers who go in and out of factory gates, the farmers who feed the world, and the entrepreneurs who create the future.

My parents were also proud to live in his America. I will never forget their reaction the day the Berlin Wall, thanks to Reagan, fell. My parents had lost their country to Fidel Castro's Communism. They had spent thirty years physically separated from their homeland, their friends, and their relatives. For my parents' generation of exiles, and for an entire generation of Americans whose hopes and dreams had been shattered by Communism, nothing could match the joy, the jubilation, and the hope that they felt watching the symbol of Communism come down. What others had believed impossible, Ronald Reagan had understood to be, not just possible, but inevitable. If America chose to be America, Communism did not stand a chance.

Formed by Reagan's own presidency, I ran for president in 2016, optimistic about America's future. In what country other than the United States could the son of a bartender and a maid rise to become a senator and declare his candidacy for the presidency? I believed America was still, as Reagan said, "mighty in its youth and powerful in its purpose," and that our task was to focus this buoyant energy to solve the problems of the twenty-first century. But one thing that became quite clear over the course of that campaign—and the years that followed—is that not all Americans share that optimism. Many Americans feel the "Shining City on the Hill" is a distant memory, or, even worse, a place where they are not welcome.

Coming away from the campaign, I remain convinced that America has more to learn from Ronald Reagan than we could ever imagine. Not because his solutions for America can be cut and pasted onto our national discourse today; he wouldn't believe that. But because by following his lead, we can humbly understand the challenges that face our nation, stand confident in the timeless principles we know in our heart to be true, and remain optimistic as we apply those principles to the challenges of today.

Reading Reagan's essays, I was struck by the questions he posed in his speech to the Building and Construction Trades Department of the AFL-CIO:

The main source of strength in this fight is going to be the people themselves. The idea is to unleash the American worker, encourage the American investor, and let each of us produce more to make a better life for all. After all, why should we pay for some luxuries that

are not truly essential to our well-being, pay by way of a subsidy
when the man and his wife in Peoria are out of work? Why should
we subsidize increased production of some things that we already
have in surplus? And why should we go in debt to pay for school
lunches for children of upper-income families when borrowing by
government may cost you your job? We not only shouldn't do those
things, we no longer can afford to do them.

I wonder what Reagan would think about the questions we ask ourselves today. Why is a great nation reliant upon a near-peer adversary
for the production of basic pharmaceutical ingredients? Why has our
national investment in the plants, property, and equipment that allow
workers across our nation to produce more to make a better life for all
plummeted while returns to Wall Street have tripled?

In that speech, Reagan says that we will not be able to make things
right overnight. But he made a critical point when he said, "Our destiny is not our fate. It is our choice." Politics is about the choices we
make as a society. All of us as Americans have an obligation to concep-
tualize a common good and take action to ensure that common good
is achieved.

Nothing was more important to Reagan's sense of a common good
than winning the Cold War and ultimately ending the specter of mutually assured destruction. Reagan understood that the challenges of
the world were complex. As he said in 1982 at the Palace of Westminster:

We have not inherited an easy world. If developments like the In-
dustrial Revolution, which began here in England, and the gifts of
science and technology have made life much easier for us, they have
also made it more dangerous. There are threats now to our freedom,

indeed to our very existence, that other generations could never even have imagined.

Imagine what Reagan would think of the challenges of the technological revolution and mass globalization. We can be confident he would have known that global security requires a strong and present United States engaged in global affairs. That we cannot be ambivalent to the cause of freedom. Reagan understood that peace could only come through strength, but that the purpose of that strength is to maximize the possibility that it would never be used. That the true mark of national strength is found not on the battlefield, but in the hearts and minds of the people. And that making the case for our values with timidity would only make us more vulnerable in the end.

I think Reagan would join me in believing that the biggest threat to America's values today is our national divisiveness. Reagan lived through some of the most divisive times in our nation's history. He knew the solution to division was gratitude for our good fortune to live in the freest nation on earth—a nation built on the hope that we could make it an even greater and fairer land. He was fond of saying, "All great change in America begins at the dinner table." But today a lot of us don't seem interested in sitting down at the same table with our fellow countrymen. Americans are the children of pilgrims, immigrants, and slaves. Together we have solved great challenges and achieved great things. What unifies us as a people is our patriotic love for this inheritance and a commitment that we will continue to do the hard work of perfecting our nation.

This spirit is too often lost in our national debates, where instead of coming to the table we return to our corners and fight our partisan battles. We aren't going to solve our problems by having one side lay down its arms; Reagan certainly wouldn't have believed so. We need to make the case for our nation's goodness, and make that case with optimism and confidence.

In 1984, Reagan described the spirit of America seen as the Olympic torch made its way across our country:

Each new story was typical of this land of ours. There was Ansel Stubbs, a youngster of ninety-nine, who passed the torch in Kansas to four-year-old Katie Johnson. In Pineville, Kentucky, it came at one a.m., so hundreds of people lined the streets with candles. In Tupelo, Mississippi, at seven a.m. on a Sunday morning, a robed church choir sang "God Bless America" as the torch went by.

That torch went through the Cumberland Gap, past the Martin Luther King, Jr., Memorial, down the Santa Fe Trail, and alongside Billy the Kid's grave.

In Richardson, Texas, it was carried by a fourteen-year-old boy in a special wheelchair. In West Virginia the runner came across a line of deaf children and let each one pass the torch for a few feet, and at the end these youngsters' hands talked excitedly in their sign language. Crowds spontaneously began singing "America the Beautiful" or "The Battle Hymn of the Republic."

And then, in San Francisco, a Vietnamese immigrant, his little son held on his shoulders, dodged photographers and policemen to cheer a nineteen-year-old black man pushing an eighty-eight-year-old white woman in a wheelchair as she carried the torch.

My friends, that's America.

It's time to return to the optimism and clarity of Reagan's America. There was nothing weak in its kindness or naïve in its optimism. Some of America's greatest days came because of the strength, conviction, and courage of Ronald Reagan. He did his part. He made a difference just as we all now must make ours. It is the duty of each generation of Americans to make our country stronger, to make our country freer, and to pass on the privilege of citizenship to generations yet to come.

THE
Heart
OF A
Great Nation

1

BEGINNINGS

By the time he was elected president in November 1980, Ronald Wilson Reagan had been a sports announcer, a Hollywood actor, a union leader, a longtime corporate spokesman for one of the biggest companies in America, and the twice-elected governor of California. He was a prominent figure in the still-young conservative movement, and his support of conservative Barry Goldwater in the 1964 presidential race, followed by Reagan's own unsuccessful bid for the Republican Party's nomination in 1976, pushed the party to the right.

Reagan's nomination and victory in 1980 cemented the party's conservatism. But his message of hope—he campaigned on a theme of a "new beginning"—had broader electoral appeal. He won the popular vote and the electoral college by wide margins in 1980 and again in 1984.

"An Era of National Renewal"

Just before noon on January 20, 1981, Reagan took the presidential oath of office at the U.S. Capitol—the first time, as he noted in the inaugural address reprinted here in full, that the oath was administered on the building's West Front, the side with the view of the National Mall and the capital's major monuments. His heartening first speech as president set the tone for his administration, explaining the need for major reforms while linking his plans to the country's ideals and its people's dreams. During the inaugural ceremony, fifty-two Americans who had been held hostage in Iran for 444 days were released, but confirmation did not come in time for Reagan to announce the news during his address as he had hoped.

Senator Hatfield, Mr. Chief Justice, Mr. President, Vice President Bush, Vice President Mondale, Senator Baker, Speaker O'Neill, Reverend Moomaw, and my fellow citizens:

To a few of us here today this is a solemn and most momentous occasion, and yet in the history of our nation it is a commonplace occurrence. The orderly transfer of authority as called for in the Constitution routinely takes place, as it has for almost two centuries, and few of us stop to think how unique we really are. In the eyes of many in the world, this every-four-year ceremony we accept as normal is nothing less than a miracle.

Mr. President, I want our fellow citizens to know how much you did to carry on this tradition. By your gracious cooperation in the transition process, you have shown a watching world that we are a united people pledged to maintaining a political system which guarantees individual liberty to a greater degree than any other, and I thank you and your people for all your help in maintaining the continuity which is the bulwark of our republic.

The business of our nation goes forward. These United States are confronted with an economic affliction of great proportions. We suffer from the longest and one of the worst sustained inflations in our national history. It distorts our economic decisions, penalizes thrift, and crushes the struggling young and the fixed-income elderly alike. It threatens to shatter the lives of millions of our people.

Idle industries have cast workers into unemployment, human misery, and personal indignity. Those who do work are denied a fair return for their labor by a tax system which penalizes successful achievement and keeps us from maintaining full productivity.

But great as our tax burden is, it has not kept pace with public spending. For decades we have piled deficit upon deficit, mortgaging our future and our children's future for the temporary convenience of the present. To continue this long trend is to guarantee tremendous social, cultural, political, and economic upheavals.

You and I, as individuals, can, by borrowing, live beyond our means, but for only a limited period of time. Why, then, should we think that collectively, as a nation, we're not bound by that same limitation? We must act today in order to preserve tomorrow. And let there be no misunderstanding: We are going to begin to act, beginning today.

The economic ills we suffer have come upon us over several decades. They will not go away in days, weeks, or months, but they will go away. They will go away because we as Americans have the capacity now, as we've had in the past, to do whatever needs to be done to preserve this last and greatest bastion of freedom.

In this present crisis, government is not the solution to our problem; government is the problem. From time to time we've been tempted to believe that society has become too complex to be managed by self-rule, that government by an elite group is superior to government for, by, and of the people. Well, if no one among us is capable of governing himself, then who among us has the capacity to govern someone else? All of us together, in and out of government, must bear the burden. The solutions we seek must be equitable, with no one group singled out to pay a higher price.

We hear much of special interest groups. Well, our concern must be for a special interest group that has been too long neglected. It knows no sectional boundaries or ethnic and racial divisions, and it crosses political party lines. It is made up of men and women who raise our food, patrol our streets, man our mines and factories, teach our children, keep our homes, and heal us when we're sick—professionals, industrialists, shopkeepers, clerks, cabbies, and truck drivers. They are, in short, "We the People," this breed called Americans.

Well, this administration's objective will be a healthy, vigorous, growing economy that provides equal opportunities for all Americans with no barriers born of bigotry or discrimination. Putting America back to work means putting all Americans back to work. Ending inflation means freeing all Americans from the terror of runaway living costs. All must share in the productive work of this "new beginning," and all must share in the bounty of a revived economy. With the idealism and fair play which are the core of our system and our strength, we can have a strong and prosperous America, at peace with itself and the world.

So, as we begin, let us take inventory. We are a nation that has a government—not the other way around. And this makes us special among the nations of the earth. Our government has no power except that granted it by the people. It is time to check and reverse the growth of government, which shows signs of having grown beyond the consent of the governed.

It is my intention to curb the size and influence of the federal establishment and to demand recognition of the distinction between the powers granted to the federal government and those reserved to the states or to the people. All of us need to be reminded that the federal government did not create the states; the states created the federal government.

Now, so there will be no misunderstanding, it's not my intention to do away with government. It is rather to make it work—work with us, not over us; to stand by our side, not ride on our back. Government can and must provide opportunity, not smother it; foster productivity, not stifle it.

If we look to the answer as to why for so many years we achieved so much, prospered as no other people on earth, it was because here in this land we unleashed the energy and individual genius of man to a greater extent than has ever been done before. Freedom and the dignity of the individual have been more available and assured here than in any other place on earth. The price for this freedom at times has been high, but we have never been unwilling to pay that price.

It is no coincidence that our present troubles parallel and are proportionate to the intervention and intrusion in our lives that result from unnecessary and excessive growth of government. It is time for us to realize that we're too great a nation to limit ourselves to small dreams. We're not, as some would have us believe, doomed to an inevitable decline. I do not believe in a fate that will fall on us no matter what we do. I do believe in a fate that will fall on us if we do nothing. So, with all the creative energy at our command, let us begin an era of national renewal. Let us renew our determination, our courage, and our strength. And let us renew our faith and our hope.

We have every right to dream heroic dreams. Those who say that we're in a time when there are not heroes, they just don't know where to look. You can see heroes every day going in and out of factory gates. Others, a handful in number, produce enough food to feed all of us and then the world beyond. You meet heroes across a counter, and they're on both sides of that counter. There are entrepreneurs with faith in themselves and faith in an idea who create new jobs, new wealth and opportunity. They're individuals and families whose taxes support the government and whose voluntary gifts support church, charity, culture, art, and education. Their patriotism is quiet, but deep. Their values sustain our national life.

Now, I have used the words "they" and "their" in speaking of these heroes. I could say "you" and "your," because I'm addressing the heroes of whom I speak—you, the citizens of this blessed land. Your dreams, your hopes, your goals are going to be the dreams, the hopes, and the goals of this administration, so help me God.

We shall reflect the compassion that is so much a part of your makeup. How can we love our country and not love our countrymen; and loving them, reach out a hand when they fall, heal them when they're sick, and provide opportunity to make them self-sufficient so they will be equal in fact and not just in theory?

Can we solve the problems confronting us? Well, the answer is an unequivocal and emphatic "yes." To paraphrase Winston Churchill, I did not take the oath I've just taken with the intention of presiding over the dissolution of the world's strongest economy.

In the days ahead I will propose removing the roadblocks that have slowed our economy and reduced productivity. Steps will be taken aimed at restoring the balance between the various levels of government. Progress may be slow, measured in inches and feet, not miles, but we will progress. It is time to reawaken this industrial giant, to get government back within its means, and to lighten our punitive tax burden. And these will be our first priorities, and on these principles there will be no compromise.

On the eve of our struggle for independence a man who might have been one of the greatest among the Founding Fathers, Dr. Joseph Warren, president of the Massachusetts Congress, said to his fellow Americans, "Our country is in danger, but not to be despaired of. . . .

On you depend the fortunes of America. You are to decide the important questions upon which rests the happiness and the liberty of millions yet unborn. Act worthy of yourselves."

Well, I believe we, the Americans of today, are ready to act worthy of ourselves, ready to do what must be done to ensure happiness and liberty for ourselves, our children, and our children's children. And as we renew ourselves here in our own land, we will be seen as having greater strength throughout the world. We will again be the exemplar of freedom and a beacon of hope for those who do not now have freedom.

To those neighbors and allies who share our freedom, we will strengthen our historic ties and assure them of our support and firm commitment. We will match loyalty with loyalty. We will strive for mutually beneficial relations. We will not use our friendship to impose on their sovereignty, for our own sovereignty is not for sale.

As for the enemies of freedom, those who are potential adversaries, they will be reminded that peace is the highest aspiration of the American people. We will negotiate for it, sacrifice for it; we will not surrender for it, now or ever.

Our forbearance should never be misunderstood. Our reluctance for conflict should not be misjudged as a failure of will. When action is required to preserve our national security, we will act. We will maintain sufficient strength to prevail if need be, knowing that if we do so we have the best chance of never having to use that strength.

Above all, we must realize that no arsenal or no weapon in the arsenals of the world is so formidable as the will and moral courage of free men and women. It is a weapon our adversaries in today's world do not have. It is a weapon that we as Americans do have. Let that be understood by those who practice terrorism and prey upon their neighbors.

I'm told that tens of thousands of prayer meetings are being held on this day, and for that I'm deeply grateful. We are a nation under God, and I believe God intended for us to be free. It would be fitting and good, I think, if on each Inaugural Day in future years it should be declared a day of prayer.

This is the first time in our history that this ceremony has been held, as you've been told, on this West Front of the Capitol. Standing here, one faces a magnificent vista, opening up on this city's special beauty and history. At the end of this open mall are those shrines to the giants on whose shoulders we stand.

Directly in front of me, the monument to a monumental man, George Washington, father of our country. A man of humility who came to greatness reluctantly. He led America out of revolutionary victory into infant nationhood. Off to one side, the stately memorial to Thomas Jefferson. The Declaration of Independence flames with his eloquence. And then, beyond the Reflecting Pool, the dignified columns of the Lincoln Memorial. Whoever would understand in his heart the meaning of America will find it in the life of Abraham Lincoln.

Beyond those monuments to heroism is the Potomac River, and on the far shore the sloping hills of Arlington National Cemetery, with its row upon row of simple white markers bearing crosses or Stars of David. They add up to only a tiny fraction of the price that has been paid for our freedom.

Each one of those markers is a monument to the kind of hero I spoke of earlier. Their lives ended in places called Belleau Wood, the Argonne, Omaha Beach, Salerno, and halfway around the world on Guadalcanal, Tarawa, Pork Chop Hill, the Chosin Reservoir, and in a hundred rice paddies and jungles of a place called Vietnam.

Under one such marker lies a young man, Martin Treptow, who left his job in a small-town barbershop in 1917 to go to France with the famed Rainbow Division. There, on the western front, he was killed trying to carry a message between battalions under heavy artillery fire.

We're told that on his body was found a diary. On the flyleaf under the heading "My Pledge," he had written these words: "America must win this war. Therefore I will work, I will save, I will sacrifice, I will endure, I will fight cheerfully and do my utmost, as if the issue of the whole struggle depended on me alone."

The crisis we are facing today does not require of us the kind of sacrifice that Martin Treptow and so many thousands of others were called upon to make. It does require, however, our best effort and our willingness to believe in ourselves and to believe in our capacity to perform great deeds, to believe that together with God's help we can and will resolve the problems which now confront us.

And after all, why shouldn't we believe that? We are Americans.

God bless you, and thank you.

"Mountains Yet to Climb"

Reagan's second term officially began on January 20, 1985; since that was a Sunday, he took the oath of office in private, in the White House. The next day, shortly before noon, he repeated the oath in a public ceremony at the Capitol—held indoors because of extreme cold weather—and delivered the following inaugural address.

Senator Mathias, Chief Justice Burger, Vice President Bush, Speaker O'Neill, Senator Dole, reverend clergy, and members of my family and friends and my fellow citizens. . . .

There are no words adequate to express my thanks for the great honor that you've bestowed on me. I'll do my utmost to be deserving of your trust.

This is, as Senator Mathias told us, the fiftieth time that we, the people, have celebrated this historic occasion. When the first president,

George Washington, placed his hand upon the Bible, he stood less than a single day's journey by horseback from raw, untamed wilderness. There were four million Americans in a union of thirteen states. Today, we are sixty times as many in a union of fifty states. We've lighted the world with our inventions, gone to the aid of mankind wherever in the world there was a cry for help, journeyed to the moon and safely returned. So much has changed, and yet we stand together as we did two centuries ago.

When I took this oath four years ago, I did so in a time of economic stress. Voices were raised saying that we had to look to our past for the greatness and glory. But we, the present-day Americans, are not given to looking backward. In this blessed land, there is always a better tomorrow.

Four years ago, I spoke to you of a new beginning, and we have accomplished that. But in another sense, our new beginning is a continuation of that beginning created two centuries ago when, for the first time in history, government, the people said, was not our master, it is our servant; its only power that which we the people allow it to have.

That system has never failed us, but for a time we failed the system. We asked things of government that government was not equipped to give. We yielded authority to the national government that properly belonged to states or to local governments or to the people themselves. We allowed taxes and inflation to rob us of our earnings and savings and watched the great industrial machine that had made us the most productive people on earth slow down and the number of unemployed increase.

By 1980 we knew it was time to renew our faith, to strive with all our strength toward the ultimate in individual freedom, consistent with an orderly society.

We believed then and now: There are no limits to growth and human progress when men and women are free to follow their dreams.

And we were right to believe that. Tax rates have been reduced, inflation cut dramatically, and more people are employed than ever before in our history.

We are creating a nation once again vibrant, robust, and alive. But there are many mountains yet to climb. We will not rest until every American enjoys the fullness of freedom, dignity, and opportunity as our birthright. It is our birthright as citizens of this great republic.

And if we meet this challenge, these will be years when Americans have restored their confidence and tradition of progress; when our values of faith, family, work, and neighborhood were restated for a modern age; when our economy was finally freed from government's grip; when we made sincere efforts at meaningful arms reductions and, by rebuilding our defenses, our economy, and developing new technologies, helped preserve peace in a troubled world; when America courageously supported the struggle for individual liberty, self-government, and free enterprise throughout the world and turned the tide of history away from totalitarian darkness and into the warm sunlight of human freedom.

My fellow citizens, our nation is poised for greatness. We must do what we know is right, and do it with all our might. Let history say of us, "These were golden years—when the American Revolution was reborn, when freedom gained new life, and America reached for her best."

Our two-party system has solved us—served us, I should say, well over the years, but never better than in those times of great challenge when we came together not as Democrats or Republicans, but as Americans united in a common cause.

Two of our Founding Fathers, a Boston lawyer named Adams and a Virginia planter named Jefferson, members of that remarkable group who met in Independence Hall and dared to think they could start the world over again, left us an important lesson. They had become, in the years then in government, bitter political rivals in the presidential election of 1800. Then, years later, when both were retired and age had softened their anger, they began to speak to each other again through letters. A bond was reestablished between those two who had helped create this government of ours.

In 1826, the fiftieth anniversary of the Declaration of Independence, they both died. They died on the same day, within a few hours of each other, and that day was the Fourth of July.

In one of those letters exchanged in the sunset of their lives, Jefferson wrote, "It carries me back to the times when, beset with difficulties and dangers, we were fellow laborers in the same cause, struggling for what is most valuable to man, his right of self-government. Laboring always at the same oar, with some wave ever ahead threatening to overwhelm us, and yet passing harmless . . . we rode through the storm with heart and hand."

Well, with heart and hand let us stand as one today—one people under God, determined that our future shall be worthy of our past. As we do, we must not repeat the well-intentioned errors of our past. We must never again abuse the trust of working men and women by sending their earnings on a futile chase after the spiraling demands of a bloated federal establishment. You elected us in 1980 to end this prescription for disaster, and I don't believe you reelected us in 1984 to reverse course.

At the heart of our efforts is one idea vindicated by twenty-five straight months of economic growth: Freedom and incentives unleash the drive and entrepreneurial genius that are the core of human progress. We have begun to increase the rewards for work, savings, and investment; reduce the increase in the cost and size of government and its interference in people's lives.

We must simplify our tax system, make it more fair, and bring the rates down for all who work and earn. We must think anew and move with a new boldness, so every American who seeks work can find work, so the least among us shall have an equal chance to achieve the greatest things—to be heroes who heal our sick, feed the hungry, protect peace among nations, and leave this world a better place.

The time has come for a new American emancipation—a great national drive to tear down economic barriers and liberate the spirit of enterprise in the most distressed areas of our country. My friends, together we can do this, and do it we must, so help me God.

From new freedom will spring new opportunities for growth, a more productive, fulfilled, and united people, and a stronger America—an America that will lead the technological revolution and also open its mind and heart and soul to the treasures of literature, music, and poetry, and the values of faith, courage, and love.

A dynamic economy, with more citizens working and paying taxes, will be our strongest tool to bring down budget deficits. But an almost unbroken fifty years of deficit spending has finally brought us to a time of reckoning. We've come to a turning point, a moment for hard decisions. I have asked the cabinet and my staff a question and now I put the same question to all of you. If not us, who? And if not now, when? It must be done by all of us going forward with a program aimed at reaching a balanced budget. We can then begin reducing the national debt.

I will shortly submit a budget to the Congress aimed at freezing government program spending for the next year. Beyond this, we must take further steps to permanently control government's power to tax and spend. We must act now to protect future generations from government's desire to spend its citizens' money and tax them into servitude when the bills come due. Let us make it unconstitutional for the federal government to spend more than the federal government takes in.

We have already started returning to the people and to state and local governments responsibilities better handled by them. Now, there is a place for the federal government in matters of social compassion.

But our fundamental goals must be to reduce dependency and upgrade the dignity of those who are infirm or disadvantaged. And here, a growing economy and support from family and community offer our best chance for a society where compassion is a way of life, where the old and infirm are cared for, the young and, yes, the unborn protected, and the unfortunate looked after and made self-sufficient.

Now, there is another area where the federal government can play a part. As an older American, I remember a time when people of different race, creed, or ethnic origin in our land found hatred and prejudice installed in social custom and, yes, in law. There's no story more heartening in our history than the progress that we've made toward the brotherhood of man that God intended for us. Let us resolve there will be no turning back or hesitation on the road to an America rich in dignity and abundant with opportunity for all our citizens.

Let us resolve that we, the people, will build an American opportunity society in which all of us—white and black, rich and poor, young and old—will go forward together, arm in arm. Again, let us remember that though our heritage is one of bloodlines from every corner of the earth, we are all Americans, pledged to carry on this last, best hope of man on earth.

I've spoken of our domestic goals and the limitations we should put on our national government. Now let me turn to a task that is the primary responsibility of national government—the safety and security of our people.

Today, we utter no prayer more fervently than the ancient prayer for peace on earth. Yet history has shown that peace does not come, nor will our freedom be preserved, by goodwill alone. There are those in the world who scorn our vision of human dignity and freedom. One nation, the Soviet Union, has conducted the greatest military buildup in the history of man, building arsenals of awesome offensive weapons.

We've made progress in restoring our defense capability. But much remains to be done. There must be no wavering by us, nor any doubts by others, that America will meet her responsibilities to remain free, secure, and at peace.

There is only one way safely and legitimately to reduce the cost of national security, and that is to reduce the need for it. And this we're trying to do in negotiations with the Soviet Union. We're not just discussing limits on a further increase of nuclear weapons; we seek, instead, to reduce their number. We seek the total elimination one day of nuclear weapons from the face of the earth.

Now, for decades, we and the Soviets have lived under the threat of mutual assured destruction—if either resorted to the use of nuclear weapons, the other could retaliate and destroy the one who had started it. Is there either logic or morality in believing that if one side threatens to kill tens of millions of our people, our only recourse is to threaten killing tens of millions of theirs?

I have approved a research program to find, if we can, a security shield that will destroy nuclear missiles before they reach their target. It wouldn't kill people; it would destroy weapons. It wouldn't militarize space; it would help demilitarize the arsenals of earth. It would render nuclear weapons obsolete. We will meet with the Soviets, hoping that we can agree on a way to rid the world of the threat of nuclear destruction.

We strive for peace and security, heartened by the changes all around us. Since the turn of the century, the number of democracies in the world has grown fourfold. Human freedom is on the march, and nowhere more so than in our own hemisphere. Freedom is one of the deepest and noblest aspirations of the human spirit. People, worldwide, hunger for the right of self-determination, for those inalienable rights that make for human dignity and progress.

America must remain freedom's staunchest friend, for freedom is our best ally and it is the world's only hope to conquer poverty and preserve peace. Every blow we inflict against poverty will be a blow against its dark allies of oppression and war. Every victory for human freedom will be a victory for world peace.

So, we go forward today, a nation still mighty in its youth and powerful in its purpose. With our alliances strengthened, with our economy leading the world to a new age of economic expansion, we look to a future rich in possibilities. And all of this is because we worked and acted together, not as members of political parties but as Americans.

My friends, we live in a world that's lit by lightning. So much is changing and will change, but so much endures and transcends time.

History is a ribbon, always unfurling. History is a journey. And as we continue our journey, we think of those who traveled before us. We stand again at the steps of this symbol of our democracy—well, we would have been standing at the steps if it hadn't gotten so cold. [*Laughter*] Now we're standing inside this symbol of our democracy, and we see and hear again the echoes of our past: a general falls to his knees in the hard snow of Valley Forge; a lonely president paces the darkened halls and ponders his struggle to preserve the Union; the men of the Alamo call out encouragement to each other; a settler pushes west and sings a song, and the song echoes out forever and fills the unknowing air.

It is the American sound. It is hopeful, bighearted, idealistic, daring, decent, and fair. That's our heritage, that's our song. We sing it still. For all our problems, our differences, we are together as of old. We raise our voices to the God who is the Author of this most tender music. And may He continue to hold us close as we fill the world with our sound—in unity, affection, and love—one people under God, dedicated to the dream of freedom that He has placed in the human heart, called upon now to pass that dream on to a waiting and hopeful world.

God bless you, and God bless America.

2

THE ECONOMY, FREE MARKETS, AND FREE ENTERPRISE

In the 1970s, the economic situation in the United States, as in much of the world, was dismal: Energy crises contributed to stagnant growth and high unemployment, which combined with runaway inflation to create the paralyzing problem economists dubbed "stagflation." In what came to be known as his "malaise" speech, President Jimmy Carter in 1979 diagnosed a national lack of confidence. But Carter proved unable to offer decisive leadership, and by early 1980 the U.S. economy had slumped into a recession.

Ronald Reagan campaigned against Carter's economic record and fecklessness. (A favorite line: "A recession is when your neighbor loses his job. A depression is when you lose yours. Recovery is when Jimmy Carter loses his.") The essence of the Reagan plan for economic renewal was to lower taxes, reduce wasteful and ineffective government spending, and rein in regulation.

"We're Out of Time"

President Reagan's first televised Oval Office address, delivered from behind the Resolute Desk on the night of February 5, 1981, was a somber, clear-eyed explanation of the economic crisis, remarkable for its plainspokenness.

I'm speaking to you tonight to give you a report on the state of our nation's economy. I regret to say that we're in the worst economic mess since the Great Depression.

A few days ago I was presented with a report I'd asked for, a comprehensive audit, if you will, of our economic condition. You won't like it. I didn't like it. But we have to face the truth and then go to work to turn things around. And make no mistake about it, we can turn them around.

I'm not going to subject you to the jumble of charts, figures, and economic jargon of that audit, but rather will try to explain where we are, how we got there, and how we can get back. First, however, let me just give a few attention-getters from the audit.

The federal budget is out of control, and we face runaway deficits of almost $80 billion for this budget year that ends September 30. That deficit is larger than the entire federal budget in 1957, and so is the almost $80 billion we will pay in interest this year on the national debt.

Twenty years ago, in 1960, our federal government payroll was less than $13 billion. Today it is $75 billion. During these twenty years our population has only increased by 23.3 percent. The federal budget has gone up 528 percent.

Now, we've just had two years of back-to-back double-digit

inflation—13.3 percent in 1979, 12.4 percent last year. The last time this happened was in World War I.

In 1960 mortgage interest rates averaged about 6 percent. They're two and a half times as high now, 15.4 percent.

The percentage of your earnings the federal government took in taxes in 1960 has almost doubled.

And finally there are seven million Americans caught up in the personal indignity and human tragedy of unemployment. If they stood in a line, allowing three feet for each person, the line would reach from the coast of Maine to California.

Well, so much for the audit itself. Let me try to put this in personal terms. Here is a dollar such as you earned, spent, or saved in 1960. And here is a quarter, a dime, and a penny—thirty-six cents. That's what this 1960 dollar is worth today. And if the present world inflation rate should continue three more years, that dollar of 1960 will be worth a quarter. What initiative is there to save? And if we don't save we're short of the investment capital needed for business and industry expansion. Workers in Japan and West Germany save several times the percentage of their income that Americans do.

What's happened to that American dream of owning a home? Only ten years ago a family could buy a home, and the monthly payment averaged little more than a quarter—twenty-seven cents out of each dollar earned. Today, it takes forty-two cents out of every dollar of income. So, fewer than one out of eleven families can afford to buy their first new home.

Regulations adopted by government with the best of intentions have added $666 to the cost of an automobile. It is estimated that altogether regulations of every kind, on shopkeepers, farmers, and major industries, add $100 billion or more to the cost of the goods and services we buy. And then another $20 billion is spent by government handling the paperwork created by those regulations.

I'm sure you're getting the idea that the audit presented to me found government policies of the last few decades responsible for our economic troubles. We forgot or just overlooked the fact that government—any government—has a built-in tendency to grow. Now, we all had a hand in looking to government for benefits, as if government had some source of revenue other than our earnings. Many, if not most, of the things we thought of or that government offered to us seemed attractive.

In the years following the Second World War it was easy, for a while at least, to overlook the price tag. Our income more than doubled in the 25 years after the war. We increased our take-home pay in those 25 years by more than we had amassed in all the preceding 150 years put together. Yes, there was some inflation, 1 or 1.5 percent a year. That didn't bother us. But if we look back at those golden years, we recall that even then voices had been raised, warning that inflation, like radioactivity, was cumulative and that once started it could get out of control.

Some government programs seemed so worthwhile that borrowing to fund them didn't bother us. By 1960 our national debt stood at $284 billion. Congress in 1971 decided to put a ceiling of $400 billion on our ability to borrow. Today the debt is $934 billion. So-called temporary increases or extensions in the debt ceiling have been allowed twenty-one times in these ten years, and now I've been forced to ask for another increase in the debt ceiling or the government will be unable to function past the middle of February—and I've only been here sixteen days. Before we reach the day when we can reduce the debt ceiling, we may in spite of our best efforts see a national debt in excess of a trillion dollars. Now, this is a figure that's literally beyond our comprehension.

We know now that inflation results from all that deficit spending. Government has only two ways of getting money other than raising taxes. It can go into the money market and borrow, competing with its own citizens and driving up interest rates, which it has done, or it can print money, and it's done that. Both methods are inflationary.

We're victims of language. The very word "inflation" leads us to think of it as just high prices. Then, of course, we resent the person who puts on the price tags, forgetting that he or she is also a victim of inflation. Inflation is not just high prices; it's a reduction in the value of our money. When the money supply is increased but the goods and services available for buying are not, we have too much money chasing too few goods. Wars are usually accompanied by inflation. Everyone is working or fighting, but production is of weapons and munitions, not things we can buy and use.

Now, one way out would be to raise taxes so that government need not borrow or print money. But in all these years of government growth, we've reached, indeed surpassed, the limit of our people's tolerance or ability to bear an increase in the tax burden. Prior to World War II, taxes were such that on the average we only had to work just a little over one month each year to pay our total federal, state, and local tax bill. Today we have to work four months to pay that bill.

Some say shift the tax burden to business and industry, but business doesn't pay taxes. Oh, don't get the wrong idea. Business is being taxed, so much so that we're being priced out of the world market. But business must pass its costs of operations—and that includes taxes—on to the customer in the price of the product. Only people pay taxes, all the taxes. Government just uses business in a kind of sneaky way to help collect the taxes. They're hidden in the price; we aren't aware of how much tax we actually pay.

Today this once-great industrial giant of ours has the lowest rate of gain in productivity of virtually all the industrial nations with whom we must compete in the world market. We can't even hold our own market here in America against foreign automobiles, steel, and a number of other products. Japanese production of automobiles is almost twice as great per worker as it is in America. Japanese steelworkers out-produce their American counterparts by about 25 percent.

Now, this isn't because they're better workers. I'll match the American working man or woman against anyone in the world. But we have to give them the tools and equipment that workers in the other industrial nations have.

We invented the assembly line and mass production, but punitive tax policies and excessive and unnecessary regulations plus government borrowing have stifled our ability to update plant and equipment. When capital investment is made, it's too often for some unproductive alterations demanded by government to meet various of its regulations. Excessive taxation of individuals has robbed us of incentive and made overtime unprofitable.

We once produced about 40 percent of the world's steel. We now produce 19 percent. We were once the greatest producer of automobiles, producing more than all the rest of the world combined. That is no longer true, and in addition, the "Big Three," the major auto companies in our land, have sustained tremendous losses in the past year and have been forced to lay off thousands of workers.

All of you who are working know that even with cost-of-living pay raises, you can't keep up with inflation. In our progressive tax system, as you increase the number of dollars you earn, you find yourself moved up into higher tax brackets, paying a higher tax rate just for trying to hold your own. The result? Your standard of living is going down.

Over the past decades we've talked of curtailing government spending so that we can then lower the tax burden. Sometimes we've even taken a run at doing that. But there were always those who told us that taxes couldn't be cut until spending was reduced. Well, you know, we can lecture our children about extravagance until we run out of voice and breath. Or we can cure their extravagance by simply reducing their allowance.

It's time to recognize that we've come to a turning point. We're threatened with an economic calamity of tremendous proportions, and the old business-as-usual treatment can't save us. Together, we must chart a different course.

We must increase productivity. That means making it possible for industry to modernize and make use of the technology which we ourselves invented. That means putting Americans back to work. And that means above all bringing government spending back within government revenues, which is the only way, together with increased productivity, that we can reduce and, yes, eliminate inflation.

In the past we've tried to fight inflation one year and then, with unemployment increased, turn the next year to fighting unemployment with more deficit spending as a pump primer. So, again, up goes inflation. It hasn't worked. We don't have to choose between inflation and unemployment—they go hand in hand. It's time to try something different, and that's what we're going to do.

I've already placed a freeze on hiring replacements for those who retire or leave government service. I've ordered a cut in government travel, the number of consultants to the government, and the buying of office equipment and other items. I've put a freeze on pending regulations and set up a task force under Vice President Bush to review regulations with an eye toward getting rid of as many as possible. I have decontrolled oil [i.e., eliminated price controls on oil that had contributed to the 1970s energy crises], which should result in more domestic production and less dependence on foreign oil. And I'm eliminating that ineffective Council on Wage and Price Stability.

But it will take more, much more. And we must realize there is no quick fix. At the same time, however, we cannot delay in implementing an economic program aimed at both reducing tax rates to stimulate productivity and reducing the growth in government spending to reduce unemployment and inflation.

On February 18, I will present in detail an economic program to Congress embodying the features I've just stated. It will propose budget cuts in virtually every department of government. It is my belief that these actual budget cuts will only be part of the savings. As our cabinet secretaries take charge of their departments, they will search out areas of waste, extravagance, and costly overhead which could yield additional and substantial reductions.

Now, at the same time we're doing this, we must go forward with a tax relief package. I shall ask for a 10 percent reduction across the board in personal income tax rates for each of the next three years. Proposals will also be submitted for accelerated depreciation allowances for business to provide necessary capital so as to create jobs.

Now, here again, in saying this, I know that language, as I said earlier, can get in the way of a clear understanding of what our program is intended to do. "Budget cuts" can sound as if we're going to reduce total government spending to a lower level than was spent the year before. Well, this is not the case. The budgets will increase as our population increases, and each year we'll see spending increases to match that growth. Government revenues will increase as the economy grows, but the burden will be lighter for each individual, because the economic base will have been expanded by reason of the reduced rates.

Now, let me show you a chart that I've had drawn to illustrate how this can be.

Here you see two trend lines. The bottom line shows the increase in tax revenues. The red line on top is the increase in government spending. Both lines turn upward, reflecting the giant tax increase already built into the system for this year, 1981, and the increases in spending built into the '81 and '82 budgets and on into the future. As you can see, the spending line rises at a steeper slant than the revenue line. And that gap between those lines illustrates the increasing deficits we've been running, including this year's $80 billion deficit.

Now, in the second chart, the lines represent the positive effects when Congress accepts our economic program. Both lines continue to rise, allowing for necessary growth, but the gap narrows as spending cuts continue over the next few years until finally the two lines come together, meaning a balanced budget.

I am confident that my administration can achieve that. At that point tax revenues, in spite of rate reductions, will be increasing faster than spending, which means we can look forward to further reductions in the tax rates. . . .

Our spending cuts will not be at the expense of the truly needy. We will, however, seek to eliminate benefits to those who are not really qualified by reason of need. . . .

Our basic system is sound. We can, with compassion, continue to meet our responsibility to those who, through no fault of their own, need our help. We can meet fully the other legitimate responsibilities of government. We cannot continue any longer our wasteful ways at the expense of the workers of this land or of our children.

Since 1960 our government has spent $5.1 trillion. Our debt has grown by $648 billion. Prices have exploded by 178 percent. How much better off are we for all that? Well, we all know we're very much worse off. When we measure how harshly these years of inflation, lower productivity, and un-controlled government growth have affected our lives, we know we must act and act now. We must not be timid. We will restore the freedom of all men and women to excel and to create. We will unleash the energy and genius of the American people, traits which have never failed us.

To the Congress of the United States, I extend my hand in cooper-ation, and I believe we can go forward in a bipartisan manner. I've found a real willingness to cooperate on the part of Democrats and members of my own party.

To my colleagues in the executive branch of government and to all federal employees, I ask that we work in the spirit of service.

I urge those great institutions in America, business and labor, to be guided by the national interest, and I'm confident they will. The only special interest that we will serve is the interest of all the people.

We can create the incentives which take advantage of the genius of our economic system—a system, as Walter Lippmann observed more than forty years ago, which for the first time in history gave men "a way of producing wealth in which the good fortune of others multiplied their own."

Our aim is to increase our national wealth so all will have more, not just redistribute what we already have, which is just a sharing of scarcity. We can begin to reward hard work and risk-taking, by forcing this government to live within its means.

Over the years we've let negative economic forces run out of control. We stalled the judgment day, but we no longer have that luxury. We're out of time.

And to you, my fellow citizens, let us join in a new determination to rebuild the foundation of our society, to work together, to act responsibly. Let us do so with the most profound respect for that which must be preserved as well as with sensitive understanding and compassion for those who must be protected.

We can leave our children with an unrepayable, massive debt and a shattered economy, or we can leave them liberty in a land where every individual has the opportunity to be whatever God intended us to be. All it takes is a little common sense and recognition of our own ability. Together we can forge a new beginning for America.

Thank you, and good night.

"There's Nothing Wrong with America That Together We Can't Fix"

In his first policy address before a joint session of Congress, on the evening of February 18, 1981, President Reagan "painted a pretty grim picture" of the economy. But, he said, "it is within our power to change this picture, and we can act with hope." For nearly half an hour, the president offered details of his proposal to cut taxes, reduce government spending (except on the military), and ease the burden of regulations. He concluded with this request to Congress.

This, then, is our proposal—America's new beginning: a program for economic recovery. I don't want it to be simply the plan of my administration. I'm here tonight to ask you to join me in making it our plan. Together we can embark on this road. [*Applause*]

Thank you very much. I should have arranged to quit right here. [*Laughter*]

Well, together we can embark on this road, not to make things easy, but to make things better. Our social, political, and cultural, as well as our economic institutions can no longer absorb the repeated shocks that have been dealt them over the past decades. Can we do the job? The answer is yes. But we must begin now.

We're in control here. There's nothing wrong with America that together we can't fix. I'm sure there'll be some who raise the old familiar cry, "Don't touch my program; cut somewhere else." I hope I've made it plain that our approach has been evenhanded, that only the programs for the truly deserving needy remain untouched. The question is, are we simply going to go down the same path we've gone down before, carving out one special program here, another special program there? I don't think that's what the American people expect of us. More important, I don't think that's what they want. They're ready to return to the source of our strength.

The substance and prosperity of our nation is built by wages brought home from the factories and the mills, the farms, and the shops. They are the services provided in ten thousand corners of America; the interest on the thrift of our people and the returns for their risk-taking. The production of America is the possession of those who build, serve, create, and produce.

For too long now, we've removed from our people the decisions on how to dispose of what they created. We've strayed from first principles. We must alter our course.

The taxing power of government must be used to provide revenues for legitimate government purposes. It must not be used to regulate the economy or bring about social change. We've tried that, and surely we must be able to see it doesn't work.

Spending by government must be limited to those functions which are the proper province of government. We can no longer afford things simply because we think of them. Next year we can reduce the budget by $41.4 billion, without harm to government's legitimate purposes or to our responsibility to all who need our benevolence. This, plus the reduction in tax rates, will help bring an end to inflation.

In the health and social services area alone, the plan we're proposing will substantially reduce the need for 465 pages of law, 1,400 pages of regulations, 5,000 federal employees who presently administer 7,600 separate grants in about 25,000 separate locations. Over 7 million man and woman hours of work by state and local officials are required to fill out government forms.

I would direct a question to those who have indicated already an unwillingness to accept such a plan: Have they an alternative which offers a greater chance of balancing the budget, reducing and eliminating inflation, stimulating the creation of jobs, and reducing the tax burden? And, if they haven't, are they suggesting we can continue on the present course without coming to a day of reckoning? If we don't do this, inflation and the growing tax burden will put an end to everything we believe in and our dreams for the future.

We don't have an option of living with inflation and its attendant tragedy, millions of productive people willing and able to work but unable to find a buyer for their work in the job market. We have an alternative, and that is the program for economic recovery.

True, it'll take time for the favorable effects of our proposal to be felt. So, we must begin now. The people are watching and waiting. They don't demand miracles. They do expect us to act. Let us act together.

Thank you, and good night.

"Unleash the American Worker"

Speaking to a conference of labor union officials—the Building and Construction Trades Department of the AFL-CIO—President Reagan on the afternoon of March 30, 1981, argued that his economic plan would help American workers. He alluded to his membership in the Screen Actors Guild, the labor union for TV and movie actors that repeatedly elected him its president in the 1940s and '50s. After finishing this speech, while walking from the Washington Hilton to the presidential limousine, Reagan was shot by John Hinckley Jr.

There's been a lot of talk in the last several weeks here in Washington about communication and the need to communicate, and the story that I haven't told for a long time—but somehow it's been brought back to me since I've been here—about communication and some of the basic rules of communication.

It was told to me the first time by Danny Villanueva, who used to placekick for the Los Angeles Rams and then later became a sports announcer, and Danny told me that one night as a sports announcer, he was having a young ballplayer with the Los Angeles Dodgers over to the house for dinner. And the young wife was bustling about getting the dinner ready while he and the ballplayer were talking sports, and the baby started to cry. And over her shoulder, the wife said to her husband, "Change the baby." And this young ballplayer was embarrassed in front of Danny, and he said to his wife, "What do you mean, change the baby? I'm a ballplayer. That's not my line of work." And she turned around, put her hands on her hips, and she communicated. [*Laughter*] She said, "Look, buster, you lay the diaper out like a diamond, you put second base on home plate, put the baby's bottom on the pitcher's mound, hook up first and third, slide home underneath, and if it starts to rain, the game ain't called; you start all over again." [*Laughter*] So, I'm going to try to communicate a little bit today.

I'm pleased to take part in this national conference of the Building and Construction Trades Department of the AFL-CIO. And I hope you'll forgive me if I point with some pride to the fact that I'm the first president of the United States to hold a lifetime membership in an AFL-CIO union. . . . Members of your organization have played and do play a great part in the building of America. They also are an important part of the industry in which my union plays a part. Now, it's true that greasepaint and make-believe are not tools of your members' trade, but we all know the meaning of work and of family and of country.

For two decades or more, I participated in renegotiating our basic contract when it came renewal time. And here, too, we have much in common. Sitting at the negotiating table, we were guided by three principles in our demands: Is it good for our people? Is it fair to the other fellow and to the customer? And is it good for the industry?

Samuel Gompers, who founded the American Federation of Labor and who literally gave his life to that cause, said, "Doing for people what they can and ought to do for themselves is a dangerous experiment. In the last analysis the welfare of the workers depends upon their own initiative. Whatever is done under the guise of philanthropy or social morality which in any way lessens initiative is the greatest crime that can be committed against the toilers. Let social busybodies and professional public morals experts in their fads reflect upon the perils they rashly invite under the pretense of social welfare."

Samuel Gompers was repudiating the socialist philosophy when he made that statement. No one worked harder to get or believed more in a fair shake for the people who sweat as the fuel of our country, but he didn't believe that this should or could come from government compulsion.

America depends on the work of labor, and the economy we build should reward and encourage that labor as our hope for the future. We've strayed far from the path that was charted by this man who believed so much in the freedom and dignity of the worker. We are in today's economic mess precisely because our leaders have forgotten that we built this great nation on rewarding the work ethic instead of punishing it.

We've gone astray from first principles. We've lost sight of the rule that individual freedom and ingenuity are at the very core of everything that we've accomplished. Government's first duty is to protect the people, not run their lives. . . .

Every American and especially all the working people of our country have an enormous stake in what we do. You pay the most taxes. You believe in a work ethic but subsidize a government that does not. You, who have traditionally saved to provide for your futures, today cannot save. You, who most want to work, are most likely to be laid off. You, through taxes on your hard-earned wages, pay for what could be as much as $25 billion each year in federal waste, abuse, and outright fraud in government programs. Franklin Delano Roosevelt spoke of "the forgotten man at the bottom of the economic pyramid." Well, today it's safe to say that the people at both ends of the pyramid are getting attention. The man who's forgotten is the fellow who built it.

Such a man wrote his congressman a few weeks back, and that letter landed on my desk. I've gotten tens of thousands of letters about our plan for economic recovery. I appreciate all of them, but a few of them really stand out, and this man's letter is one of them.

He's an unemployed factory worker from Illinois, the Peoria area, but he worked in construction for ten years before that. His income right now is totally dependent on unemployment and supplemental benefits from the company he worked for. He and his wife have only been married three months, but she's been laid off too. He wrote to say that if spending cuts in government affect his benefits, it'll be hard for his family, but they'll make it. And shades of Sam Gompers, he ended his letter saying that when the opponents of our economic plan start lobbying against it—and let me quote—he said, "Let me know that there is someone out here who's seen what they can do and is willing to stake his future on trying a different approach."

That man has faith in America and faith in what the American people can do if the government will only let them do it. And that man, like most of America, wants a change. . . .

The main source of strength in this fight is going to be the people themselves. The idea is to unleash the American worker, encourage the American investor, and let each of us produce more to make a better life for all. After all, why should we pay for some luxuries that are not truly essential to our well-being, pay by way of a subsidy when the man and his wife in Peoria are out of work? Why should we subsidize increased production of some things that we already have in surplus? And why should we go in debt to pay for school lunches for children of upper-income families when borrowing by government may cost you your job? We not only shouldn't do those things; we no longer can afford to do them.

We'll continue to fulfill our obligations to those who must depend on the rest of us. Those who are deserving can rest assured that they'll not be cut adrift, but the rest of us will feel the impact of the budget cuts, which have been distributed through the economy, as evenly as possible. . . .

Now, I know that we can't make things right overnight. But we will make them right. Our destiny is not our fate. It is our choice. And I'm asking you as I ask all Americans, in these months of decision, please join me as we take this new path. You and your forebears built this nation. Now, please help us rebuild it, and together we'll make America great again.

Thank you very much.

"They Look to Us to Meet the Great Challenge"

President Reagan's first speech after the attempt on his life was back at the Capitol, where he addressed a joint session of Congress on the evening of April 28, 1981. Invoking NASA's recent launching of a space shuttle into orbit for the first time, the president concluded with this appeal to Congress to act on his economic program.

Tonight, I renew my call for us to work as a team, to join in cooperation so that we find answers which will begin to solve all our economic problems and not just some of them. The economic recovery package that I've outlined to you over the past weeks is, I deeply believe, the only answer that we have left.

Reducing the growth of spending, cutting marginal tax rates, providing relief from overregulation, and following a noninflationary and predictable monetary policy are interwoven measures which will ensure that we have addressed each of the severe dislocations which threaten our economic future. These policies will make our economy stronger, and the stronger economy will balance the budget, which we're committed to do by 1984.

When I took the oath of office, I pledged loyalty to only one special interest group—"We the People." Those people—neighbors and friends, shopkeepers and laborers, farmers and craftsmen—do not have infinite patience. As a matter of fact, some eighty years ago, Teddy Roosevelt wrote these instructive words in his first message to the Congress: "The American people are slow to wrath, but when their wrath is once kindled, it burns like a consuming flame." Well, perhaps that kind of wrath will be deserved if our answer to these serious problems is to repeat the mistakes of the past.

The old and comfortable way is to shave a little here and add a little there. Well, that's not acceptable anymore. I think this great and historic Congress knows that way is no longer acceptable. [*Applause*] Thank you very much.

I think you've shown that you know the one sure way to continue the inflationary spiral is to fall back into the predictable patterns of old economic practices. Isn't it time that we tried something new?

When you allowed me to speak to you here in these chambers a little earlier, I told you that I wanted this program for economic recovery to be ours—yours and mine. I think the bipartisan substitute bill has achieved that purpose. It moves us toward economic vitality.

Just two weeks ago, you and I joined millions of our fellow Americans in marveling at the magic, historical moment that John Young and Bob Crippen created in their space shuttle, *Columbia*. The last manned effort was almost six years ago, and I remembered on this more recent day, over the years, how we'd all come to expect technological precision of our men and machines. And each amazing achievement became commonplace, until the next new challenge was raised.

With the space shuttle we tested our ingenuity once again, moving beyond the accomplishments of the past into the promise and uncertainty of the future. Thus, we not only planned to send up a 122-foot aircraft 170 miles into space, but we also intended to make it maneuverable and return it to Earth, landing 98 tons of exotic metals delicately on a remote, dry lake bed. The space shuttle did more than prove our technological abilities. It raised our expectations once more. It started us dreaming again.

The poet Carl Sandburg wrote, "The republic is a dream. Nothing happens unless first a dream." And that's what makes us, as Americans, different. We've always reached for a new spirit and aimed at a higher goal. We've been courageous and determined, unafraid and bold. Who among us wants to be first to say we no longer have those qualities, that we must limp along, doing the same things that have brought us our present misery?

I believe that the people you and I represent are ready to chart a new course. They look to us to meet the great challenge, to reach beyond the commonplace and not fall short for lack of creativity or courage.

Someone you know [Henry David Thoreau] has said that he who would have nothing to do with thorns must never attempt to gather flowers. Well, we have much greatness before us. We can restore our economic strength and build opportunities like none we've ever had before.

As Carl Sandburg said, all we need to begin with is a dream that we can do better than before. All we need to have is faith, and that dream will come true. All we need to do is act, and the time for action is now.

Thank you. Good night.

"They . . . Will Be Terminated"

On the morning of August 3, 1981, the Professional Air Traffic Controllers Organization (PATCO) went on strike. While it was legal for the union to organize and bargain, its members were forbidden from striking. President Reagan, who had clashed with striking public-sector unions when he was governor of California, took swift action against PATCO. That same morning, in remarks delivered in the White House Rose Garden alongside the attorney general and the secretary of transportation, he issued the ultimatum below. Apparently believing the president was bluffing, most of the strikers did not return to work. They were fired en masse and PATCO was decertified.

This morning at seven a.m. the union representing those who man America's air traffic control facilities called a strike. This was the culmination of seven months of negotiations between the Federal Aviation Administration and the union. At one point in these negotiations agreement was reached and signed by both sides, granting a $40 million increase in salaries and benefits. This is twice what other government employees can expect. It was granted in recognition of the difficulties inherent in the work these people perform. Now, however, the union demands are seventeen times what had been agreed to—$681 million. This would impose a tax burden on their fellow citizens which is unacceptable.

I would like to thank the supervisors and controllers who are on the job today, helping to get the nation's air system operating safely. In the New York area, for example, four supervisors were scheduled to report for work, and seventeen additionally volunteered. At National Airport a traffic controller told a newsperson he had resigned from the union and reported to work because, "How can I ask my kids to obey the law if I don't?" This is a great tribute to America.

Let me make one thing plain. I respect the right of workers in the private sector to strike. Indeed, as president of my own union, I led the first strike ever called by that union. I guess I'm maybe the first one to ever hold this office who is a lifetime member of an AFL-CIO union. But we cannot compare labor-management relations in the private sector with government. Government cannot close down the assembly line. It has to provide without interruption the protective services which are government's reason for being.

It was in recognition of this that the Congress passed a law forbidding strikes by government employees against the public safety. Let me read the solemn oath taken by each of these employees, a sworn affidavit, when they accepted their jobs: "I am not participating in any strike against the government of the United States or any agency thereof, and I will not so participate while an employee of the government of the United States or any agency thereof."

It is for this reason that I must tell those who fail to report for duty this morning they are in violation of the law, and if they do not report for work within forty-eight hours, they have forfeited their jobs and will be terminated. . . .

[*In response to a question from a reporter:*] With all this talk of penalties and everything else, I hope that you'll emphasize, again, the possibility of termination, because I believe that there are a great many of those people—and they're fine people—who have been swept up in this and probably have not really considered the result—the fact that they had taken an oath, the fact that this is now in violation of the law. . . . And I am hoping that they will in a sense remove themselves from the lawbreaker situation by returning to their posts. I have no way to know whether this had been conveyed to them by their union leaders, who had been informed that this would be the result of a strike. . . .

[*Question from a reporter: "Mr. President, why have you taken such strong action as your first action? Why not some lesser action at this point?"*]

What lesser action can there be? The law is very explicit. They are violating the law. And as I say, we called this to the attention of their leadership. Whether this was conveyed to the membership before they voted to strike, I don't know. But this is one of the reasons why there can be no further negotiation while this situation continues. You can't sit and negotiate with a union that's in violation of the law.

[*Secretary of Transportation Drew Lewis: "And their oath."*]

And their oath.

"Free Trade Is in All Our Interests"

The president delivered these remarks on agriculture and trade on October 20, 1982, before an audience of four thousand at a farm owned by the Werries family in Chapin, Illinois. Afterward, he briefly drove a green John Deere tractor with the help of farmer John Werries.

Year after year, here in the Midwest you produce from your rich, black earth a bountiful harvest called the American equivalent of the oil riches in the Persian Gulf. The farmers of Illinois are among the most hardworking people anywhere. And to produce this abundance you carry an extraordinary burden for the nation and the world. On behalf of the 231 million Americans whose cupboards you fill and for the millions more worldwide that you save from hunger, I bring you thanks. . . .

We've lifted the weight of America's foreign policy from your already overburdened shoulders. We ended the Soviet grain embargo. . . .

Our farmers, I know, are among our most patriotic citizens. I know you care about freedom and a strong America. But American farmers once had a 70 percent share of the Soviet grain market. When the embargo was imposed [by President Carter following the Russian invasion of Afghanistan in 1979], the Soviets still got their grain, but they bought it from our eager competitors. Today, we've worked our way back to a 35 percent share, but we have a long way to go to regain lost ground. We still are suffering the loss of about eighty thousand potential jobs; farm prices are lower; and our economy is weaker.

You have to fight the weather. You have to fight insects. You fight all kinds of natural disasters that can happen in farming. You shouldn't have to fight your own government. And you're not going to have to.

That embargo was bad foreign policy. It was bad domestic policy. And I'm proud that we were able to take it off. For every $1 billion in additional farm exports, our economy gains an additional billion dollars and thirty-five thousand jobs in farm-related activities. . . .

Nothing means more to the health of American agriculture than restoring our reputation as a reliable supplier. To do this, we've committed your government to an export policy with three key points. First, there will be no restriction on farm products because of rising domestic prices. Second, farm exports will not be singled out as an instrument of foreign policy except in extreme situations, which I think you would all understand—such as a war or something of that kind— and then that would only be as part of a broad trade embargo supported by our trading partners. And, third, world markets must be freed of trade barriers and unfair trade practices.

Free trade is in all our interests, but because of foreign subsidies and protections, our farmers are being pitted against the economic strength of the national treasuries of other countries. All nations, particularly our friends in Europe and Japan, must be made to understand that trade is a two-way proposition. And Secretary Block has already announced our new blended credit program to encourage long-term growth for our farm exports.

"My Goal Is an America Bursting with Opportunity"

President Reagan wanted to follow up his 1981 tax cut with a broad tax reform, transforming "a system that's become an endless source of confusion and resentment into one that is clear, simple, and fair for all." The excerpt below is drawn from his May 28, 1985, tele-vised Oval Office address making the case for such a reform—one that would especially strengthen families and small businesses. By October of the following year, the president had signed a tax reform bill into law.

Over the course of this century, our tax system has been modified dozens of times and in hundreds of ways, yet most of those changes didn't improve the system. They made it more like Washington itself—complicated, unfair, cluttered with gobbledygook and loopholes designed for those with the power and influence to hire high-priced legal and tax advisers.

But there's more to it than that. Some years ago a historian, I believe, said that every time in the past when a government began taxing above a certain level of the people's earnings, trust in government began to erode. He said it would begin with efforts to avoid paying the full tax. This would become outright cheating and, eventually, a distrust and contempt of government itself until there would be a breakdown in law and order.

Well, how many times have we heard people brag about clever schemes to avoid paying taxes or watched luxuries casually written off to be paid for by somebody else? That somebody being you. I believe that, in both spirit and substance, our tax system has come to be un-American.

Death and taxes may be inevitable, but unjust taxes are not. The first American revolution was sparked by an unshakable conviction—taxation without representation is tyranny. Two centuries later, a second American revolution for hope and opportunity is gathering force again—a peaceful revolution, but born of popular resentment against a tax system that is unwise, unwanted, and unfair. . . .

I'll start by answering one question on your minds: Will our proposal help you? You bet it will. We call it America's tax plan because it will reduce tax burdens on the working people of this country, close loopholes that benefit a privileged few, simplify a code so complex even Albert Einstein reportedly needed help on his 1040 form, and lead us into a future of greater growth and opportunity for all. . . .

I believe the worth of any economic policy must be measured by the strength of its commitment to American families, the bedrock of our society. There is no instrument of hard work, savings, and job creation as effective as the family. There is no cultural institution as ennobling as family life. And there is no superior, indeed no equal, means to rear the young, protect the weak, or attend the elderly. None.

Yet past government policies betrayed families and family values. They permitted inflation to push families relentlessly into higher and higher tax brackets. And not only did the personal exemption fail to keep pace with inflation; in real dollars its actual value dropped dramatically over the last thirty years.

The power to tax is the power to destroy. For three decades families have paid the freight for the special interests. Now families are in trouble. As one man from Memphis, Tennessee, recently wrote, "The taxes that are taken out of my check is money that I need, not extra play money. Please do all that you can to make the tax system more equitable toward the family." Well, sir, that's just what we intend to do—to pass the strongest pro-family initiative in postwar history. . . . We're offering a ladder of opportunity for every family that feels trapped, a ladder of opportunity to grab hold of and to climb out of poverty forever.

Comparing the distance between the present system and our proposal is like comparing the distance between a Model T and the space shuttle. And I should know—I've seen both. . . .

My goal is an America bursting with opportunity, an America that celebrates freedom every day by giving every citizen an equal chance, an America that is once again the youngest nation on earth—her spirit unleashed and breaking free. . . .

The pessimists will give a hundred reasons why this historic proposal won't pass and can't work. Well, they've been opposing progress and predicting disaster for four years now. Yet here we are tonight a stronger, more united, more confident nation than at any time in recent memory.

Remember, there are no limits to growth and human progress when men and women are free to follow their dreams. The American dream belongs to you; it lives in millions of different hearts; it can be fulfilled in millions of different ways. And with you by our side, we're not going to stop moving and shaking this town until that dream is real for every American, from the sidewalks of Harlem to the mountaintops of Hawaii.

My fellow citizens, let's not let this magnificent moment slip away. Tax relief is in sight. Let's make it a reality. Let's not let prisoners of mediocrity wear us down. Let's not let the special interest raids of the few rob us of all our dreams.

In these last four years, we've made a fresh start together. In these next four, we can begin a new chapter in our history—freedom's finest hour. We can do it. And if you help, we will do it this year.

Thank you. God bless you, and good night.

"Knock Down the Barriers to Progress That Government Itself Has Created"

On the afternoon of March 12, 1986, while awarding the annual National Medals of Science and Technology to twenty-six individuals in the East Room of the White House, President Reagan offered these remarks about discovery, innovation, and technological progress.

Thank you, and welcome to the White House. To paraphrase an earlier president, this must be one of the most extraordinary collections of talent and human intelligence that has ever come together in one room in the White House, with the possible exception of when Thomas Jefferson dined alone. [*Laughter*]

You know, a favorite story of mine is about one of the first times the White House played host to an event concerning science and technology, and that was back in '76–1876. A demonstration of a recently invented device was put on here for President Rutherford B. Hayes. "That's an amazing invention," he said, "but who would ever want to use them?" He was talking about the telephone. [*Laughter*] I thought at the time when I heard him that he might be mistaken. [*Laughter*] We've come a long way from those times. But I sometimes feel that, just like President Hayes, some of the journalists who cover our everyday political affairs here in Washington have a tendency to miss the real news: the transforming discoveries and achievements that you and your colleagues are making every day.

I remember just a little over five years ago when all the headlines were of shortages. Every morning it seemed we read some new scare story telling us that the earth's resources were about to run out for good, leaving our world poorer and shrinking our hopes for the future. But at the same time, scientists, inventors, and entrepreneurs were mining the most abundant resource in the world: the human mind and imagination. Men and women such as you, with the spirit of discovery, enterprise, and achievement, have been opening up new worlds of possibility and transforming all our lives for the better.

Whole industries have sprung up around what were only, years ago, merely ideas in the minds of scientists and inventors. New grains and agriculture techniques have alleviated hunger. New vaccines have conquered some of mankind's most dreaded diseases. Quantum leaps in technology are making possible greater prosperity and personal fulfillment than mankind has ever known. In the computer industry, for instance, miraculous advances in productivity are now almost commonplace. Let me give you an example, although I'm sure you could provide many more. In one semiconductor plant in Pennsylvania in 1957, each worker produced five transistors a day for $7.50 apiece. Today each worker produces over a million semiconductors every day, each one costing a fraction of a penny.

Some say that about 90 percent of all scientific knowledge has been generated in the last thirty years alone, and we'll likely double it by the end of the century. Such an explosion of knowledge creates an unprecedented opportunity to expand the global economy, to bring prosperity and hope to those corners of the world that for too long have known only deprivation and want. The United States must take the lead in making this happen. And you who are on the cutting edge of human achievement understand that freedom is not a luxury but a necessity. Freedom to think, freedom to imagine and create—these are not privileges, but the very source of our life's bread and the hope of mankind's future. How can government aid the cause of human progress? Well, in 1985 alone we invested over $49 billion in research and development. Now, this is an important role, but it's even more important to knock down the barriers to progress that government itself has created. And that's why we've rolled back needless government regulations, cut tax rates—and we plan to cut them again. . . .

But as we look at the record of scientific achievement, there remains one area crying out for attention. I believe that our nuclear dilemma presents us with some of the major unfinished business of science. We have begun research on a nonnuclear defense against nuclear attack. As I said before, yesterday's impossibilities have become commonplace realities today. Why should we start thinking small now? In protecting mankind from the peril of nuclear destruction, we must be ambitious. We can't lock ourselves into a fatalistic acceptance of a world held in jeopardy. In this area, more especially, we must approach the future with vision and hope that reach for the greatest possibilities. Only if we try can we succeed. You know, people who say it can't be done—they remind me of a story, too. At my age practically everything reminds me of a story. [*Laughter*]

Back in 1842 the royal astronomer in Great Britain studied Charles Babbage's new analytical engine, the forerunner of the modern computer, and pronounced it worthless. His foresight was almost equal to a half century later, when the head of the U.S. Patent Office advised President McKinley to abolish the Patent Office because, he said,

"Everything that can be invented has already been invented." [*Laughter*]
Well, if science has taught us anything, it's taught us not to be modest
in our aspirations. The fact, I have to confess, is that fact is my secret
agenda for bringing you all here today. I'm going to ask all of you to
turn your attention to the budget problem.

Well, congratulations! You're all heroes in the cause of human progress. God bless you all. And now I will step away from the podium, and
we shall have the awards.

3

SELF-GOVERNMENT

Although the phrase "small-government conservative" is sometimes used nowadays to describe President Reagan, and was for years enthusiastically adopted by many Republicans who admired him, that label grossly oversimplifies his views.

It would be closer to truth to say that Reagan wanted effective government, and that he believed—for a host of constitutional, practical, and moral reasons—that power and responsibility should be kept as close to the people as possible while allowing government to fulfill its important functions.

The New Federalism

During his time as governor of California, Reagan supported reforms that would restore authority to local government that had been seriously eroded by state and federal mandates. He later extended this idea under the rubric "new federalism," which he explained to reporters in the November 19, 1981, Oval Office interview excerpted here.

[*Reporter: "Mr. President, in your dream of the future of American federalism, what domestic functions do you believe should be federal, as opposed to state and local, responsibilities?"*]

Well, the first one, of course, is national security. That is the prime responsibility of the national government. . . .

But I would think that first of all, education—we built the greatest school system the world has ever seen and built it at the local level and the local school district level. And then the federal government got into the school business only by having preempted so much of the tax resources, and those tax resources that grew with the economy faster than something like the property tax, which is the principal basis for educational funding. Then they got into it through that money thing, having preempted the money, created the problem, and then they said, "Well, now we want to help you." But in return for the help, they wanted to also regulate, and have interfered to a large extent.

Welfare—welfare is presently administered at the local level. It is, in most states, done at the county level. They have a county welfare department, but they do it under regulations imposed from Washington. And I can tell you, those regulations would line the walls of this room, and they're constantly changing. They have got employees at the county level that do nothing but try to keep up and inform the workers of what the new regulations are. . . .

[*Reporter: "Mr. President, without being too general, I wonder if you could sum up for us some sort of philosophical thing, just what you see as the new federalism? Just a brief—(inaudible)."*]

Again, as I say, start with the Constitution. . . . Then find those functions—maybe we'd do well if we looked at the past. I know that everyone used to say I'm trying to take the country back—no, only as far as the Constitution. Find out those things that are, today, more or less administered in partnership at the local level and yet under federal control, and see if you need that extra layer of bureaucracy on top.

I would think that this would include such things as welfare; certainly, it would include education. And then with this, under this federalism, review again what legitimately and honestly belongs at the federal level and at the local level in the system of taxes.

Back when I was growing up, the governments of the United States, between them, only took a dime out of every dollar earned. Only a third of that or less went to the federal government; two-thirds to local and state government. Today, they are taking more than forty cents out of every dollar, and two-thirds of that goes to the federal government. It's just reversed, the other way around.

And have this fairness in revenues so that wherever possible, you can have the responsibility for raising the money and the responsibility for performing the function in the hands of the same government.

"The Constitutional Balance Envisioned by the Founding Fathers"

In his first State of the Union address, delivered on January 26, 1982, and excerpted here, President Reagan spelled out how and why he hoped to devolve power from the federal government to state and local governments.

Our next major undertaking must be a program . . . to make government again accountable to the people, to make our system of federalism work again.

Our citizens feel they've lost control of even the most basic decisions made about the essential services of government, such as schools, welfare, roads, and even garbage collection. And they're right. A maze of interlocking jurisdictions and levels of government confronts average citizens in trying to solve even the simplest of problems. They don't know where to turn for answers, who to hold accountable, who to praise, who to blame, who to vote for or against. The main reason for this is the overpowering growth of federal grants-in-aid programs during the past few decades.

In 1960 the federal government had 132 categorical grant programs, costing $7 billion. When I took office, there were approximately 500, costing nearly a hundred billion dollars—13 programs for energy, 36 for pollution control, 66 for social services, 90 for education. And here in the Congress, it takes at least 166 committees just to try to keep track of them.

You know and I know that neither the president nor the Congress can properly oversee this jungle of grants-in-aid; indeed, the growth of these grants has led to the distortion in the vital functions of government. As one Democratic governor put it recently, the national government should be worrying about "arms control, not potholes."

The growth in these federal programs has—in the words of one intergovernmental commission—made the federal government "more pervasive, more intrusive, more unmanageable, more ineffective and costly, and above all, more [un]accountable." Let's solve this problem with a single, bold stroke: the return of some $47 billion in federal programs to state and local government, together with the means to finance them and a transition period of nearly ten years to avoid unnecessary disruption. . . .

Hand in hand with this program to strengthen the discretion and flexibility of state and local governments, we're proposing legislation for an experimental effort to improve and develop our depressed urban areas in the 1980s and '90s. This legislation will permit states and localities to apply to the federal government for designation as urban enterprise zones. A broad range of special economic incentives in the zones will help attract new business, new jobs, new opportunity to America's inner cities and rural towns. Some will say our mission is to save free enterprise. Well, I say we must free enterprise so that together we can save America.

Some will also say our states and local communities are not up to the challenge of a new and creative partnership. Well, that might have been true twenty years ago, before reforms like reapportionment and the Voting Rights Act, the ten-year extension of which I strongly support. It's no longer true today. This administration has faith in state and local governments and the constitutional balance envisioned by the Founding Fathers. We also believe in the integrity, decency, and sound, good sense of grassroots Americans.

Our faith in the American people is reflected in another major endeavor. Our private sector initiatives task force is seeking out successful community models of school, church, business, union, foundation, and civic programs that help community needs. Such groups are almost invariably far more efficient than government in running social programs.

We're not asking them to replace discarded and often discredited government programs dollar for dollar, service for service. We just want to help them perform the good works they choose and help others to profit by their example. Three hundred and eighty-five thousand corporations and private organizations are already working on social programs ranging from drug rehabilitation to job training, and thousands more Americans have written us asking how they can help. The volunteer spirit is still alive and well in America.

"Restore the Partnership"

This toast President Reagan delivered at a February 23, 1982, dinner honoring the nation's governors makes the case for a "revitalized federalism." The charming story about bureaucratic goofiness that the president tells is one that, on another occasion, he claimed was an "actual incident."

Well, your advice and counsel during these past days and in the year since I came to office have been invaluable as we've worked to renew the health and promise of this country. And together, we've begun restoring the partnership between the levels of American government.

I'm aware that some of you feel caught between yesterday's call for greater autonomy and tomorrow's fear of being left alone with problems you didn't create. To you I give this pledge: The federal government will not turn its back on people, communities, or states in need of help.

We will not create winners and losers, turning states and regions against each other. Our goal has been and will remain to bring prosperity to all Americans in every part of our country.

The reforms that we've proposed won't work miracles, but they will bring progress. They don't confuse the ideals of federal assistance with the failed realities of bureaucracy.

You know, I have to stop and tell you one of my favorite stories about bureaucracy. There was a man in Washington whose job was sitting at a desk in his particular department. And papers came to his desk, and he decided where they should go and initialed them and sent them on. And one day a classified paper came to him, but he read it and figured out where it should go, initialed it, and sent it on. And a couple of days later it came back to him, saying, "You were not supposed to read this." [*Laughter*] "Erase your initials, and initial the erasure." [*Laughter*]

Well, sometimes you recognize that programs that have helped will wipe away those that have failed or made matters worse, is what it is—what we're aiming at. In this centennial year of the birth of Franklin Roosevelt, a former governor, we should read again his words with regard to our need to restore economic sanity to Washington and power and resources to you. He said, "Civilization cannot go back. Civilization must not stand still. It is our task to perfect, to improve, to alter when necessary, but, in all cases, to go forward."

FDR also expressed his belief in giving back to the states authorities which he said had been unjustly usurped by the federal government. And I figure if we give enough of them back, then I'm going to be able to go to the ranch more often. [*Laughter*]

But we of this era must understand that we, too, have come upon a new day. We must change the way that we view government's role in our rapidly changing society. Roosevelt's challenge is our challenge tonight and in the weeks and months ahead. We must summon the courage to move forward. Governor [Richard] Snelling [of Vermont] put it very well when he said, "Either you believe in democracy or you don't." Well, I do, and I know you do, too.

Our program for economic recovery and our proposal to restore the partnership between state, local, and federal government are born from that belief. They spring from an abiding faith in the American people and in our ability to govern ourselves.

"This Is Something That's Been a Dream of Mine"

On July 6, 1982, President Reagan made these remarks about his new federalism plan to a group of state and local government officials gathered in Los Angeles.

This is not a budget-balancing gimmick. This is something that's been a dream of mine. It goes back a great many years, and particularly back to the days when I was a governor growing increasingly frustrated with federal red tape.

And we came up with the concept. We didn't present it as a finished plan, as some of you know, but we presented it as a plan as a beginning place for consultations with local officials, mayors, with state legislators, with county officials, and, of course, with members of the Congress.

I have to say that I think the most reluctance we normally run into— and that is to be expected—is at the national level, where there is a built-in resistance to giving up activities or power at any time. Now, sometimes some of them are very sincere. They look at it and think, "Well, if we're asked to raise the funds as Congress, then we can't turn these funds over without exerting some control over how it is spent."

Of course, our answer to that is: Let's look forward to a day where they're not raising those funds, where the tax sources which were usurped by the federal government at the same time it usurped so many, once, state and local functions—they usurped the tax sources also. And so, the thing is to accompany the functions with the resources to pay for them.

Now, I'm going to be very brief here in my remarks, because I think we're going to have a dialogue. . . . But, you know, traveling the mashed-potato circuit for many years—and I know that many of you have done the same thing—I have often quoted Thomas Jefferson in my protestations, then, against government intervention and big government, particularly, intervening. His line when he said, "Were we directed from Washington when to sow and when to reap, we should soon want for [i.e., lack] bread." And yet I never have put that—I had put that in the context of—as I'm sure many of you have—of intervention by, particularly, the federal government in things that were not its proper province. Would you like to hear that put in the context in which he said it? Because it's even more timely than it was in that supposed context in which I myself used it and perhaps many of you: "Were not this great country already divided into states, that division must be made, that each might do for itself what concerns itself directly and what it can do so much better than distant authority. Every state is again divided into counties, each to take care of what lies within its local bounds; each county again into townships or wards to handle minute details. Were we directed from Washington when to sow and when to reap, we should soon want for bread."

So, we can claim that Jefferson was the first one to present the present federal program.

And, as I say, I know that you must share in that frustration too. I could go on citing anecdotes here and examples of the frustration I felt sometimes at the federal government's insistence on doing it that way. And yet, I can understand now, being there, how, once they're entrusted with that, they feel that whatever problem comes up must be nationwide. They lose sight of the great diversity of this country. So, they pass a rule that's supposed to fit—I won't say South Succotash, Wisconsin, anymore, because everybody's started trying to find South Succotash [*laughter*]—but to fit all these diverse fifty states and all the local communities within them.

"It Will Permanently Diminish the Sum Total of American Democracy"

President Reagan nominated Robert Bork to the U.S. Supreme Court on July 31, 1987. The nomination was immediately attacked by Senate Democrats and their allies, who badly misrepresented Judge Bork's views. In this October 14, 1987, Oval Office address in defense of the nomination, the president warned about the ill effects of the "ugly spectacle" and articulated his understanding of the proper role and responsibility of the judiciary in our system of government. The next week, the Senate rejected the Bork nomination in a 58–42 vote.

As you know, I have selected one of the finest judges in America's history, Robert Bork, for the Supreme Court. You've heard that this nomination is a lost cause. You've also heard that I am determined to fight right down to the final ballot on the Senate floor. I'm doing this because what's now at stake in this battle must never in our land of freedom become a lost cause. And whether lost or not, we Americans must never give up this particular battle: the independence of our judiciary.

Back in July when I nominated Judge Bork, I thought the

confirmation process would go forward with a calm and sensible exchange of views. Unfortunately, the confirmation process became an ugly spectacle, marred by distortions and innuendos, and casting aside the normal rules of decency and honesty. As Judge Bork said last Friday, and I quote, "The process of confirming Justices for our nation's highest court has been transformed in a way that should not and, indeed, must not be permitted to occur again. The tactics and techniques of national political campaigns have been unleashed on the process of confirming judges. That is not simply disturbing; it is dangerous. Federal judges are not appointed to decide cases according to the latest opinion polls; they are appointed to decide cases impartially, according to law. But when judicial nominees are assessed and treated like political candidates, the effect will be to chill the climate in which judicial deliberations take place, to erode public confidence in the impartiality of courts, and to endanger the independence of the judiciary."

Judge Bork said he had no illusions about the difficulty of the task before us, but he also said, and I agree, that a crucial principle is at stake. And we will fight for every vote to maintain that principle. It is the process that is used to determine the fitness of those men and women selected to serve on our courts, those people who guard the basic liberties that we all cherish and have been the beacon of freedom for over two centuries.

If the campaign of distortion and disinformation used by opponents of this nominee is allowed to succeed, it will represent more than a temporary setback for one candidate or the administration. It will permanently diminish the sum total of American democracy; it will call into question the idea of free, fair, and civil exchange; and it will mean that on critical issues like the fight against crime and drugs and keeping those who are unelected from unconstitutionally taking power into their own hands, each of us and each of our children will be the losers.

During the hearings, one of Judge Bork's critics said that among the functions of the court was reinterpreting the Constitution so that it would not remain, in his words, "frozen into ancient error because it is so hard to amend." Well, that to my mind is the issue, plain and simple. Too many theorists believe that the courts should save the country from the Constitution. Well, I believe it's time to save the Constitution from them. The principal errors in recent years have had nothing to do with the intent of the framers who finished their work two hundred years ago last month. They've had to do with those who have looked upon the courts as their own special province to impose by judicial fiat what they could not accomplish at the polls. They've had to do with judges who too often have made law enforcement a game where clever lawyers try to find ways to trip up the police on the rules. . . .

In the next several days, your senators will cast a vote on the Bork nomination. It is more than just one vote on one man: It's a decision on the future of our judicial system. The purpose of the Senate debate is to allow all sides to be heard. Honorable men and women should not be afraid to change their minds based on that debate.

I hope that in the days and weeks ahead you will let them know that the confirmation process must never again be compromised with high-pressure politics. Tell them that America stands for better than that and that you expect them to stand for America. Remind them that there is a thing we call the Constitution and to serve under it is a sacred trust, that they have sworn themselves to that trust, and that not just for this nomination or any nomination but for the sake of the independence of the American system of justice for generations to come. Now is the time to uphold that trust, no matter how powerful are those in opposition.

There is a vision for America that we all share, an America where the Constitution is held in high esteem, where all our citizens are treated equally under the law, where the legislature makes the law and the judges interpret the law, and where the right of the people to self-government is respected.

Thank you, and God bless you all.

4

PEACE THROUGH STRENGTH

Although President Reagan dearly wanted to reduce federal spending and balance the budget, his military buildup made that impossible. But he deemed the protection of U.S. national security the primary obligation of the federal government. "Peace is made by the fact of strength—economic, military, and strategic," he said in a TV address two weeks before the 1980 election. "Peace is lost when such strength disappears or—just as bad—is seen by an adversary as disappearing. We must build peace upon strength. There is no other way. . . . Only if we are strong will peace be strong."

"Peace, Security, and
Freedom across the Globe"

In dramatic remarks delivered at the National Press Club in Wash-
ington, DC, on the morning of November 18, 1981, President Rea-
gan revealed that he had secretly opened high-level diplomatic
correspondence with the leader of the Soviet Union, and proposed
Strategic Arms Reduction Talks (START).

Officers, ladies and gentlemen of the National Press Club, and, as
of a very short time ago, fellow members:

Back in April while in the hospital I had, as you can readily understand, a lot of time for reflection. And one day I decided to send a
personal, handwritten letter to Soviet president Leonid Brezhnev reminding him that we had met about ten years ago in San Clemente,
California, as he and President Nixon were concluding a series of meetings that had brought hope to all the world. Never had peace and goodwill seemed closer at hand.

I'd like to read you a few paragraphs from that letter: "Mr. President:
When we met, I asked if you were aware that the hopes and aspirations
of millions of people throughout the world were dependent on the decisions that would be reached in those meetings. You took my hand in
both of yours and assured me that you were aware of that and that you
were dedicated with all your heart and soul and mind to fulfilling those
hopes and dreams."

I went on in my letter to say, "The people of the world still share
that hope. Indeed, the peoples of the world, despite differences in racial
and ethnic origin, have very much in common. They want the dignity

of having some control over their individual lives, their destiny. They want to work at the craft or trade of their own choosing and to be fairly rewarded. They want to raise their families in peace without harming anyone or suffering harm themselves. Government exists for their convenience, not the other way around.

"If they are incapable, as some would have us believe, of self-government, then where among them do we find any who are capable of governing others?

"Is it possible that we have permitted ideology, political and economic philosophies, and governmental policies to keep us from considering the very real, everyday problems of our peoples? Will the average Soviet family be better off or even aware that the Soviet Union has imposed a government of its own choice on the people of Afghanistan? Is life better for the people of Cuba because the Cuban military dictate who shall govern the people of Angola?

"It is often implied that such things have been made necessary because of territorial ambitions of the United States; that we have imperialistic designs, and thus constitute a threat to your own security and that of the newly emerging nations. Not only is there no evidence to support such a charge; there is solid evidence that the United States, when it could have dominated the world with no risk to itself, made no effort whatsoever to do so.

"When World War II ended, the United States had the only undamaged industrial power in the world. Our military might was at its peak, and we alone had the ultimate weapon, the nuclear weapon, with the unquestioned ability to deliver it anywhere in the world. If we had sought world domination then, who could have opposed us?

"But the United States followed a different course, one unique in all the history of mankind. We used our power and wealth to rebuild the war-ravaged economies of the world, including those of the nations who had been our enemies. May I say, there is absolutely no substance to charges that the United States is guilty of imperialism or attempts to impose its will on other countries, by use of force."

I continued my letter by saying—or concluded my letter, I should say—by saying, "Mr. President, should we not be concerned with eliminating the obstacles which prevent our people, those you and I represent, from achieving their most cherished goals?"

Well, it's in the same spirit that I want to speak today to this audience and the people of the world about America's program for peace and the coming negotiations which begin November 30 in Geneva, Switzerland. Specifically, I want to present our program for preserving peace in Europe and our wider program for arms control.

Twice in my lifetime, I have seen the peoples of Europe plunged into the tragedy of war. Twice in my lifetime, Europe has suffered destruction and military occupation in wars that statesmen proved powerless to prevent, soldiers unable to contain, and ordinary citizens unable to escape. And twice in my lifetime, young Americans have bled their lives into the soil of those battlefields not to enrich or enlarge our domain, but to restore the peace and independence of our friends and allies.

All of us who lived through those troubled times share a common resolve that they must never come again. And most of us share a common appreciation of the Atlantic Alliance that has made a peaceful, free, and prosperous Western Europe in the postwar era possible.

But today, a new generation is emerging on both sides of the Atlantic. Its members were not present at the creation of the North Atlantic Alliance. Many of them don't fully understand its roots in defending freedom and rebuilding a war-torn continent. Some young people question why we need weapons, particularly nuclear weapons, to deter war and to assure peaceful development. They fear that the accumulation of weapons itself may lead to conflagration. Some even propose unilateral disarmament.

I understand their concerns. Their questions deserve to be answered.

But we have an obligation to answer their questions on the basis of judgment and reason and experience. Our policies have resulted in the longest European peace in this century. Wouldn't a rash departure from these policies, as some now suggest, endanger that peace?

From its founding, the Atlantic Alliance has preserved the peace through unity, deterrence, and dialogue. First, we and our allies have stood united by the firm commitment that an attack upon any one of us would be considered an attack upon us all. Second, we and our allies have deterred aggression by maintaining forces strong enough to ensure that any aggressor would lose more from an attack than he could possibly gain. And third, we and our allies have engaged the Soviets in a dialogue about mutual restraint and arms limitations, hoping to reduce the risk of war and the burden of armaments and to lower the barriers that divide East from West.

These three elements of our policy have preserved the peace in Europe for more than a third of a century. They can preserve it for generations to come, so long as we pursue them with sufficient will and vigor.

Today, I wish to reaffirm America's commitment to the Atlantic Alliance and our resolve to sustain the peace. And from my conversations with allied leaders, I know that they also remain true to this tried and proven course.

NATO's policy of peace is based on restraint and balance. No NATO weapons, conventional or nuclear, will ever be used in Europe except in response to attack. NATO's defense plans have been responsible and restrained. The allies remain strong, united, and resolute. But the momentum of the continuing Soviet military buildup threatens both the conventional and the nuclear balance.

Consider the facts. Over the past decade, the United States reduced the size of its armed forces and decreased its military spending. The Soviets steadily increased the number of men under arms. They now number more than double those of the United States. Over the same period, the Soviets expanded their real military spending by about one-third. The Soviet Union increased its inventory of tanks to some fifty thousand, compared to our eleven thousand. Historically a land power, they transformed their navy from a coastal defense force to an open-ocean fleet, while the United States, a sea power with transoceanic alliances, cut its fleet in half.

During a period when NATO deployed no new intermediate-range nuclear missiles and actually withdrew 1,000 nuclear warheads, the Soviet Union deployed more than 750 nuclear warheads on the new SS-20 missiles alone.

Our response to this relentless buildup of Soviet military power has been restrained but firm. We have made decisions to strengthen all three legs of the strategic triad: sea-, land-, and air-based. We have proposed a defense program in the United States for the next five years which will remedy the neglect of the past decade and restore the eroding balance on which our security depends.

I would like to discuss more specifically the growing threat to Western Europe which is posed by the continuing deployment of certain Soviet intermediate-range nuclear missiles. The Soviet Union has three different type such missile systems: the SS-20, the SS-4, and the SS-5, all with the range capable of reaching virtually all of Western Europe. There are other Soviet weapons systems which also represent a major threat.

Now, the only answer to these systems is a comparable threat to Soviet threats, to Soviet targets; in other words, a deterrent preventing the use of these Soviet weapons by the counterthreat of a like response against their own territory. At present, however, there is no equivalent deterrent to these Soviet intermediate missiles. And the Soviets continue to add one new SS-20 a week.

To counter this, the allies agreed in 1979, as part of a two-track decision, to deploy as a deterrent land-based cruise missiles and Pershing

II missiles capable of reaching targets in the Soviet Union. These missiles are to be deployed in several countries of Western Europe. This relatively limited force in no way serves as a substitute for the much larger strategic umbrella spread over our NATO allies. Rather, it provides a vital link between conventional shorter-range nuclear forces in Europe and intercontinental forces in the United States.

Deployment of these systems will demonstrate to the Soviet Union that this link cannot be broken. Deterring war depends on the perceived ability of our forces to perform effectively. The more effective our forces are, the less likely it is that we'll have to use them. So, we and our allies are proceeding to modernize NATO's nuclear forces of intermediate range to meet increased Soviet deployments of nuclear systems threatening Western Europe.

Let me turn now to our hopes for arms control negotiations. There's a tendency to make this entire subject overly complex. I want to be clear and concise. I told you of the letter I wrote to President Brezhnev last April. Well, I've just sent another message to the Soviet leadership. It's a simple, straightforward, yet historic message. The United States proposes the mutual reduction of conventional intermediate-range nuclear and strategic forces. Specifically, I have proposed a four-point agenda to achieve this objective in my letter to President Brezhnev.

The first and most important point concerns the Geneva negotiations. As part of the 1979 two-track decision, NATO made a commitment to seek arms control negotiations with the Soviet Union on intermediate-range nuclear forces. The United States has been preparing for these negotiations through close consultation with our NATO partners.

We're now ready to set forth our proposal. I have informed President Brezhnev that when our delegation travels to the negotiations on intermediate-range, land-based nuclear missiles in Geneva on the thirtieth of this month, my representatives will present the following proposal: The United States is prepared to cancel its deployment of Pershing II and ground-launch cruise missiles if the Soviets will dismantle their SS-20, SS-4, and SS-5 missiles. This would be a historic step. With Soviet agreement, we could together substantially reduce the dread threat of nuclear war which hangs over the people of Europe. This, like the first footstep on the moon, would be a giant step for mankind.

Now, we intend to negotiate in good faith and go to Geneva willing to listen to and consider the proposals of our Soviet counterparts, but let me call to your attention the background against which our proposal is made.

During the past six years, while the United States deployed no new intermediate-range missiles and withdrew 1,000 nuclear warheads from Europe, the Soviet Union deployed 750 warheads on mobile, accurate ballistic missiles. They now have 1,100 warheads on the SS-20s, SS-4s, and 5s. And the United States has no comparable missiles. Indeed, the United States dismantled the last such missile in Europe over fifteen years ago.

As we look to the future of the negotiations, it's also important to address certain Soviet claims, which left unrefuted could become critical barriers to real progress in arms control.

The Soviets assert that a balance of intermediate-range nuclear forces already exists. That assertion is wrong. By any objective measure, as this chart indicates, the Soviet Union has developed an increasingly overwhelming advantage. They now enjoy a superiority on the order of six to one. The red is the Soviet buildup; the blue is our own. That is 1975, and that is 1981.

Now, Soviet spokesmen have suggested that moving their SS-20s behind the Ural Mountains will remove the threat to Europe. Well, as this map demonstrates, the SS-20s, even if deployed behind the Urals, will have a range that puts almost all of Western Europe—the great cities:

Rome, Athens, Paris, London, Brussels, Amsterdam, Berlin, and so many more—all of Scandinavia, all of the Middle East, all of northern Africa, all within range of these missiles which, incidentally, are mobile and can be moved on shorter notice. These little images mark the present location which would give them a range clear out into the Atlantic.

The second proposal that I've made to President Brezhnev concerns strategic weapons. The United States proposes to open negotiations on strategic arms as soon as possible next year.

I have instructed Secretary [of State Alexander] Haig to discuss the timing of such meetings with Soviet representatives. Substance, however, is far more important than timing. As our proposal for the Geneva talks this month illustrates, we can make proposals for genuinely serious reductions, but only if we take the time to prepare carefully.

The United States has been preparing carefully for resumption of strategic arms negotiations because we don't want a repetition of past disappointments. We don't want an arms control process that sends hopes soaring only to end in dashed expectations.

Now, I have informed President Brezhnev that we will seek to negotiate substantial reductions in nuclear arms which would result in levels that are equal and verifiable. Our approach to verification will be to emphasize openness and creativity, rather than the secrecy and suspicion which have undermined confidence in arms control in the past.

While we can hope to benefit from work done over the past decade in strategic arms negotiations, let us agree to do more than simply begin where these previous efforts left off. We can and should attempt major qualitative and quantitative progress. Only such progress can fulfill the hopes of our own people and the rest of the world. And let us see how far we can go in achieving truly substantial reductions in our strategic arsenals.

To symbolize this fundamental change in direction, we will call these negotiations START—Strategic Arms Reduction Talks.

The third proposal I've made to the Soviet Union is that we act to achieve equality at lower levels of conventional forces in Europe. The defense needs of the Soviet Union hardly call for maintaining more combat divisions in East Germany today than were in the whole Allied invasion force that landed in Normandy on D-Day. The Soviet Union could make no more convincing contribution to peace in Europe, and in the world, than by agreeing to reduce its conventional forces significantly and constrain the potential for sudden aggression.

Finally, I have pointed out to President Brezhnev that to maintain peace we must reduce the risks of surprise attack and the chance of war arising out of uncertainty or miscalculation.

I am renewing our proposal for a conference to develop effective measures that would reduce these dangers. At the current Madrid meeting of the Conference on Security and Cooperation in Europe, we're laying the foundation for a Western-proposed conference on disarmament in Europe. This conference would discuss new measures to enhance stability and security in Europe. Agreement in this conference is within reach. I urge the Soviet Union to join us and many other nations who are ready to launch this important enterprise.

All of these proposals are based on the same fair-minded principles—substantial, militarily significant reduction in forces, equal ceilings for similar types of forces, and adequate provisions for verification.

My administration, our country, and I are committed to achieving arms reductions agreements based on these principles. Today I have outlined the kinds of bold, equitable proposals which the world expects of us. But we cannot reduce arms unilaterally. Success can only come if the Soviet Union will share our commitment, if it will demonstrate that its often-repeated professions of concern for peace will be matched by positive action.

Preservation of peace in Europe and the pursuit of arms reduction talks are of fundamental importance. But we must also help to bring peace and security to regions now torn by conflict, external intervention, and war.

The American concept of peace goes well beyond the absence of war. We foresee a flowering of economic growth and individual liberty in a world at peace.

At the economic summit conference in Cancún, I met with the leaders of twenty-one nations and sketched out our approach to global economic growth. We want to eliminate the barriers to trade and investment which hinder these critical incentives to growth, and we're working to develop new programs to help the poorest nations achieve self-sustaining growth.

And terms like "peace" and "security," we have to say, have little meaning for the oppressed and the destitute. They also mean little to the individual whose state has stripped him of human freedom and dignity. Wherever there is oppression, we must strive for the peace and security of individuals as well as states. We must recognize that progress and the pursuit of liberty is a necessary complement to military security. Nowhere has this fundamental truth been more boldly and clearly stated than in the Helsinki Accords of 1975. These accords have not yet been translated into living reality.

Today I've announced an agenda that can help to achieve peace, security, and freedom across the globe. In particular, I have made an important offer to forgo entirely deployment of new American missiles in Europe if the Soviet Union is prepared to respond on an equal footing.

There is no reason why people in any part of the world should have to live in permanent fear of war or its specter. I believe the time has come for all nations to act in a responsible spirit that doesn't threaten other states. I believe the time is right to move forward on arms control and the resolution of critical regional disputes at the conference table. Nothing will have a higher priority for me and for the American people over the coming months and years.

Addressing the United Nations twenty years ago, another American president described the goal that we still pursue today. He said, "If we all can persevere, if we can look beyond our shores and ambitions, then surely the age will dawn in which the strong are just and the weak secure and the peace preserved."

He didn't live to see that goal achieved. I invite all nations to join with America today in the quest for such a world.

Thank you.

"Why Can't We Reduce the Number of Horrendous Weapons?"

In 1932, Eureka College in Illinois awarded Ronald Reagan a bachelor's degree in economics and sociology. Twenty-five years later, he returned to accept an honorary degree. And on May 9, 1982, fifty years after his own graduation, President Reagan used the occasion of a Eureka commencement address, delivered in a fitness center named after him, to lay out a five-point plan for the future of U.S.-Soviet relations.

We are now approaching an extremely important phase in East-West relations as the current Soviet leadership is succeeded by a new generation. Both the current and the new Soviet leadership should realize aggressive policies will meet a firm Western response. On the other hand, a Soviet leadership devoted to improving its people's lives, rather than expanding its armed conquests, will find a sympathetic partner in the West. The West will respond with expanded trade and other forms of cooperation. But all of this depends on Soviet actions.

Standing in the Athenian marketplace two thousand years ago, Demosthenes said, "What sane man would let another man's words rather than his deeds proclaim who is at peace and who is at war with him?"

Peace is not the absence of conflict, but the ability to cope with conflict by peaceful means. I believe we can cope. I believe that the West can fashion a realistic, durable policy that will protect our interests and keep the peace, not just for this generation but for your children and your grandchildren.

I believe such a policy consists of five points: military balance, economic security, regional stability, arms reductions, and dialogue. Now, these are the means by which we can seek peace with the Soviet Union in the years ahead. Today, I want to set this five-point program to guide the future of our East-West relations, set it out for all to hear and see.

First, a sound East-West military balance is absolutely essential. Last week NATO published a comprehensive comparison of its forces with those of the Warsaw Pact. Its message is clear: During the past decade, the Soviet Union has built up its forces across the board. During that same period, the defense expenditures of the United States declined in real terms. The United States has already undertaken steps to recover from that decade of neglect. And I should add that the expenditures of our European allies have increased slowly but steadily, something we often fail to recognize here at home.

The second point on which we must reach consensus with our allies deals with economic security. Consultations are under way among Western nations on the transfer of militarily significant technology and the extension of financial credits to the East, as well as on the question of energy dependence on the East, that energy dependence of Europe. We recognize that some of our allies' economic requirements are distinct from our own. But the Soviets must not have access to Western technology with military applications, and we must not subsidize the

Soviet economy. The Soviet Union must make the difficult choices brought on by its military budgets and economic shortcomings.

The third element is regional stability with peaceful change. Last year, in a speech in Philadelphia and in the summit meetings at Cancún, I outlined the basic American plan to assist the developing world. These principles for economic development remain the foundation of our approach. They represent no threat to the Soviet Union. Yet in many areas of the developing world we find that Soviet arms and Soviet-supported troops are attempting to destabilize societies and extend Moscow's influence.

High on our agenda must be progress toward peace in Afghanistan. The United States is prepared to engage in a serious effort to negotiate an end to the conflict caused by the Soviet invasion of that country. We are ready to cooperate in an international effort to resolve this problem, to secure a full Soviet withdrawal from Afghanistan, and to ensure self-determination for the Afghan people.

In southern Africa, working closely with our Western allies and the African states, we've made real progress toward independence for Namibia. These negotiations, if successful, will result in peaceful and secure conditions throughout southern Africa. The simultaneous withdrawal of Cuban forces from Angola is essential to achieving Namibian independence, as well as creating long-range prospects for peace in the region.

Central America also has become a dangerous point of tension in East-West relations. The Soviet Union cannot escape responsibility for the violence and suffering in the region caused by accelerated transfer of advanced military equipment to Cuba.

However, it was in Western Europe—or Eastern Europe, I should say—that the hopes of the 1970s were greatest, and it's there that they have been the most bitterly disappointed. There was hope that the people of Poland could develop a freer society. But the Soviet Union has refused to allow the people of Poland to decide their own fate, just as it refused to allow the people of Hungary to decide theirs in 1956, or the people of Czechoslovakia in 1968.

If martial law in Poland is lifted, if all the political prisoners are released, and if a dialogue is restored with the Solidarity union, the United States is prepared to join in a program of economic support. Water cannons and clubs against the Polish people are hardly the kind of dialogue that gives us hope. It's up to the Soviets and their client regimes to show good faith by concrete actions.

The fourth point is arms reduction. I know that this weighs heavily on many of your minds. In our 1931 *Prism* [the Eureka College yearbook], we quoted Carl Sandburg, who in his own beautiful way quoted the Mother Prairie, saying, "Have you seen a red sunset drip over one of my cornfields, the shore of night stars, the wave lines of dawn up a wheat valley?" What an idyllic scene that paints in our minds—and what a nightmarish prospect that a huge mushroom cloud might someday destroy such beauty. My duty as president is to ensure that the ultimate nightmare never occurs, that the prairies and the cities and the people who inhabit them remain free and untouched by nuclear conflict.

I wish more than anything there were a simple policy that would eliminate that nuclear danger. But there are only difficult policy choices through which we can achieve a stable nuclear balance at the lowest possible level.

I do not doubt that the Soviet people, and, yes, the Soviet leaders, have an overriding interest in preventing the use of nuclear weapons. The Soviet Union within the memory of its leaders has known the devastation of total conventional war and knows that nuclear war would be even more calamitous. And yet, so far, the Soviet Union has used arms control negotiations primarily as an instrument to restrict U.S. defense programs and, in conjunction with their own arms buildup, a means to enhance Soviet power and prestige.

Unfortunately, for some time suspicions have grown that the Soviet Union has not been living up to its obligations under existing arms control treaties. There is conclusive evidence the Soviet Union has provided toxins to the Laotians and Vietnamese for use against defenseless villagers in Southeast Asia. And the Soviets themselves are employing chemical weapons on the freedom fighters in Afghanistan.

We must establish firm criteria for arms control in the 1980s if we're to secure genuine and lasting restraint on Soviet military programs. . . . We must seek agreements which are verifiable, equitable, and militarily significant. Agreements that provide only the appearance of arms control breed dangerous illusions. . . .

Since the first days of my administration, we've been working on our approach to the crucial issue of strategic arms and the control and negotiations for control of those arms with the Soviet Union. The study and analysis required has been complex and difficult. It had to be undertaken deliberately, thoroughly, and correctly. We've laid a solid basis for these negotiations. We're consulting with congressional leaders and with our allies, and we are now ready to proceed.

The main threat to peace posed by nuclear weapons today is the growing instability of the nuclear balance. This is due to the increasingly destructive potential of the massive Soviet buildup in its ballistic missile force.

Therefore, our goal is to enhance deterrence and achieve stability through significant reductions in the most destabilizing nuclear systems, ballistic missiles, and especially the giant intercontinental ballistic missiles, while maintaining a nuclear capability sufficient to deter conflict, to underwrite our national security, and to meet our commitment to allies and friends.

For the immediate future, I'm asking my START . . . negotiating team to propose to their Soviet counterparts a practical, phased reduction plan. The focus of our efforts will be to reduce significantly the most destabilizing systems, the ballistic missiles, the number of warheads they carry, and their overall destructive potential.

At the first phase, or the end of the first phase of START, I expect ballistic missile warheads, the most serious threat we face, to be reduced to equal levels, equal ceilings, at least a third below the current levels. To enhance stability, I would ask that no more than half of those warheads be land-based. I hope that these warhead reductions, as well as significant reductions in missiles themselves, could be achieved as rapidly as possible.

In a second phase, we'll seek to achieve an equal ceiling on other elements of our strategic nuclear forces, including limits on the ballistic missile throw-weight at less than current American levels. In both phases, we shall insist on verification procedures to ensure compliance with the agreement.

This, I might say, will be the twentieth time that we have sought such negotiations with the Soviet Union since World War II. The monumental task of reducing and reshaping our strategic forces to enhance stability will take many years of concentrated effort. But I believe that it will be possible to reduce the risks of war by removing the instabilities that now exist and by dismantling the nuclear menace.

I have written to President Brezhnev and directed Secretary Haig to approach the Soviet government concerning the initiation of formal negotiations on the reduction of strategic nuclear arms, START, at the earliest opportunity. We hope negotiations will begin by the end of June.

We will negotiate seriously, in good faith, and carefully consider all proposals made by the Soviet Union. If they approach these negotiations in the same spirit, I'm confident that together we can achieve an agreement of enduring value that reduces the number of nuclear weapons, halts the growth in strategic forces, and opens the way to even more far-reaching steps in the future. . . .

The fifth and final point I propose for East-West relations is dialogue. I've always believed that people's problems can be solved when people talk to each other instead of about each other. And I've already expressed my own desire to meet with President Brezhnev in New York next month. If this can't be done, I'd hope we could arrange a future meeting where positive results can be anticipated. And when we sit down, I'll tell President Brezhnev that the United States is ready to build a new understanding based upon the principles I've outlined today.

I'll tell him that his government and his people have nothing to fear from the United States. The free nations living at peace in the world community can vouch for the fact that we seek only harmony. And I'll ask President Brezhnev why our two nations can't practice mutual restraint. Why can't our peoples enjoy the benefits that would flow from real cooperation? Why can't we reduce the number of horrendous weapons?

Perhaps I should also speak to him of this school and these graduates who are leaving it today—of your hopes for the future, of your deep desire for peace, and yet your strong commitment to defend your values if threatened. Perhaps if he someday could attend such a ceremony as this, he'd better understand America. In the only system he knows, you would be here by the decision of government, and on this day the government representatives would be here telling most, if not all, of you where you were going to report to work tomorrow.

But as we go to Europe for the talks and as we proceed in the important challenges facing this country, I want you to know that I will be thinking of you and of Eureka and what you represent. In one of my yearbooks, I remember reading that "the work of the prairie is to be the soil for the growth of a strong Western culture." I believe Eureka is fulfilling that work. You, the members of the 1982 graduating class, are this year's harvest.

I spoke of the difference between our two countries. I try to follow the humor of the Russian people. We don't hear much about the Russian people. We hear about the Russian leaders. But you can learn a lot, because they do have a sense of humor, and you can learn from the jokes they're telling. And one of the most recent jokes I found kind of, well, personally interesting. Maybe [it] might—tell you something about their country.

The joke they tell is that an American and a Russian were arguing about the differences between our two countries. And the American said, "Look, in my country I can walk into the Oval Office; I can hit the desk with my fist and say, 'President Reagan, I don't like the way you're governing the United States.'" And the Russian said, "I can do that." The American said, "What?" He says, "I can walk into the Kremlin, into Brezhnev's office. I can pound Brezhnev's desk, and I can say, 'Mr. President, I don't like the way Ronald Reagan is governing the United States.'" [*Laughter*]

Eureka as an institution and you as individuals are sustaining the best of Western man's ideals. As a fellow graduate and in the office I hold, I'll do my best to uphold these same ideals.

To the class of '82, congratulations, and God bless you.

"A Paper Castle That Will Be Blown Away by the Winds of War"

On June 17, 1982, President Reagan for the first time addressed the United Nations General Assembly in New York, as part of a special session the UN was hosting that summer on the subject of disarmament. Lou Cannon, a White House correspondent for the Washington Post *who would later become a Reagan biographer, described*

this as "the most harshly worded address ever delivered to the
world body by an American president"—harsh in its criticism of
both the Soviet Union and any disarmament process that put talk
before verifiable action.

Mr. Secretary-General, Mr. President, distinguished delegates, ladies and gentlemen:

I speak today as both a citizen of the United States and of the world. I come with the heartfelt wishes of my people for peace, bearing honest proposals and looking for genuine progress.

[The late UN secretary-general] Dag Hammarskjöld said twenty-four years ago this month, "We meet in a time of peace, which is no peace." His words are as true today as they were then. More than a hundred disputes have disturbed the peace among nations since World War II, and today the threat of nuclear disaster hangs over the lives of all our people. The Bible tells us there will be a time for peace, but so far this century mankind has failed to find it.

The United Nations is dedicated to world peace, and its charter clearly prohibits the international use of force. Yet the tide of belligerence continues to rise. The charter's influence has weakened even in the four years since the first special session on disarmament. We must not only condemn aggression; we must enforce the dictates of our charter and resume the struggle for peace.

The record of history is clear: Citizens of the United States resort to force reluctantly and only when they must. Our foreign policy, as President Eisenhower once said, "is not difficult to state. We are for peace first, last, and always for very simple reasons." We know that only in a peaceful atmosphere, a peace with justice, one in which we can be confident, can America prosper as we have known prosperity in the past, he said.

He said to those who challenge the truth of those words, let me point out, at the end of World War II, we were the only undamaged industrial power in the world. Our military supremacy was unquestioned. We had harnessed the atom and had the ability to unleash its destructive force anywhere in the world. In short, we could have achieved world domination, but that was contrary to the character of our people. Instead, we wrote a new chapter in the history of mankind.

We used our power and wealth to rebuild the war-ravaged economies of the world, both East and West, including those nations who had been our enemies. We took the initiative in creating such international institutions as this United Nations, where leaders of goodwill could come together to build bridges for peace and prosperity.

America has no territorial ambitions. We occupy no countries, and we have built no walls to lock our people in. Our commitment to self-determination, freedom, and peace is the very soul of America. That commitment is as strong today as it ever was.

The United States has fought four wars in my lifetime. In each, we struggled to defend freedom and democracy. We were never the aggressors. America's strength and, yes, her military power have been a force for peace, not conquest; for democracy, not despotism; for freedom, not tyranny. Watching, as I have, succeeding generations of American youth bleed their lives onto far-flung battlefields to protect our ideals and secure the rule of law, I have known how important it is to deter conflict. But since coming to the presidency, the enormity of the responsibility of this office has made my commitment even deeper. I believe that responsibility is shared by all of us here today.

On our recent trip to Europe, my wife, Nancy, told me of a bronze statue, twenty-two feet high, that she saw on a cliff on the coast of France. The beach at the base of the cliff is called Saint Laurent, but countless American family Bibles have written it in on the flyleaf and know it as Omaha Beach. The pastoral quiet of that French countryside is in marked contrast to the bloody violence that took place there on a June day thirty-eight years ago when the Allies stormed the continent. At the end of just one day of battle, 10,500 Americans were wounded, missing, or killed in what became known as the Normandy landing.

The statue atop that cliff is called The Spirit of American Youth Rising from the Waves. Its image of sacrifice is almost too powerful to describe.

The pain of war is still vivid in our national memory. It sends me to this special session of the United Nations eager to comply with the plea of Pope Paul VI when he spoke in this chamber nearly seventeen years ago. "If you want to be brothers," His Holiness said, "let the arms fall from your hands." Well, we Americans yearn to let them go. But we need more than mere words, more than empty promises, before we can proceed.

We look around the world and see rampant conflict and aggression. There are many sources of this conflict—expansionist ambitions, local rivalries, the striving to obtain justice and security. We must all work to resolve such discords by peaceful means and to prevent them from escalation.

In the nuclear era, the major powers bear a special responsibility to ease these sources of conflict and to refrain from aggression. And that's why we're so deeply concerned by Soviet conduct. Since World War II, the record of tyranny has included Soviet violation of the Yalta agreements leading to domination of Eastern Europe, symbolized by the Berlin Wall—a grim, gray monument to repression that I visited just a week ago. It includes the takeovers of Czechoslovakia, Hungary, and Afghanistan; and the ruthless repression of the proud people of Poland. Soviet-sponsored guerrillas and terrorists are at work in Central and South America, in Africa, the Middle East, in the Caribbean, and in Europe, violating human rights and unnerving the world with violence.

Communist atrocities in Southeast Asia, Afghanistan, and elsewhere continue to shock the free world as refugees escape to tell of their horror.

The decade of so-called détente witnessed the most massive Soviet buildup of military power in history. They increased their defense spending by 40 percent while American defense actually declined in the same real terms. Soviet aggression and support for violence around the world have eroded the confidence needed for arms negotiations. While we exercised unilateral restraint, they forged ahead and today possess nuclear and conventional forces far in excess of an adequate deterrent capability.

Soviet oppression is not limited to the countries they invade. At the very time the Soviet Union is trying to manipulate the peace movement in the West, it is stifling a budding peace movement at home. In Moscow, banners are scuttled, buttons are snatched, and demonstrators are arrested when even a few people dare to speak about their fears.

Eleanor Roosevelt, one of our first ambassadors to this body, reminded us that the high-sounding words of tyrants stand in bleak contradiction to their deeds. "Their promises," she said, "are in deep contrast to their performances."

My country learned a bitter lesson in this century: The scourge of tyranny cannot be stopped with words alone. So, we have embarked on an effort to renew our strength that had fallen dangerously low. We refuse to become weaker while potential adversaries remain committed to their imperialist adventures.

My people have sent me here today to speak for them as citizens of the world, which they truly are, for we Americans are drawn from every nationality represented in this chamber today. We understand that men and women of every race and creed can and must work together for peace. We stand ready to take the next steps down the road of cooperation through verifiable arms reduction.

Agreements on arms control and disarmament can be useful in reinforcing peace; but they're not magic. We should not confuse the signing of agreements with the solving of problems. Simply collecting agreements will not bring peace. Agreements genuinely reinforce peace only when they are kept. Otherwise we're building a paper castle that will be blown away by the winds of war.

Let me repeat, we need deeds, not words, to convince us of Soviet sincerity, should they choose to join us on this path.

Since the end of World War II, the United States has been the leader in serious disarmament and arms control proposals. In 1946, in what became known as the Baruch Plan, the United States submitted a proposal for control of nuclear weapons and nuclear energy by an international authority. The Soviets rejected this plan. In 1955 President Eisenhower made his Open Skies proposal, under which the United States and the Soviet Union would have exchanged blueprints of military establishments and provided for aerial reconnaissance. The Soviets rejected this plan.

In 1963 the Limited Test Ban Treaty came into force. This treaty ended nuclear weapons testing in the atmosphere, outer space, or underwater by participating nations. In 1970 the Treaty on the Non-Proliferation of Nuclear Weapons took effect. The United States played a major role in this key effort to prevent the spread of nuclear explosives and to provide for international safeguards on civil nuclear activities.

My country remains deeply committed to those objectives today, and to strengthening the nonproliferation framework. This is essential to international security. In the early 1970s, again at United States urging, agreements were reached between the United States and the USSR providing for ceilings on some categories of weapons. They could have been more meaningful if Soviet actions had shown restraint and commitment to stability at lower levels of force.

The United Nations designated the 1970s as the first disarmament decade. But good intentions were not enough. In reality that ten-year period included an unprecedented buildup in military weapons and the flaring of aggression and use of force in almost every region of the world. We are now in the second disarmament decade. The task at hand is to assure civilized behavior among nations, to unite behind an agenda of peace.

Over the past seven months, the United States has put forward a broad-based, comprehensive series of proposals to reduce the risk of war. We have proposed four major points as an agenda for peace: elimination of land-based, intermediate-range missiles; a one-third reduction in strategic ballistic missile warheads; a substantial reduction in NATO and Warsaw Pact ground and air forces; and new safeguards to reduce the risk of accidental war. We urge the Soviet Union today to join with us in this quest. We must act not for ourselves alone, but for all mankind.

On November 18 of last year, I announced United States objectives in arms control agreements. They must be equitable and militarily significant. They must stabilize forces at lower levels, and they must be verifiable. The United States and its allies have made specific, reasonable, and equitable proposals.

In February, our negotiating team in Geneva offered the Soviet Union a draft treaty on intermediate-range nuclear forces. We offered to cancel deployment of our Pershing II ballistic missiles and ground-launched cruise missiles in exchange for Soviet elimination of the SS-20, SS-4, and SS-5 missiles. This proposal would eliminate with one stroke those systems about which both sides have expressed the greatest concern.

The United States is also looking forward to beginning negotiations on strategic arms reductions with the Soviet Union in less than two weeks. We will work hard to make these talks an opportunity for real progress in our quest for peace.

On May 9 I announced a phased approach to the reduction of strategic arms. In a first phase, the number of ballistic missile warheads on each side would be reduced to about five thousand. No more than half the remaining warheads would be on land-based missiles. All ballistic missiles would be reduced to an equal level, at about one-half the current United States number. In the second phase, we would reduce each side's overall destructive power to equal levels, including a mutual ceiling on ballistic missile throw-weight below the current U.S. level. We are also prepared to discuss other elements of the strategic balance.

Before I returned from Europe last week, I met in Bonn with the leaders of the North Atlantic Treaty Organization. We agreed to introduce a major new Western initiative for the Vienna negotiations on Mutual Balanced Force Reductions. Our approach calls for common, collective ceilings for both NATO and the Warsaw Treaty Organization. After seven years, there would be a total of 700,000 ground forces and 900,000 ground and air force personnel combined. It also includes a package of associated measures to encourage cooperation and verify compliance.

We urge the Soviet Union and members of the Warsaw Pact to view our Western proposal as a means to reach agreement in Vienna after nine long years of inconclusive talks. We also urge them to implement the 1975 Helsinki agreement on security and cooperation in Europe.

Let me stress that for agreements to work, both sides must be able to verify compliance. The building of mutual confidence in compliance can only be achieved through greater openness. I encourage the special session on disarmament to endorse the importance of these principles in arms control agreements. I have instructed our representatives at the forty-nation Committee on Disarmament to renew emphasis on verification and compliance. Based on a U.S. proposal, a committee has been formed to examine these issues as they relate to restrictions on nuclear testing.

We are also pressing the need for effective verification provisions in agreements banning chemical weapons. The use of chemical and biological weapons has long been viewed with revulsion by civilized nations. No peacemaking institution can ignore the use of those dread weapons and still live up to its mission. The need for a truly effective and verifiable chemical weapons agreement has been highlighted by recent events. The Soviet Union and their allies are violating the Geneva Protocol of 1925, related rules of international law, and the 1972 Biological Weapons Convention. There is conclusive evidence that the Soviet government has provided toxins for use in Laos and Kampuchea [Cambodia], and are themselves using chemical weapons against freedom fighters in Afghanistan.

We have repeatedly protested to the Soviet government, as well as to the governments of Laos and Vietnam, their use of chemical and toxin weapons. We call upon them now to grant full and free access to their countries or to territories they control so that United Nations experts can conduct an effective, independent investigation to verify cessation of these horrors.

Evidence of noncompliance with existing arms control agreements underscores the need to approach negotiation of any new agreements with care. The democracies of the West are open societies. Information on our defenses is available to our citizens, our elected officials, and the world. We do not hesitate to inform potential adversaries of our military forces and ask in return for the same information concerning theirs.

The amount and type of military spending by a country is important for the world to know, as a measure of its intentions and the threat that country may pose to its neighbors. The Soviet Union and other closed societies go to extraordinary lengths to hide their true military spending, not only from other nations but from their own people. This practice contributes to distrust and fear about their intentions.

Today, the United States proposes an international conference on military expenditures to build on the work of this body in developing a common system for accounting and reporting. We urge the Soviet Union, in particular, to join this effort in good faith, to revise the universally discredited official figures it publishes, and to join with us in giving the world a true account of the resources we allocate to our armed forces.

Last Friday in Berlin, I said that I would leave no stone unturned in the effort to reinforce peace and lessen the risk of war. It's been clear to me steps should be taken to improve mutual communication, confidence, and lessen the likelihood of misinterpretation. I have, therefore, directed the exploration of ways to increase understanding and communication between the United States and the Soviet Union in times of peace and of crisis.

We will approach the Soviet Union with proposals for reciprocal exchanges in such areas as advance notification of major strategic exercises that otherwise might be misinterpreted; advance notification of ICBM launches within, as well as beyond, national boundaries; and an expanded exchange of strategic forces data.

While substantial information on U.S. activities and forces in these areas already is provided, I believe that jointly and regularly sharing information would represent a qualitative improvement in the strategic nuclear environment and would help reduce the chance of misunderstandings. I call upon the Soviet Union to join the United States in exploring these possibilities to build confidence, and I ask for your support of our efforts.

One of the major items before this conference is the development of a comprehensive program of disarmament. We support the effort to chart a course of realistic and effective measures in the quest for peace.

I have come to this hall to call for international recommitment to the basic tenet of the United Nations Charter—that all members practice tolerance and live together in peace as good neighbors under the rule of law, forsaking armed force as a means of settling disputes between nations. America urges you to support the agenda for peace that I have outlined today. We ask you to reinforce the bilateral and multilateral arms control negotiations between members of NATO and the Warsaw Pact and to rededicate yourselves to maintaining international peace and security, and removing threats to peace.

We, who have signed the UN Charter, have pledged to refrain from the threat or use of force against the territory or independence of any state. In these times when more and more lawless acts are going unpunished—as some members of this very body show a growing disregard for the UN Charter—the peace-loving nations of the world must condemn aggression and pledge again to act in a way that is worthy of the ideals that we have endorsed. Let us finally make the charter live.

In late spring, thirty-seven years ago, representatives of fifty nations gathered on the other side of this continent, in the San Francisco Opera House. The League of Nations had crumbled, and World War II still raged. But those men and nations were determined to find peace. The result was this charter for peace that is the framework of the United Nations.

President Harry Truman spoke of the revival of an old faith. He said the everlasting moral force of justice prompting that United Nations conference—such a force remains strong in America and in other countries where speech is free and citizens have the right to gather and make their opinions known. And President Truman said, "If we should pay merely lip service to inspiring ideals, and later do violence to simple justice, we would draw down upon us the bitter wrath of generations yet unborn." Those words of Harry Truman have special meaning for us today as we live with the potential to destroy civilization.

"We must learn to live together in peace," he said. "We must build a new world—a far better world." What a better world it would be if the guns were silent, if neighbor no longer encroached on neighbor, and all peoples were free to reap the rewards of their toil and determine their own destiny and system of government, whatever their choice.

During my recent audience with His Holiness Pope John Paul II, I gave him the pledge of the American people to do everything possible for peace and arms reduction. The American people believe forging real and lasting peace to be their sacred trust. Let us never forget that such a peace would be a terrible hoax if the world were no longer blessed with freedom and respect for human rights.

"The United Nations," Hammarskjöld said, "was born out of the cataclysms of war. It should justify the sacrifices of all those who have died for freedom and justice. It is our duty to the past." Hammarskjöld said, "And it is our duty to the future so to serve both our nations and the world."

As both patriots of our nations and the hope of all the world, let those of us assembled here in the name of peace deepen our understandings, renew our commitment to the rule of law, and take new and bolder steps to calm an uneasy world. Can any delegate here deny that in so doing he would be doing what the people, the rank and file of his own country or her own country, want him or her to do? Isn't it time for us to really represent the deepest, most heartfelt yearnings of all of our people?

Let no nation abuse this common longing to be free of fear. We must not manipulate our people by playing upon their nightmares. We must serve mankind through genuine disarmament. With God's help we can secure life and freedom for generations to come.

Thank you very much.

"I Believe Our Strategy for
Peace Will Succeed"

*President Reagan's televised Oval Office address on November 22,
1982, was a masterly example of his explanatory style. He took
complicated strategic and technical matters and explained them
with convincing clarity—making the case not only for the new MX
intercontinental ballistic missile, but also for his general approach
to nuclear deterrence and arms reductions.*

Good evening.

The week before last was an especially moving one here in Washington. The Vietnam veterans finally came home once and for all to America's heart. [The Vietnam Veterans Memorial was dedicated on November 13, 1982.] They were welcomed with tears, with pride, and with a monument to their great sacrifice. Many of their names, like those of our republic's greatest citizens, are now engraved in stone in this city that belongs to all of us. On behalf of the nation, let me again thank the Vietnam veterans from the bottom of my heart for their courageous service to America.

Seeing those moving scenes, I know mothers of a new generation must have worried about their children and about peace. And that's what I'd like to talk to you about tonight—the future of our children in a world where peace is made uneasy by the presence of nuclear weapons.

A year ago, I said the time was right to move forward on arms control. I outlined several proposals and said nothing would have a higher priority in this administration. Now, a year later, I want to report on those proposals and on other efforts we're making to ensure the safety of our children's future.

The prevention of conflict and the reduction of weapons are the most important public issues of our time. Yet, on no other issue are there more misconceptions and misunderstandings. You, the American people, deserve an explanation from your government on what our policy is on these issues. Too often, the experts have been content to discuss grandiose strategies among themselves and cloud the public debate in technicalities no one can understand. The result is that many Americans have become frightened. And let me say, fear of the unknown is entirely understandable. Unfortunately, much of the information emerging in this debate bears little semblance to the facts.

To begin, let's go back to what the world was like at the end of World War II. The United States was the only undamaged industrial power in the world. Our military power was at its peak, and we alone had the atomic weapon. But we didn't use this wealth and this power to bully; we used it to rebuild. We raised up the war-ravaged economies, including the economies of those who had fought against us. At first, the peace of the world was unthreatened, because we alone were left with any real power, and we were using it for the good of our fellow man. Any potential enemy was deterred from aggression because the cost would have far outweighed the gain.

As the Soviets' power grew, we still managed to maintain the peace. The United States had established a system of alliances, with NATO as the centerpiece. In addition, we grew even more respected as a world leader with a strong economy and deeply held moral values.

With our commitment to help shape a better world, the United States also pursued, and always pursued, every diplomatic channel for peace. And for at least thirty years after World War II, the United States still continued to possess a large military advantage over the Soviet Union. Our strength deterred—that is, prevented—aggression against us.

This nation's military objective has always been to maintain peace by preventing war. This is neither a Democratic nor a Republican policy. It's supported by our allies. And most important of all, it's worked for nearly forty years.

What do we mean when we speak of "nuclear deterrence"? Certainly, we don't want such weapons for their own sake. We don't desire excessive forces or what some people have called "overkill." Basically, it's a matter of others knowing that starting a conflict would be more costly to them than anything they might hope to gain. And, yes, it is sadly ironic that in these modern times, it still takes weapons to prevent war. I wish it did not.

We desire peace. But peace is a goal, not a policy. Lasting peace is what we hope for at the end of our journey; it doesn't describe the steps we must take nor the paths we should follow to reach that goal.

I intend to search for peace along two parallel paths: deterrence and arms reductions. I believe these are the only paths that offer any real hope for an enduring peace.

And let me say I believe that if we follow prudent policies, the risk of nuclear conflict will be reduced. Certainly, the United States will never use its forces except in response to attack. Through the years, Soviet leaders have also expressed a sober view of nuclear war. And if we maintain a strong deterrent, they are exceedingly unlikely to launch an attack. . . .

The Soviet military buildup must not be ignored. We've recognized the problem and, together with our allies, we've begun to correct the imbalance. Look at this chart of projected real defense spending for the next several years. Here is the Soviet line. Let us assume the Soviets' rate of spending remains at the level they've followed since the 1960s. The blue line is the United States. If my defense proposals are passed, it will still take five years before we come close to the Soviet level. Yet, the modernization of our strategic and conventional forces will assure that deterrence works and peace prevails.

Our deployed nuclear forces were built before the age of microcir-cuits. It's not right to ask our young men and women in uniform to maintain and operate such antiques. Many have already given their lives to missile explosions and aircraft accidents caused by the old age of their equipment. We must replace and modernize our forces, and that's why I decided to proceed with the production and deployment of the new ICBM known as the MX.

Three earlier presidents worked to develop this missile. Based on the best advice that I could get, I concluded that the MX is the right missile at the right time. On the other hand, when I arrived in office I felt the proposal on where and how to base the missile simply cost too much in terms of money and the impact on our citizens' lives. I've concluded, however, it's absolutely essential that we proceed to produce this missile and that we base it in a series of closely based silos at Warren Air Force Base, near Cheyenne, Wyoming.

This plan requires only half as many missiles as the earlier plan and will fit in an area of only twenty square miles. It is the product of around-the-clock research that has been underway since I directed a search for a better, cheaper way. I urge the members of Congress who must pass this plan to listen and examine the facts before they come to their own conclusion.

Some may question what modernizing our military has to do with peace. Well, as I explained earlier, a secure force keeps others from threatening us, and that keeps the peace. And just as important, it also increases the prospects of reaching significant arms reductions with the Soviets, and that's what we really want.

The United States wants deep cuts in the world's arsenal of weap-ons, but unless we demonstrate the will to rebuild our strength and restore the military balance, the Soviets, since they're so far ahead, have little incentive to negotiate with us. Let me repeat that point because it goes to the heart of our policies. Unless we demonstrate the will to rebuild our strength, the Soviets have little incentive to negotiate. If we hadn't begun to modernize, the Soviet negotiators would know we had nothing to bargain with except talk. They would know we were bluffing without a good hand, because they know what cards we hold just as we know what's in their hand.

You may recall that in 1969 the Soviets didn't want to negotiate a treaty banning antiballistic missiles. It was only after our Senate narrowly voted to fund an antiballistic missile program that the Soviets agreed to negotiate. We then reached an agreement. We also know that one-sided arms control doesn't work. We've tried time and time again to set an example by cutting our own forces in the hope that the Soviets would do likewise. The result has always been that they keep building.

I believe our strategy for peace will succeed. Never before has the United States proposed such a comprehensive program of nuclear arms control. Never in our history have we engaged in so many negotiations with the Soviets to reduce nuclear arms and to find a stable peace. What we are saying to them is this: We will modernize our military in order to keep the balance for peace, but wouldn't it be better if we both simply reduced our arsenals to a much lower level? . . .

In 1977, when the last administration proposed more limited reductions, the Soviet Union refused even to discuss them. This time their reaction has been quite different. Their opening position is a serious one, and even though it doesn't meet our objective of deep reductions, there's no question we're heading in the right direction. One reason for this change is clear. The Soviet Union knows that we are now serious about our own strategic programs and that they must be prepared to negotiate in earnest. . . .

Earlier, I spoke of America's contributions to peace following World War II, of all we did to promote peace and prosperity for our fellow man. Well, we're still those same people. We still seek peace above all else.

I want to remind our own citizens and those around the world of this tradition of American goodwill, because I am concerned about the effects the nuclear fear is having on our people. The most upsetting letters I receive are from schoolchildren who write to me as a class assignment. It's evident they've discussed the most nightmarish aspects of a nuclear holocaust in their classrooms. Their letters are often full of terror. Well, this should not be so.

The philosopher Spinoza said, "Peace is a virtue, a state of mind, a disposition for benevolence, confidence, justice." Well, those are the qualities we want our children to inherit, not fear. They must grow up confident if they're to meet the challenges of tomorrow as we will meet the challenges of today.

I began these remarks speaking of our children. I want to close on the same theme. Our children should not grow up frightened. They should not fear the future. We're working to make it peaceful and free. I believe their future can be the brightest, most exciting of any generation. We must reassure them and let them know that their parents and the leaders of this world are seeking, above all else, to keep them safe and at peace. I consider this to be a sacred trust.

My fellow Americans, on this Thanksgiving when we have so much to be grateful for, let us give special thanks for our peace, our freedom, and our good people.

I've always believed that this land was set aside in an uncommon way, that a divine plan placed this great continent between the oceans to be found by a people from every corner of the earth who had a special love of faith, freedom, and peace.

Let us reaffirm America's destiny of goodness and goodwill. Let us work for peace and, as we do, let us remember the lines of the famous old hymn: "O God of Love, O King of Peace, make wars throughout the world to cease."

Thank you. Good night, and God bless you.

The "Star Wars" Speech

In a half-hour televised Oval Office address on the evening of March 23, 1983, President Reagan set forth an idea that would change the dynamics of the Cold War: the creation of a defensive system capable of tracking and destroying enemy ballistic missiles before they reached U.S. or allied targets. If such a system could be built, it would render obsolete the strategic concept of "mutual assured destruction" under which the world's two superpowers had, as Reagan said elsewhere, long held "each other hostage to nuclear terror and destruction," a policy he considered "downright immoral." The Reagan administration's antimissile program was called the Strategic Defense Initiative—although when critics mockingly called it the "Star Wars" program, that nickname stuck.

My fellow Americans, thank you for sharing your time with me tonight.

The subject I want to discuss with you, peace and national security, is both timely and important. Timely, because I've reached a decision which offers a new hope for our children in the twenty-first century, a decision I'll tell you about in a few minutes. And important because there's a very big decision that you must make for yourselves. This subject involves the most basic duty that any president and any people share, the duty to protect and strengthen the peace.

At the beginning of this year, I submitted to the Congress a defense budget which reflects my best judgment of the best understanding of the experts and specialists who advise me about what we and our allies must do to protect our people in the years ahead. That budget is much more than a long list of numbers, for behind all the numbers lies

America's ability to prevent the greatest of human tragedies and preserve our free way of life in a sometimes dangerous world. It is part of a careful, long-term plan to make America strong again after too many years of neglect and mistakes.

Our efforts to rebuild America's defenses and strengthen the peace began two years ago, when we requested a major increase in the defense program. Since then, the amount of those increases we first proposed has been reduced by half, through improvements in management and procurement and other savings.

The budget request that is now before the Congress has been trimmed to the limits of safety. Further deep cuts cannot be made without seriously endangering the security of the nation. The choice is up to the men and women you've elected to the Congress, and that means the choice is up to you.

Tonight, I want to explain to you what this defense debate is all about and why I'm convinced that the budget now before the Congress is necessary, responsible, and deserving of your support. And I want to offer hope for the future. . . .

The defense policy of the United States is based on a simple premise: The United States does not start fights. We will never be an aggressor. We maintain our strength in order to deter and defend against aggression—to preserve freedom and peace.

Since the dawn of the atomic age, we've sought to reduce the risk of war by maintaining a strong deterrent and by seeking genuine arms control. "Deterrence" means simply this: making sure any adversary who thinks about attacking the United States, or our allies, or our vital interests, concludes that the risks to him outweigh any potential gains. Once he understands that, he won't attack. We maintain the peace through our strength; weakness only invites aggression.

This strategy of deterrence has not changed. It still works. But what it takes to maintain deterrence has changed. It took one kind of military force to deter an attack when we had far more nuclear weapons than any other power; it takes another kind now that the Soviets, for example, have enough accurate and powerful nuclear weapons to destroy virtually all of our missiles on the ground. Now, this is not to say that the Soviet Union is planning to make war on us. Nor do I believe a war is inevitable—quite the contrary. But what must be recognized is that our security is based on being prepared to meet all threats.

There was a time when we depended on coastal forts and artillery batteries, because, with the weaponry of that day, any attack would have had to come by sea. Well, this is a different world, and our defenses must be based on recognition and awareness of the weaponry possessed by other nations in the nuclear age.

We can't afford to believe that we will never be threatened. There have been two world wars in my lifetime. We didn't start them and, indeed, did everything we could to avoid being drawn into them. But we were ill-prepared for both. Had we been better prepared, peace might have been preserved.

For twenty years the Soviet Union has been accumulating enormous military might. They didn't stop when their forces exceeded all requirements of a legitimate defensive capability. And they haven't stopped now. During the past decade and a half, the Soviets have built up a massive arsenal of new strategic nuclear weapons—weapons that can strike directly at the United States.

As an example, the United States introduced its last new intercontinental ballistic missile, the Minute Man III, in 1969, and we're now dismantling our even older Titan missiles. But what has the Soviet Union done in these intervening years? Well, since 1969 the Soviet Union has built five new classes of ICBMs, and upgraded these eight times. As a result, their missiles are much more powerful and accurate than they were several years ago, and they continue to develop more, while ours are increasingly obsolete.

The same thing has happened in other areas. Over the same period, the Soviet Union built 4 new classes of submarine-launched ballistic missiles and over 60 new missile submarines. We built 2 new types of submarine missiles and actually withdrew 10 submarines from strategic missions. The Soviet Union built over 200 new Backfire bombers, and their brand-new Blackjack bomber is now under development. We haven't built a new long-range bomber since our B-52s were deployed about a quarter of a century ago, and we've already retired several hundred of those because of old age. Indeed, despite what many people think, our strategic forces only cost about 15 percent of the defense budget.

Another example of what's happened: In 1978 the Soviets had 600 intermediate-range nuclear missiles based on land and were beginning to add the SS-20—a new, highly accurate, mobile missile with 3 warheads. We had none. Since then the Soviets have strengthened their lead. By the end of 1979, when Soviet leader Brezhnev declared "a balance now exists," the Soviets had over 800 warheads. We still had none. A year ago this month, Mr. Brezhnev pledged a moratorium, or freeze, on SS-20 deployment. But by last August, their 800 warheads had become more than 1,200. We still had none. Some freeze. At this time Soviet Defense Minister Ustinov announced "approximate parity of forces continues to exist." But the Soviets are still adding an average of 3 new warheads a week, and now have 1,300. These warheads can reach their targets in a matter of a few minutes. We still have none. So far, it seems that the Soviet definition of parity is a box score of 1,300 to nothing, in their favor.

So, together with our NATO allies, we decided in 1979 to deploy new weapons, beginning this year, as a deterrent to their SS-20s and as an incentive to the Soviet Union to meet us in serious arms control negotiations. We will begin that deployment late this year. At the same time, however, we're willing to cancel our program if the Soviets will dismantle theirs. This is what we've called a zero-zero plan. The Soviets are now at the negotiating table—and I think it's fair to say that without our planned deployments, they wouldn't be there.

Now, let's consider conventional forces. Since 1974 the United States has produced 3,050 tactical combat aircraft. By contrast, the Soviet Union has produced twice as many. When we look at attack submarines, the United States has produced 27 while the Soviet Union has produced 61. For armored vehicles, including tanks, we have produced 11,200. The Soviet Union has produced 54,000—nearly 5 to 1 in their favor. Finally, with artillery, we've produced 950 artillery and rocket launchers while the Soviets have produced more than 13,000—a staggering 14-to-1 ratio.

There was a time when we were able to offset superior Soviet numbers with higher quality, but today they are building weapons as sophisticated and modern as our own. . . .

Some people may still ask: Would the Soviets ever use their formidable military power? Well, again, can we afford to believe they won't? There is Afghanistan. And in Poland, the Soviets denied the will of the people and in so doing demonstrated to the world how their military power could also be used to intimidate.

The final fact is that the Soviet Union is acquiring what can only be considered an offensive military force. They have continued to build far more intercontinental ballistic missiles than they could possibly need simply to deter an attack. Their conventional forces are trained and equipped not so much to defend against an attack as they are to permit sudden, surprise offensives of their own.

Our NATO allies have assumed a great defense burden, including the military draft in most countries. We're working with them and our other friends around the world to do more. Our defensive strategy means we need military forces that can move very quickly, forces that are trained and ready to respond to any emergency.

Every item in our defense program—our ships, our tanks, our planes, our funds for training and spare parts—is intended for one all-important purpose: to keep the peace. Unfortunately, a decade of neglecting our military forces had called into question our ability to do that.

When I took office in January 1981, I was appalled by what I found: American planes that couldn't fly and American ships that couldn't sail for lack of spare parts and trained personnel, and insufficient fuel and ammunition for essential training. The inevitable result of all this was poor morale in our armed forces, difficulty in recruiting the brightest young Americans to wear the uniform, and difficulty in convincing our most experienced military personnel to stay on.

There was a real question then about how well we could meet a crisis. And it was obvious that we had to begin a major modernization program to ensure we could deter aggression and preserve the peace in the years ahead.

We had to move immediately to improve the basic readiness and staying power of our conventional forces, so they could meet—and therefore help deter—a crisis. We had to make up for lost years of investment by moving forward with a long-term plan to prepare our forces to counter the military capabilities our adversaries were developing for the future.

I know that all of you want peace, and so do I. I know too that many of you seriously believe that a nuclear freeze would further the cause of peace. But a freeze now would make us less, not more, secure and would raise, not reduce, the risks of war. It would be largely unverifiable and would seriously undercut our negotiations on arms reduction. It would reward the Soviets for their massive military buildup while preventing us from modernizing our aging and increasingly vulnerable forces. With their present margin of superiority, why should they agree to arms reductions knowing that we were prohibited from catching up?

Believe me, it wasn't pleasant for someone who had come to Washington determined to reduce government spending, but we had to move forward with the task of repairing our defenses or we would lose our ability to deter conflict now and in the future. We had to demonstrate to any adversary that aggression could not succeed, and that the only real solution was substantial, equitable, and effectively verifiable arms reduction—the kind we're working for right now in Geneva.

Thanks to your strong support, and bipartisan support from the Congress, we began to turn things around. Already, we're seeing some very encouraging results. Quality recruitment and retention are up dramatically—more high school graduates are choosing military careers, and more experienced career personnel are choosing to stay. Our men and women in uniform at last are getting the tools and training they need to do their jobs. . . .

Now, thus far tonight I've shared with you my thoughts on the problems of national security we must face together. My predecessors in the Oval Office have appeared before you on other occasions to describe the threat posed by Soviet power and have proposed steps to address that threat. But since the advent of nuclear weapons, those steps have been increasingly directed toward deterrence of aggression through the promise of retaliation.

This approach to stability through offensive threat has worked. We and our allies have succeeded in preventing nuclear war for more than three decades. In recent months, however, my advisers, including in particular the Joint Chiefs of Staff, have underscored the necessity to break out of a future that relies solely on offensive retaliation for our security.

Over the course of these discussions, I've become more and more deeply convinced that the human spirit must be capable of rising above dealing with other nations and human beings by threatening their existence. Feeling this way, I believe we must thoroughly examine every opportunity for reducing tensions and for introducing greater stability into the strategic calculus on both sides.

One of the most important contributions we can make is, of course, to lower the level of all arms, and particularly nuclear arms. We're engaged right now in several negotiations with the Soviet Union to bring about a mutual reduction of weapons. I will report to you a week from tomorrow my thoughts on that score. But let me just say, I'm totally committed to this course.

If the Soviet Union will join with us in our effort to achieve major arms reduction, we will have succeeded in stabilizing the nuclear balance. Nevertheless, it will still be necessary to rely on the specter of retaliation, on mutual threat. And that's a sad commentary on the human condition. Wouldn't it be better to save lives than to avenge them? Are we not capable of demonstrating our peaceful intentions by applying all our abilities and our ingenuity to achieving a truly lasting stability? I think we are. Indeed, we must.

After careful consultation with my advisers, including the Joint Chiefs of Staff, I believe there is a way. Let me share with you a vision of the future which offers hope. It is that we embark on a program to counter the awesome Soviet missile threat with measures that are defensive. Let us turn to the very strengths in technology that spawned our great industrial base and that have given us the quality of life we enjoy today.

What if free people could live secure in the knowledge that their security did not rest upon the threat of instant U.S. retaliation to deter a Soviet attack, that we could intercept and destroy strategic ballistic missiles before they reached our own soil or that of our allies?

I know this is a formidable, technical task, one that may not be accomplished before the end of this century. Yet, current technology has attained a level of sophistication where it's reasonable for us to begin this effort. It will take years, probably decades of effort on many fronts.

There will be failures and setbacks, just as there will be successes and breakthroughs. And as we proceed, we must remain constant in preserving the nuclear deterrent and maintaining a solid capability for flexible response. But isn't it worth every investment necessary to free the world from the threat of nuclear war? We know it is.

In the meantime, we will continue to pursue real reductions in nuclear arms, negotiating from a position of strength that can be ensured only by modernizing our strategic forces. At the same time, we must take steps to reduce the risk of a conventional military conflict escalating to nuclear war by improving our nonnuclear capabilities.

America does possess—now—the technologies to attain very significant improvements in the effectiveness of our conventional, nonnuclear forces. Proceeding boldly with these new technologies, we can significantly reduce any incentive that the Soviet Union may have to threaten attack against the United States or its allies.

As we pursue our goal of defensive technologies, we recognize that our allies rely upon our strategic offensive power to deter attacks against them. Their vital interests and ours are inextricably linked. Their safety and ours are one. And no change in technology can or will alter that reality. We must and shall continue to honor our commitments.

I clearly recognize that defensive systems have limitations and raise certain problems and ambiguities. If paired with offensive systems, they can be viewed as fostering an aggressive policy, and no one wants that. But with these considerations firmly in mind, I call upon the scientific community in our country, those who gave us nuclear weapons, to turn their great talents now to the cause of mankind and world peace, to give us the means of rendering these nuclear weapons impotent and obsolete.

Tonight, consistent with our obligations of the ABM treaty and recognizing the need for closer consultation with our allies, I'm taking an important first step. I am directing a comprehensive and intensive

effort to define a long-term research and development program to begin to achieve our ultimate goal of eliminating the threat posed by
strategic nuclear missiles. This could pave the way for arms control
measures to eliminate the weapons themselves. We seek neither military superiority nor political advantage. Our only purpose—one all
people share—is to search for ways to reduce the danger of nuclear war.

My fellow Americans, tonight we're launching an effort which holds
the promise of changing the course of human history. There will be
risks, and results take time. But I believe we can do it. As we cross this
threshold, I ask for your prayers and your support.

Thank you, good night, and God bless you.

"We in the West Have Much to Do, and We Must Do It Together"

*On the afternoon of May 8, 1985—the fortieth anniversary of V-E
Day—President Reagan addressed the European Parliament at
the Palais de l'Europe in Strasbourg, France. He sought to remind
the listeners of the history, ideals, and responsibilities shared by the
United States and European democracies, and to explain shifts in
U.S. policy toward the Soviet Union. His remarks, excerpted here,
were met with occasional boos, and some members of the audience
made a show of walking out. ("I've learned something useful," Reagan ad-libbed in response. "Maybe if I talk long enough in my own
congress, some of those will walk out.")*

Thank you, ladies and gentlemen. It is an honor to be with you on
this day.

We mark today the anniversary of the liberation of Europe from tyrants who had seized this continent and plunged it into a terrible war. Forty years ago today, the guns were stilled and peace began, a peace that has become the longest of this century.

On this day forty years ago, they swarmed onto the boulevards of Paris, rallied under the Arc de Triomphe, and sang the "Marseillaise." They were out there in the open and free air. And now, on this day forty years ago, Winston Churchill walked out onto a balcony in Whitehall and said to the people of Britain, "This is your victory." And the crowd yelled back, in an unforgettable moment of love and gratitude, "No, it is yours." Londoners tore the blackout curtains from their windows, put floodlights on the great symbols of English history. And for the first time in nearly six years, Big Ben, Buckingham Palace, and St. Paul's Cathedral were illuminated against the sky.

Across the ocean, a half a million New Yorkers flooded Times Square and laughed and posed for the cameras. In Washington, our new president, Harry Truman, called reporters into his office and said, "The flags of freedom fly all over Europe."

On that day forty years ago, I was at my post in an Army Air Corps installation in Culver City, California. Passing a radio, I heard the words, "Ladies and gentlemen, the war in Europe is over." I felt a chill, as if a gust of cold wind had just swept past, and even though for America there was still a war in the Pacific front, I realized I would never forget that moment.

This day can't help but be emotional, for in it we feel the long tug of memory. We're reminded of shared joy and shared pain. A few weeks ago in California, an old soldier with tears in his eyes said, "It was such a different world then. It's almost impossible to describe it to someone who wasn't there. But when they finally turned the lights on in the cities again, it was like being reborn."

If it is hard to communicate the happiness of those days, it is even harder to communicate, to those who did not share it, the depth of Europe's agony. So much of it lay in ruins. Whole cities had been destroyed. Children played in the rubble and begged for food.

And by this day forty years ago, over forty million lay dead, and the survivors—they composed a continent of victims. And to this day we wonder: How did this happen? How did civilization take such a terrible turn? After all the books and documentaries, after all the histories and studies, we still wonder: How?

Hannah Arendt spoke of the "banality of evil"—the banality of the little men who did the terrible deeds. We know they were totalitarians who used the state, which they had elevated to the level of a god, to inflict war on peaceful nations and genocide on innocent peoples. We know of the existence of evil in the human heart, and we know that in Nazi Germany that evil was institutionalized, given power and direction by the state and those who did its bidding. We also know that early attempts to placate the totalitarians did not save us from war. They didn't save us from war; in fact they guaranteed war. There are lessons to be learned in this and never forgotten.

But there is a lesson, too, in another thing we saw in those days: Perhaps we can call it the commonness of virtue. The common men and women who somehow dug greatness from within their souls, the people who sang to the children during the Blitz, who joined the resistance and said no to tyranny, the people who had the courage to hide and save the Jews and the dissidents, the people who became for a moment the repositories of all the courage of the West—from a child named Anne Frank to a hero named Raoul Wallenberg. These names shine. They give us heart forever. The glow of their memories lit Europe in her darkest days.

Who can forget the hard days after the war? We can't help but look back and think life was so vivid then. There was the sense of purpose, the joy of shared effort, and later the impossible joy of our triumph.

Those were the days when the West rolled up its sleeves and repaired the damage that had been done, the days when Europe rose in glory from the ruins. Old enemies were reconciled with the European family. Together, America and Western Europe created and put into place the Marshall Plan to rebuild from the rubble. And together we created an Atlantic alliance, which proceeded not from transient interests of state, but from shared ideals. Together we created the North Atlantic Treaty Organization, a partnership aimed at seeing that the kind of tyrants that had tormented Europe would never torment her again.

NATO was a triumph of organization and effort, but it was also something very new and very different. For NATO derived its strength directly from the moral values of the people it represented, from their high ideals, their love of liberty, and their commitment to peace. But perhaps the greatest triumph of all was not in the realm of a sound defense or material achievement. No, the greatest triumph after the war is that in spite of all of the chaos, poverty, sickness, and misfortune that plagued this continent, the people of Western Europe resisted the call of new tyrants and the lure of their seductive ideologies. Your nations did not become the breeding ground for new extremist philosophies. You resisted the totalitarian temptation. Your people embraced democracy, the dream the Fascists could not kill. They chose freedom.

And today we celebrate the leaders who led the way—Churchill and Monnet, Adenauer and Schuman, De Gasperi and Spaak, Truman and Marshall. And we celebrate, too, the free political parties that contributed their share of greatness—the Liberals and the Christian Democrats, the Social Democrats and Labour and the Conservatives. Together they tugged at the same oar, and the great and mighty ship of Europe moved on.

If any doubt their success, let them look at you. In this room are those who fought on opposite sides forty years ago and their sons and daughters. Now you work together to lead Europe democratically; you buried animosity and hatred in the rubble. There is no greater testament to reconciliation and to the peaceful unity of Europe than the men and women in this chamber.

In the decades after the war, Europe knew great growth and power, amazing vitality in every area of life—from fine arts to fashion, from manufacturing to science to the world of ideas. Europe was robust and alive, and none of this was an accident. It was the natural result of freedom, the natural fruit of the democratic ideal. We in America looked at Europe and called her what she was—an economic miracle. . . .

I'm here to tell you that America remains, as she was forty years ago, dedicated to the unity of Europe. We continue to see a strong and unified Europe not as a rival but as an even stronger partner. Indeed, John F. Kennedy, in his ringing declaration of interdependence in the Freedom Bell city of Philadelphia twenty-three years ago, explicitly made this objective a key tenet of postwar American policy; that policy saw the New World and the Old as twin pillars of a larger democratic community. We Americans still see European unity as a vital force in that historic process. We favor the expansion of the European Community; we welcome the entrance of Spain and Portugal into that community, for their presence makes for a stronger Europe, and a stronger Europe is a stronger West.

Yet despite Europe's economic miracle, which brought so much prosperity to so many, despite the visionary ideas of the European leaders, despite the enlargement of democracy's frontiers within the European Community itself, I'm told that a more doubting mood is upon Europe today. I hear words like "Europessimism" and "Europaralysis." I'm told that Europe seems to have lost that sense of confidence that dominated that postwar era. Well, if there is something of a lost quality these days, is it connected to the fact that some in the past few years have begun to question the ideals and philosophies that have guided the West for centuries, that some have even come to question the moral and intellectual worth of the West?

I wish to speak, in part, to that questioning today. . . .

The leaders and people of postwar Europe had learned the lessons of their history from the failures of their predecessors. They learned that aggression feeds on appeasement and that weakness itself can be provocative. We, for our part, can learn from the success of our predecessors. We know that both conflict and aggression can be deterred, that democratic nations are capable of the resolve, the sacrifices, and the consistency of policy needed to sustain such deterrence.

From the creation of NATO in 1949 through the early 1970s, Soviet aggression was effectively deterred. The strength of Western economies, the vitality of our societies, the wisdom of our diplomacy all contributed to Soviet restraint; but certainly the decisive factor must have been the countervailing power—ultimately military, and, above all, nuclear power, which the West was capable of bringing to bear in the defense of its interests.

It was in the early 1970s that the United States lost that superiority over the Soviet Union in strategic nuclear weapons, which had characterized the postwar era. In Europe the effect of this loss was not quickly perceptible, but seen globally, Soviet conduct changed markedly and dangerously. . . .

The ineffectual Western response to Soviet adventurism of the late 1970s had many roots, not least the crisis of self-confidence within the American body politic wrought by the Vietnam experience. But just as Soviet decision-making in the earlier postwar era had taken place against a background of overwhelming American strategic power, so the decisions of the late seventies were taken in Moscow, as in Washington and throughout Europe, against a background of growing Soviet and stagnating Western nuclear strength.

One might draw the conclusion from these events that the West should reassert that nuclear superiority over the Soviet Union upon which our security and our strategy rested through the postwar era.

That is not my view. We cannot and should not seek to build our peace and freedom perpetually upon the basis of expanding nuclear arsenals.

In the short run, we have no alternative but to compete with the Soviet Union in this field, not in the pursuit of superiority but merely of balance. It is thus essential that the United States maintain a modern and survivable nuclear capability in each leg of the strategic triad—sea-, land-, and air-based. It is similarly important that France and Britain maintain and modernize their independent strategic capabilities.

Now, the Soviet Union, however, does not share our view of what constitutes a stable nuclear balance. It has chosen instead to build nuclear forces clearly designed to strike first and thus disarm their adversary. The Soviet Union is now moving toward deployment of new mobile MIRVed [multiple independent reentry vehicle] missiles, which have these capabilities plus the potential to avoid detection, monitoring, or arms control verification. In doing this the Soviet Union is undermining stability and the basis for mutual deterrence.

One can imagine several possible responses to the continued Soviet buildup of nuclear forces. On the one hand, we can ask the Soviet Union to reduce its offensive systems through equitable, verifiable arms control measures. We are pressing that case in Geneva. Thus far, however, we've heard nothing new from the other side.

A second possibility would be for the West to step up our current modernization effort to keep up with constantly accelerating Soviet deployments, not to regain superiority but merely to keep up with Soviet deployments. But is this really an acceptable alternative? Even if this course could be sustained by the West, it would produce a less stable strategic balance than the one we have today. Must we accept an endless process of nuclear arms competition? I don't think so. We need a better guarantee of peace than that.

And fortunately, there is a third possibility. It is to offset the continued Soviet offensive buildup in destabilizing weapons by developing defenses against these weapons.

In 1983 I launched a new research program—the Strategic Defense Initiative. The state of modern technology may soon make possible, for the first time, the ability to use nonnuclear systems to defeat ballistic missiles. The Soviets themselves have long recognized the value of defensive systems and have invested heavily in them. Indeed, they have spent as much on defensive systems as they have on offensive systems for more than twenty years.

Now, this research program will take time. As we proceed with it, we will remain within existing treaty constraints. We will also consult in the closest possible fashion with our allies. And when the time for decisions on the possible production and deployment of such systems comes, we must and will discuss and negotiate these issues with the Soviet Union.

Both for the short and the long term, I'm confident that the West can maintain effective military deterrence. But surely we can aspire to more than maintaining a state of highly armed truce in international politics. . . .

Let me talk about the reflections which have molded our policy toward the Soviet Union. That policy embodies the following basic elements.

While we maintain deterrence to preserve the peace, the United States will make a steady, sustained effort to reduce tensions and solve problems in its relations with the Soviet Union.

The United States is prepared to conclude fair, equitable, verifiable agreements for arms reduction, above all with regard to offensive nuclear weapons.

The United States will insist upon compliance with past agreements, both for their own sake and to strengthen confidence in the possibility of future accords.

The United States seeks no unilateral advantages and, of course, can accept none on the Soviet side.

The United States will proceed in full consultation with its allies, recognizing that our fates are intertwined and we must act in unity.

The United States does not seek to undermine or change the Soviet system nor to impinge upon the security of the Soviet Union. At the same time it will resist attempts by the Soviet Union to use or threaten force against others or to impose its system on others by force.

Ultimately, I hope the leaders of the Soviet Union will come to understand that they have nothing to gain from attempts to achieve military superiority or to spread their dominance by force but have much to gain from joining the West in mutual arms reduction and expanding cooperation. . . .

I propose that the United States and the Soviet Union take four practical steps.

First, that our two countries make a regular practice of exchanging military observers at military exercises and locations. We now follow this practice with many other nations, to the equal benefit of all parties.

Second, as I believe it is desirable for the leaders of the United States and Soviet Union to meet and tackle problems, I am also convinced that the military leaders of our nations could benefit from more contact. I therefore propose that we institute regular, high-level contacts between Soviet and American military leaders to develop better understanding and to prevent potential tragedies from occurring.

Third, I urge that the Conference on Disarmament in Europe act promptly and agree on the concrete confidence-building measures proposed by the NATO countries. The United States is prepared to discuss the Soviet proposal on nonuse of force in the context of Soviet agreement to concrete confidence-building measures.

Fourth, I believe a permanent military-to-military communications link could serve a useful purpose in this important area of our relationship. It could be the channel for exchanging notifications and other information regarding routine military activities, thereby reducing the chances of misunderstanding and misinterpretation. And over time, it might evolve into a risk-reduction mechanism for rapid communication and exchange of data in times of crisis.

These proposals are not cure-alls for our current problems. They will not compensate for the deaths which have occurred. But as terrible as past events have been, it would be more tragic if we were to make no attempt to prevent even larger tragedies from occurring through lack of contact and communication.

We in the West have much to do, and we must do it together. We must remain unified in the face of attempts to divide us and strong in spite of attempts to weaken us. And we must remember that our unity and strength are not a mere impulse of like-minded allies, but the natural result of our shared love for liberty.

Surely we have no illusions that convergence of the Communist system and the free societies of the West is likely. We're in for an extended period of competition of ideas. It is up to us in the West to answer whether or not we will make available the resources, ideas, and assistance necessary to compete with the Soviet Union in the third world. We have much in our favor, not least the experience of those states which have tried Marxism and are looking for an alternative. . . .

I want to reaffirm to the people of Europe the constancy of the American purpose. We were at your side through two great wars; we have been at your side through forty years of a sometimes painful peace. We're at your side today, because, like you, we have not veered from the ideals of the West—the ideals of freedom, liberty, and peace. Let no one—no one—doubt our purpose.

The United States is committed not only to the security of Europe; we're committed to the re-creation of a larger and more genuinely European Europe. The United States is committed not only to a partnership with Europe; the United States is committed to an end to the artificial division of Europe.

We do not deny any nation's legitimate interest in security. We share the basic aspirations of all of the peoples of Europe—freedom, prosperity, and peace. But when families are divided and people are not allowed to maintain normal human and cultural contacts, this creates international tension. Only in a system in which all feel secure and sovereign can there be a lasting and secure peace. . . .

Here in Western Europe you have created a multinational democratic community in which there is a free flow of people, of information, of goods, and of culture. West Europeans move frequently and freely in all directions, sharing and partaking of each other's ideas and culture. It is my hope that in the twenty-first century, which is only fifteen years away, all Europeans, from Moscow to Lisbon, will be able to travel without a passport; and the free flow of people and ideas will include the other half of Europe. It is my fervent wish that in the next century there will be one free Europe.

I do not believe those who say the people of Europe today are paralyzed and pessimistic. And I would say to those who think this, Europe, beloved Europe, you are greater than you know. You are the treasury of centuries of Western thought and Western culture; you are the father of Western ideals and the mother of Western faith. Europe, you have been the power and the glory of the West, and you are a moral success. In the horrors after World War II, you rejected totalitarianism; you rejected the lure of the new superman and a new Communist man; you proved that you were and are a moral triumph.

You in the West are a Europe without illusions, a Europe firmly grounded in the ideals and traditions that made her greatness, a Europe unbound and unfettered by a bankrupt ideology. You are today a new Europe on the brink of a new century, a democratic community with much to be proud of.

We have so much to do. The work ahead is not unlike the building of a great cathedral. The work is slow, complicated, and painstaking. It's passed on with pride from generation to generation. It's the work not only of leaders but of ordinary people. The cathedral evolves as it is created, with each generation adding its own vision. But the initial ideal remains constant, and the faith that drives the vision persists. The results may be slow to see, but our children and their children will trace in the air the emerging arches and spires and know the faith and dedication and love that produced them. My friends, Europe is the cathedral, and it is illuminated still.

And if you doubt your will and your spirit and your strength to stand for something, think of those people forty years ago who wept in the rubble, who laughed in the streets, who paraded across Europe, who cheered Churchill with love and devotion, who sang the "Marseillaise" down the boulevards. Spirit like that does not disappear; it cannot perish; it will not go. There is too much left unsung within it.

"Peace Is the Holy Shadow Cast by Men Treading on the Path of Virtue"

The Charter of the United Nations went into effect on October 24, 1945. On the morning of its fortieth anniversary, President Reagan addressed the UN General Assembly in New York. He pointed out that the Soviets' "expressions of peaceful intent" were belied by their aggressive actions. Then, in the excerpt below, he made the case for his antiballistic missile program, rejecting the claim that such a tool was inherently offensive. And he described concrete steps Soviet leaders could take if they genuinely wanted peace instead of costly, deadly conflict.

The United States has never sought treaties merely to paper over differences. We continue to believe that a nuclear war is one that cannot be won and must never be fought. And that is why we have sought for nearly ten years . . . radical, equitable, verifiable reductions in these vast arsenals of offensive nuclear weapons. . . .

The ballistic missile is the most awesome, threatening, and destructive weapon in the history of man. Thus, I welcome the interest of the new Soviet leadership in the reduction of offensive strategic forces. Ultimately, we must remove this menace, once and for all, from the face of the earth. Until that day, the United States seeks to escape the prison of mutual terror by research and testing that could, in time, enable us to neutralize the threat of these ballistic missiles and, ultimately, render them obsolete.

How is Moscow threatened if the capitals of other nations are protected? We do not ask the Soviet leaders, whose country has suffered so much from war, to leave their people defenseless against foreign attack. Why then do they insist that we remain undefended? Who is threatened if Western research and Soviet research, that is itself well-advanced, should develop a nonnuclear system which would threaten not human beings but only ballistic missiles? Surely, the world will sleep more secure when these missiles have been rendered useless, militarily and politically; when the sword of Damocles that has hung over our planet for too many decades is lifted by Western and Russian scientists working to shield their citizens and one day shut down space as an avenue of weapons of mass destruction. If we're destined by history to compete, militarily, to keep the peace, then let us compete in systems that defend our societies rather than weapons which can destroy us both and much of God's creation along with us.

Some eighteen years ago, then-premier Aleksei Kosygin was asked about a moratorium on the development of an antimissile defense system. The official news agency, TASS, reported that he replied with these words: "I believe the defensive systems, which prevent attack, are not the cause of the arms race, but constitute a factor preventing the death of people. Maybe an antimissile system is more expensive than an offensive system, but it is designed not to kill people, but to preserve human lives." Preserving lives—no peace is more fundamental than that. Great obstacles lie ahead, but they should not deter us. Peace is God's commandment. Peace is the holy shadow cast by men treading on the path of virtue.

But just as we all know what peace is, we certainly know what peace is not. Peace based on repression cannot be true peace, and is secure only when individuals are free to direct their own governments. Peace based on partition cannot be true peace. Put simply, nothing can justify the continuing and permanent division of the European Continent. Walls of partition and distrust must give way to greater communication for an open world. Before leaving for Geneva, I shall make new proposals to achieve this goal. Peace based on mutual fear cannot be true peace, because staking our future on a precarious balance of terror is not good enough. The world needs a balance of safety. And finally, a peace based on averting our eyes from trouble cannot be true peace. The consequences of conflict are every bit as tragic when the destruction is contained within one country.

5

CONFRONTING THE
EVIL EMPIRE

When Ronald Reagan was elected president, the playwright and dissident Václav Havel was serving time in a prison in Communist Czechoslovakia, having been convicted of subversive activities. By 1993, Havel was the democratically elected president of the new Czech Republic. "The fall of the Communist empire," Havel said, "is an event on the same scale of historical importance as the fall of the Roman Empire." Part of the credit for that epochal event, Havel believed, was due to the leadership of the U.S. president, who felt a moral obligation to oppose with vigor the ideology and actions of the Soviet Communist regime.

"The Decay of the Soviet Experiment"

In June 1982, President Reagan embarked on a ten-day trip to France, Italy, Vatican City, the United Kingdom, and West Germany. On the morning of June 8, he went horseback riding with Queen Elizabeth II on the grounds of Windsor Castle. Then, in the early afternoon, at the Palace of Westminster, he became the first U.S. president to address both houses of the Parliament of the United Kingdom. This speech is remarkable for its critique of both the material and the moral failings of the Soviet Union—at a time when few observers were able to see the former and many observers were unwilling to see the latter.

My Lord Chancellor, Mr. Speaker:

The journey of which this visit forms a part is a long one. Already it has taken me to two great cities of the West, Rome and Paris, and to the economic summit at Versailles. And there, once again, our sister democracies have proved that even in a time of severe economic strain, free peoples can work together freely and voluntarily to address problems as serious as inflation, unemployment, trade, and economic development in a spirit of cooperation and solidarity.

Other milestones lie ahead. Later this week, in Germany, we and our NATO allies will discuss measures for our joint defense and America's latest initiatives for a more peaceful, secure world through arms reductions.

Each stop of this trip is important, but among them all, this moment occupies a special place in my heart and in the hearts of my countrymen— a moment of kinship and homecoming in these hallowed halls.

Speaking for all Americans, I want to say how very much at home we feel in your house. Every American would, because this is, as we have been so eloquently told, one of democracy's shrines. Here the rights of free people and the processes of representation have been debated and refined.

It has been said that an institution is the lengthening shadow of a man. This institution is the lengthening shadow of all the men and women who have sat here and all those who have voted to send representatives here.

This is my second visit to Great Britain as president of the United States. My first opportunity to stand on British soil occurred almost a year and a half ago, when your prime minister graciously hosted a diplomatic dinner at the British embassy in Washington. Mrs. Thatcher said then that she hoped I was not distressed to find staring down at me from the grand staircase a portrait of His Royal Majesty King George III. She suggested it was best to let bygones be bygones, and in view of our two countries' remarkable friendship in succeeding years, she added that most Englishmen today would agree with Thomas Jefferson that "a little rebellion now and then is a very good thing." [*Laughter*]

Well, from here I will go to Bonn and then Berlin, where there stands a grim symbol of power untamed. The Berlin Wall, that dreadful gray gash across the city, is in its third decade. It is the fitting signature of the regime that built it.

And a few hundred kilometers behind the Berlin Wall, there is another symbol. In the center of Warsaw, there is a sign that notes the distances to two capitals. In one direction it points toward Moscow. In the other it points toward Brussels, headquarters of Western Europe's tangible unity. The marker says that the distances from Warsaw to Moscow and Warsaw to Brussels are equal. The sign makes this point: Poland is not East or West. Poland is at the center of European civilization. It has contributed mightily to that civilization. It is doing so today by being magnificently unreconciled to oppression.

Poland's struggle to be Poland and to secure the basic rights we often take for granted demonstrates why we dare not take those rights for granted. Gladstone, defending the Reform Bill of 1866, declared, "You cannot fight against the future. Time is on our side." It was easier to believe in the march of democracy in Gladstone's day—in that high noon of Victorian optimism.

We're approaching the end of a bloody century plagued by a terrible political invention—totalitarianism. Optimism comes less easily today, not because democracy is less vigorous, but because democracy's enemies have refined their instruments of repression. Yet optimism is in order, because day by day democracy is proving itself to be a not-at-all-fragile flower. From Stettin on the Baltic to Varna on the Black Sea, the regimes planted by totalitarianism have had more than thirty years to establish their legitimacy. But none—not one regime—has yet been able to risk free elections. Regimes planted by bayonets do not take root.

The strength of the Solidarity movement in Poland demonstrates the truth told in an underground joke in the Soviet Union. It is that the Soviet Union would remain a one-party nation even if an opposition party were permitted, because everyone would join the opposition party. [*Laughter*]

America's time as a player on the stage of world history has been brief. I think understanding this fact has always made you patient with your younger cousins—well, not always patient. I do recall that on one occasion, Sir Winston Churchill said in exasperation about one of our most distinguished diplomats, "He is the only case I know of a bull who carries his china shop with him." [*Laughter*]

But witty as Sir Winston was, he also had that special attribute of great statesmen—the gift of vision, the willingness to see the future based on the experience of the past. It is this sense of history, this understanding of the past, that I want to talk with you about today, for it is in remembering what we share of the past that our two nations can make common cause for the future.

We have not inherited an easy world. If developments like the Industrial Revolution, which began here in England, and the gifts of science and technology have made life much easier for us, they have also made it more dangerous. There are threats now to our freedom, indeed to our very existence, that other generations could never even have imagined.

There is first the threat of global war. No president, no congress, no prime minister, no parliament can spend a day entirely free of this threat. And I don't have to tell you that in today's world the existence of nuclear weapons could mean, if not the extinction of mankind, then surely the end of civilization as we know it. That's why negotiations on intermediate-range nuclear forces, now underway in Europe, and the START talks—Strategic Arms Reduction Talks—which will begin later this month, are not just critical to American or Western policy; they are critical to mankind. Our commitment to early success in these negotiations is firm and unshakable, and our purpose is clear: reducing the risk of war by reducing the means of waging war on both sides.

At the same time there is a threat posed to human freedom by the enormous power of the modern state. History teaches the dangers of government that overreaches—political control taking precedence over free economic growth, secret police, mindless bureaucracy, all combining to stifle individual excellence and personal freedom.

Now, I'm aware that among us here and throughout Europe there is legitimate disagreement over the extent to which the public sector should play a role in a nation's economy and life. But on one point all of us are united: our abhorrence of dictatorship in all its forms, but most particularly totalitarianism and the terrible inhumanities it has caused in our time—the great purge, Auschwitz and Dachau, the Gulag, and Cambodia.

Historians looking back at our time will note the consistent restraint and peaceful intentions of the West. They will note that it was the democracies who refused to use the threat of their nuclear monopoly in the forties and early fifties for territorial or imperial gain. Had that nuclear monopoly been in the hands of the Communist world, the map of Europe—indeed, the world—would look very different today. And certainly they will note it was not the democracies that invaded Afghanistan or suppressed Polish Solidarity or used chemical and toxin warfare in Afghanistan and Southeast Asia.

If history teaches anything, it teaches self-delusion in the face of unpleasant facts is folly. We see around us today the marks of our terrible dilemma—predictions of doomsday, antinuclear demonstrations, an arms race in which the West must, for its own protection, be an unwilling participant. At the same time we see totalitarian forces in the world who seek subversion and conflict around the globe to further their barbarous assault on the human spirit. What, then, is our course? Must civilization perish in a hail of fiery atoms? Must freedom wither in a quiet, deadening accommodation with totalitarian evil?

Sir Winston Churchill refused to accept the inevitability of war or even that it was imminent. He said, "I do not believe that Soviet Russia desires war. What they desire is the fruits of war and the indefinite expansion of their power and doctrines. But what we have to consider here today while time remains is the permanent prevention of war and the establishment of conditions of freedom and democracy as rapidly as possible in all countries."

Well, this is precisely our mission today: to preserve freedom as well as peace. It may not be easy to see; but I believe we live now at a turning point.

In an ironic sense Karl Marx was right. We are witnessing today a great revolutionary crisis, a crisis where the demands of the economic order are conflicting directly with those of the political order. But the crisis is happening not in the free, non-Marxist West, but in the home of Marxist-Leninism, the Soviet Union. It is the Soviet Union that runs against the tide of history by denying human freedom and human dignity to its citizens. It also is in deep economic difficulty. The rate of growth in the national product has been steadily declining since the fifties and is less than half of what it was then.

The dimensions of this failure are astounding: A country which employs one-fifth of its population in agriculture is unable to feed its own people. Were it not for the private sector, the tiny private sector tolerated in Soviet agriculture, the country might be on the brink of famine. These private plots occupy a bare 3 percent of the arable land but account for nearly one-quarter of Soviet farm output and nearly one-third of meat products and vegetables. Overcentralized, with little or no incentives, year after year the Soviet system pours its best resource into the making of instruments of destruction. The constant shrinkage of economic growth combined with the growth of military production is putting a heavy strain on the Soviet people. What we see here is a political structure that no longer corresponds to its economic base, a society where productive forces are hampered by political ones.

The decay of the Soviet experiment should come as no surprise to us. Wherever the comparisons have been made between free and closed societies—West Germany and East Germany, Austria and Czechoslovakia, Malaysia and Vietnam—it is the democratic countries that are prosperous and responsive to the needs of their people. And one of the simple but overwhelming facts of our time is this: Of all the millions of refugees we've seen in the modern world, their flight is always away from, not toward, the Communist world. Today on the NATO line, our military forces face east to prevent a possible invasion. On the other side of the line, the Soviet forces also face east to prevent their people from leaving.

The hard evidence of totalitarian rule has caused in mankind an uprising of the intellect and will. Whether it is the growth of the new schools of economics in America or England or the appearance of the so-called new philosophers in France, there is one unifying thread running through the intellectual work of these groups—rejection of the arbitrary power of the state, the refusal to subordinate the rights of the individual to the superstate, the realization that collectivism stifles all the best human impulses. . . .

In the Communist world as well, man's instinctive desire for freedom and self-determination surfaces again and again. To be sure, there are grim reminders of how brutally the police state attempts to snuff out this quest for self-rule—1953 in East Germany, 1956 in Hungary, 1968 in Czechoslovakia, 1981 in Poland. But the struggle continues in Poland. And we know that there are even those who strive and suffer for freedom within the confines of the Soviet Union itself. How we conduct ourselves here in the Western democracies will determine whether this trend continues.

No, democracy is not a fragile flower. Still, it needs cultivating. If the rest of this century is to witness the gradual growth of freedom and democratic ideals, we must take actions to assist the campaign for democracy.

Some argue that we should encourage democratic change in rightwing dictatorships, but not in Communist regimes. Well, to accept this preposterous notion—as some well-meaning people have—is to invite the argument that once countries achieve a nuclear capability, they should be allowed an undisturbed reign of terror over their own citizens. We reject this course.

As for the Soviet view, Chairman Brezhnev repeatedly has stressed that the competition of ideas and systems must continue and that this is entirely consistent with relaxation of tensions and peace.

Well, we ask only that these systems begin by living up to their own constitutions, abiding by their own laws, and complying with the international obligations they have undertaken. We ask only for a process, a direction, a basic code of decency, not for an instant transformation.

We cannot ignore the fact that even without our encouragement there has been and will continue to be repeated explosions against repression and dictatorships. The Soviet Union itself is not immune to this reality. Any system is inherently unstable that has no peaceful means to legitimize its leaders. In such cases, the very repressiveness of the state ultimately drives people to resist it, if necessary, by force.

While we must be cautious about forcing the pace of change, we must not hesitate to declare our ultimate objectives and to take concrete actions to move toward them. We must be staunch in our conviction that freedom is not the sole prerogative of a lucky few, but the inalienable and universal right of all human beings. So states the United Nations Universal Declaration of Human Rights, which, among other things, guarantees free elections.

The objective I propose is quite simple to state: to foster the infrastructure of democracy, the system of a free press, unions, political parties, universities, which allows a people to choose their own way to develop their own culture, to reconcile their own differences through peaceful means.

This is not cultural imperialism; it is providing the means for genuine self-determination and protection for diversity. Democracy already flourishes in countries with very different cultures and historical experiences. It would be cultural condescension, or worse, to say that any people prefer dictatorship to democracy. Who would voluntarily choose not to have the right to vote, decide to purchase government propaganda handouts instead of independent newspapers, prefer government to worker-controlled unions, opt for land to be owned by the state instead of those who till it, want government repression of religious liberty, a single political party instead of a free choice, a rigid cultural orthodoxy instead of democratic tolerance and diversity?

Since 1917 the Soviet Union has given covert political training and assistance to Marxist-Leninists in many countries. Of course, it also has promoted the use of violence and subversion by these same forces. Over the past several decades, West European and other Social Democrats, Christian Democrats, and leaders have offered open assistance to fraternal, political, and social institutions to bring about peaceful and democratic progress. Appropriately, for a vigorous new democracy, the Federal Republic of Germany's political foundations have become a major force in this effort.

We in America now intend to take additional steps, as many of our allies have already done, toward realizing this same goal. The chairmen and other leaders of the national Republican and Democratic Party organizations are initiating a study with the bipartisan American political foundation to determine how the United States can best contribute as a nation to the global campaign for democracy now gathering force. They will have the cooperation of congressional leaders of both parties, along with representatives of business, labor, and other major institutions in our society. I look forward to receiving their recommendations and to working with these institutions and the Congress in the common task of strengthening democracy throughout the world.

It is time that we committed ourselves as a nation—in both the public and private sectors—to assisting democratic development.

We plan to consult with leaders of other nations as well. There is a proposal before the Council of Europe to invite parliamentarians from democratic countries to a meeting next year in Strasbourg. That prestigious gathering could consider ways to help democratic political movements.

This November in Washington there will take place an international meeting on free elections. And next spring there will be a conference of world authorities on constitutionalism and self-government hosted by the chief justice of the United States. Authorities from a number of developing and developed countries—judges, philosophers, and politicians with practical experience—have agreed to explore how to turn principle into practice and further the rule of law.

At the same time, we invite the Soviet Union to consider with us how the competition of ideas and values—which it is committed to support—can be conducted on a peaceful and reciprocal basis. For example, I am prepared to offer President Brezhnev an opportunity to speak to the American people on our television if he will allow me the same opportunity with the Soviet people. We also suggest that panels of our newsmen periodically appear on each other's television to discuss major events.

Now, I don't wish to sound overly optimistic, yet the Soviet Union is not immune from the reality of what is going on in the world. It has happened in the past—a small ruling elite either mistakenly attempts to ease domestic unrest through greater repression and foreign adventure, or it chooses a wiser course. It begins to allow its people a voice in their own destiny. Even if this latter process is not realized soon, I believe the renewed strength of the democratic movement, complemented by a global campaign for freedom, will strengthen the prospects for arms control and a world at peace.

I have discussed on other occasions, including my address on May 9, the elements of Western policies toward the Soviet Union to safeguard our interests and protect the peace. What I am describing now is a plan and a hope for the long term—the march of freedom and democracy which will leave Marxism-Leninism on the ash heap of history as it has left other tyrannies which stifle the freedom and muzzle the self-expression of the people. And that's why we must continue our efforts to strengthen NATO even as we move forward with our Zero Option initiative in the negotiations on intermediate-range forces and our proposal for a one-third reduction in strategic ballistic missile warheads.

Our military strength is a prerequisite to peace, but let it be clear we maintain this strength in the hope it will never be used, for the ultimate determinant in the struggle that's now going on in the world will not be bombs and rockets, but a test of wills and ideas, a trial of spiritual resolve, the values we hold, the beliefs we cherish, the ideals to which we are dedicated.

The British people know that, given strong leadership, time, and a little bit of hope, the forces of good ultimately rally and triumph over evil. Here among you is the cradle of self-government, the Mother of Parliaments. Here is the enduring greatness of the British contribution to mankind, the great civilized ideas: individual liberty, representative government, and the rule of law under God.

I've often wondered about the shyness of some of us in the West about standing for these ideals that have done so much to ease the plight of man and the hardships of our imperfect world. This reluctance to use those vast resources at our command reminds me of the elderly lady whose home was bombed in the Blitz. As the rescuers moved about, they found a bottle of brandy she'd stored behind the staircase, which was all that was left standing. And since she was barely conscious, one of the workers pulled the cork to give her a taste of it. She came around immediately and said, "Here now—there now, put it back. That's for emergencies." [*Laughter*]

Well, the emergency is upon us. Let us be shy no longer. Let us go to our strength. Let us offer hope. Let us tell the world that a new age is not only possible but probable.

During the dark days of the Second World War, when this island was incandescent with courage, Winston Churchill exclaimed about Britain's adversaries, "What kind of a people do they think we are?" Well, Britain's adversaries found out what extraordinary people the British are. But all the democracies paid a terrible price for allowing the dictators to underestimate us. We dare not make that mistake again. So, let us ask ourselves, "What kind of people do we think we are?"

And let us answer, "Free people, worthy of freedom and determined not only to remain so but to help others gain their freedom as well."

Sir Winston led his people to great victory in war and then lost an election just as the fruits of victory were about to be enjoyed. But he left office honorably, and, as it turned out, temporarily, knowing that the liberty of his people was more important than the fate of any single leader. History recalls his greatness in ways no dictator will ever know. And he left us a message of hope for the future, as timely now as when he first uttered it, as opposition leader in the Commons nearly twenty-seven years ago, when he said, "When we look back on all the perils through which we have passed and at the mighty foes that we have laid low and all the dark and deadly designs that we have frustrated, why should we fear for our future? We have," he said, "come safely through the worst."

Well, the task I've set forth will long outlive our own generation. But together, we too have come through the worst. Let us now begin a major effort to secure the best—a crusade for freedom that will engage the faith and fortitude of the next generation. For the sake of peace and justice, let us move toward a world in which all people are at last free to determine their own destiny.

Thank you.

"Bleak and Brutal as the Berlin Wall Itself"

In the Westminster speech above, President Reagan referred to the Berlin Wall as "that dreadful gray gash across the city." Three days later, on June 11, 1982, he visited West Berlin and again criticized the wall and the Communist regime that built it. First, in a speech

to American military personnel stationed in West Berlin, he said,
"If I had a chance, I'd like to ask the Soviet leaders one question—in
fact, I may stuff the question in a bottle and throw it over the wall
when I go there today. I really want to hear their explanation. Why
is that wall there? Why are they so afraid of freedom on this side of
the wall? Well, the truth is, they're scared to death of it because
they know that freedom is catching, and they don't dare [let] their
people have a taste of it." Then, after visiting the wall, he delivered
these remarks at Berlin's Charlottenburg Palace.

Mr. Governing Mayor, Mr. Chancellor, Excellencies, you ladies and gentlemen:

It was one of Germany's greatest sons, Goethe, who said that "there is strong shadow where there is much light." In our times, Berlin, more than any other place in the world, is such a meeting place of light and shadow, tyranny and freedom. To be here is truly to stand on freedom's edge and in the shadow of a wall that has come to symbolize all that is darkest in the world today, to sense how shining and priceless and how much in need of constant vigilance and protection our legacy of liberty is. . . .

We Americans—we Americans are optimists, but we are also realists. We're a peaceful people, but we're not a weak or gullible people. So, we look with hope to the Soviet Union's response. But we expect positive actions rather than rhetoric as the first proof of Soviet good intentions. We expect that the response to my Berlin initiative for peace will demonstrate finally that the Soviet Union is serious about working to reduce tensions in other parts of the world as they have been able to do here in Berlin.

Peace, it has been said, is more than the absence of armed conflict. Reducing military forces alone will not automatically guarantee the long-term prospects for peace.

Several times in the 1950s and '60s the world went to the brink of war over Berlin. Those confrontations did not come because of military forces or operations alone. They arose because the Soviet Union refused to allow the free flow of peoples and ideas between East and West. And they came because the Soviet authorities and their minions repressed millions of citizens in Eastern Germany who did not wish to live under a Communist dictatorship.

So, I want to concentrate the second part of America's new Berlin initiative on ways to reduce the human barriers—barriers as bleak and brutal as the Berlin Wall itself—which divide Europe today. . . . A united, resolute Western alliance stands ready to defend itself if necessary. But we are also ready to work with the Soviet bloc in peaceful cooperation if the leaders of the East are willing to respond in kind.

Let them remember the message of Schiller that only "he who has done his best for his own time has lived for all times." Let them join with us in our time to achieve a lasting peace and a better life for tomorrow's generations on both sides of that blighted wall. And let the Brandenburg Gate become a symbol not of two separate and hostile worlds, but an open door through which ideas, free ideas, and peaceful competition flourish.

My final message is for the people of Berlin. Even before my first visit to your city, I felt a part of you, as all free men and women around the world do. We lived through the blockade and airlift with you. We witnessed the heroic reconstruction of a devastated city, and we watched the creation of your strong democratic institutions.

When I came here in 1978, I was deeply moved and proud of your success. What finer proof of what freedom can accomplish than the vibrant, prosperous island you've created in the midst of a hostile sea. Today, my reverence for your courage and accomplishment has grown even deeper.

You are a constant inspiration for us all—for our hopes and ideals, and for the human qualities of courage, endurance, and faith that are the one secret weapon of the West no totalitarian regime can ever match. As long as Berlin exists, there can be no doubt about the hope for democracy.

Yes, the hated wall still stands. But taller and stronger than that bleak barrier dividing East from West, free from oppress[ion], stands the character of the Berliners themselves. You have endured in your splendid city on the Spree, and my return visit has convinced me, in the words of the beloved old song, that "Berlin bleibt doch Berlin"—Berlin is still Berlin.

We all remember John Kennedy's stirring words when he visited Berlin. I can only add that we in America and in the West are still Berliners, too, and always will be. And I am proud to say today that it is good to be home again.

God bless you. Danke schön.

"The Aggressive Impulses of an Evil Empire"

The first two-thirds of President Reagan's March 8, 1983, speech in Orlando, spoken to the annual convention of the National Association of Evangelicals, dealt with domestic social policy. Then, in the last third, excerpted below, the speech turned to foreign policy. The president himself insisted on the inclusion of the phrase "evil empire," which had previously been cut from his Westminster address. Although this speech was roundly mocked by the liberal cognoscenti—"It was the worst presidential speech in American history, and I've seen them all," said liberal historian Henry Steele Commager—history has vindicated both its moral analysis and its rhetoric.

And this brings me to my final point today. During my first press conference as president, in answer to a direct question, I pointed out that, as good Marxist-Leninists, the Soviet leaders have openly and publicly declared that the only morality they recognize is that which will further their cause, which is world revolution. I think I should point out I was only quoting Lenin, their guiding spirit, who said in 1920 that they repudiate all morality that proceeds from supernatural ideas—that's their name for religion—or ideas that are outside class conceptions. Morality is entirely subordinate to the interests of class war. And everything is moral that is necessary for the annihilation of the old, exploiting social order, and for uniting the proletariat.

Well, I think the refusal of many influential people to accept this elementary fact of Soviet doctrine illustrates a historical reluctance to see totalitarian powers for what they are. We saw this phenomenon in the 1930s. We see it too often today.

This doesn't mean we should isolate ourselves and refuse to seek an understanding with them. I intend to do everything I can to persuade them of our peaceful intent, to remind them that it was the West that refused to use its nuclear monopoly in the forties and fifties for territorial gain and which now proposes [a] 50 percent cut in strategic ballistic missiles and the elimination of an entire class of land-based, intermediate-range nuclear missiles.

At the same time, however, they must be made to understand we will never compromise our principles and standards. We will never give away our freedom. We will never abandon our belief in God. And we will never stop searching for a genuine peace. But we can assure none of these things America stands for through the so-called nuclear freeze solutions proposed by some.

The truth is that a freeze now would be a very dangerous fraud, for that is merely the illusion of peace. The reality is that we must find peace through strength.

I would agree to a freeze if only we could freeze the Soviets' global desires. A freeze at current levels of weapons would remove any incentive for the Soviets to negotiate seriously in Geneva and virtually end our chances to achieve the major arms reductions which we have proposed. Instead, they would achieve their objectives through the freeze.

A freeze would reward the Soviet Union for its enormous and unparalleled military buildup. It would prevent the essential and long-overdue modernization of United States and allied defenses and would leave our aging forces increasingly vulnerable. And an honest freeze would require extensive prior negotiations on the systems and numbers to be limited and on the measures to ensure effective verification and compliance. And the kind of a freeze that has been suggested would be virtually impossible to verify. Such a major effort would divert us completely from our current negotiations on achieving substantial reductions.

A number of years ago, I heard a young father, a very prominent young man in the entertainment world, addressing a tremendous gathering in California. It was during the time of the Cold War, and Communism and our own way of life were very much on people's minds. And he was speaking to that subject. And suddenly, though, I heard him saying, "I love my little girls more than anything." And I said to myself, "Oh, no, don't. You can't—don't say that." But I had underestimated him. He went on: "I would rather see my little girls die now, still believing in God, than have them grow up under Communism and one day die no longer believing in God."

There were thousands of young people in that audience. They came to their feet with shouts of joy. They had instantly recognized the profound truth in what he had said, with regard to the physical and the soul and what was truly important.

Yes, let us pray for the salvation of all of those who live in that totalitarian darkness—pray they will discover the joy of knowing God. But until they do, let us be aware that while they preach the supremacy of the state, declare its omnipotence over individual man, and predict its eventual domination of all peoples on the earth, they are the focus of evil in the modern world.

It was C. S. Lewis who, in his unforgettable Screwtape Letters, wrote, "The greatest evil is not done now in those sordid 'dens of crime' that Dickens loved to paint. It is not even done in concentration camps and labor camps. In those we see its final result. But it is conceived and ordered (moved, seconded, carried, and minuted) in clear [clean], carpeted, warmed, and well-lighted offices, by quiet men with white collars and cut fingernails and smooth-shaven cheeks who do not need to raise their voice."

Well, because these "quiet men" do not "raise their voices," because they sometimes speak in soothing tones of brotherhood and peace, because, like other dictators before them, they're always making "their final territorial demand," some would have us accept them at their word and accommodate ourselves to their aggressive impulses. But if history teaches anything, it teaches that simpleminded appeasement or wishful thinking about our adversaries is folly. It means the betrayal of our past, the squandering of our freedom.

So, I urge you to speak out against those who would place the United States in a position of military and moral inferiority. You know, I've always believed that old Screwtape reserved his best efforts for those of you in the church. So, in your discussions of the nuclear freeze proposals, I urge you to beware the temptation of pride—the temptation of blithely declaring yourselves above it all and [to] label both sides equally at fault, to ignore the facts of history and the aggressive impulses of an evil empire, to simply call the arms race a giant misunderstanding and thereby remove yourself from the struggle between right and wrong and good and evil.

I ask you to resist the attempts of those who would have you with-hold your support for our efforts, this administration's efforts, to keep America strong and free, while we negotiate real and verifiable reductions in the world's nuclear arsenals and one day, with God's help, their total elimination.

While America's military strength is important, let me add here that I've always maintained that the struggle now going on for the world will never be decided by bombs or rockets, by armies or military might. The real crisis we face today is a spiritual one; at root, it is a test of moral will and faith.

Whittaker Chambers, the man whose own religious conversion made him a witness to one of the terrible traumas of our time, the Hiss-Chambers case, wrote that the crisis of the Western world exists to the degree in which the West is indifferent to God, the degree to which it collaborates in Communism's attempt to make man stand alone without God. And then he said . . . Marxism-Leninism is actually the second-oldest faith, first proclaimed in the Garden of Eden with the words of temptation, "Ye shall be as gods."

The Western world can answer this challenge, he wrote, "but only provided that its faith in God and the freedom He enjoins is as great as Communism's faith in Man."

I believe we shall rise to the challenge. I believe that Communism is another sad, bizarre chapter in human history whose last pages even now are being written. I believe this because the source of our strength in the quest for human freedom is not material, but spiritual. And because it knows no limitation, it must terrify and ultimately triumph over those who would enslave their fellow man. For in the words of Isaiah, "He giveth power to the faint; and to them that have no might He increased strength. . . . But they that wait upon the Lord shall renew their strength; they shall mount up with wings as eagles; they shall run, and not be weary. . . ."

Yes, change your world. One of our Founding Fathers, Thomas Paine, said, "We have it within our power to begin the world over again." We can do it, doing together what no one church could do by itself.

God bless you, and thank you very much.

"We Met, as We Had to Meet"

A new general secretary of the Communist Party of the Soviet Union—the country's de facto leader—came to power in March 1985: Mikhail Gorbachev. He was younger than his predecessors and seemed to be reform-minded. ("I like Mr. Gorbachev. We can do business together," said U.K. prime minister Margaret Thatcher, a close Reagan ally.) Reagan and Gorbachev agreed to meet in Geneva, Switzerland, in November 1985—the first of what would ultimately be four tremendously consequential summits between the two men. Afterward, President Reagan described the summit in an address before a joint session of Congress on the evening of November 21.

Mr. Speaker, Mr. President, members of the Congress, distinguished guests, and my fellow Americans:

It's great to be home, and Nancy and I thank you for this wonderful homecoming. And before I go on, I want to say a personal thank-you to Nancy. She was an outstanding ambassador of goodwill for all of us. She didn't know I was going to say that. Mr. Speaker, Senator Dole, I want you to know that your statements of support here were greatly appreciated. You can't imagine how much it means in dealing with the Soviets to have the Congress, the allies, and the American people firmly behind you.

I guess you know that I have just come from Geneva and talks with General Secretary Gorbachev. In the past few days, the past two days, we spent over fifteen hours in various meetings with the general secretary and the members of his official party. And approximately five of those hours were talks between Mr. Gorbachev and myself, just one-on-one. That was the best part—our fireside summit. There will be, I know, a great deal of commentary and opinion as to what the meetings produced and what they were like. There were over three thousand reporters in Geneva, so it's possible there will be three thousand opinions on what happened. So, maybe it's the old broadcaster in me, but I decided to file my own report directly to you.

We met, as we had to meet. I called for a fresh start, and we made that start. I can't claim that we had a meeting of the minds on such fundamentals as ideology or national purpose, but we understand each other better, and that's a key to peace. I gained a better perspective; I feel he did, too. It was a constructive meeting; so constructive, in fact, that I look forward to welcoming Mr. Gorbachev to the United States next year. And I have accepted his invitation to go to Moscow the following year. We arranged that out in the parking lot. I found Mr. Gorbachev to be an energetic defender of Soviet policy. He was an eloquent speaker and a good listener.

Our subject matter was shaped by the facts of this century. These past forty years have not been an easy time for the West or for the world. You know the facts; there is no need to recite the historical record. Suffice it to say that the United States cannot afford illusions about the nature of the USSR. We cannot assume that their ideology and purpose will change; this implies enduring competition. Our task is to assure that this competition remains peaceful. With all that divides us, we cannot afford to let confusion complicate things further. We must be clear with each other and direct. We must pay each other the tribute of candor.

When I took the oath of office for the first time, we began dealing with the Soviet Union in a way that was more realistic than in, say, the recent past. And so, in a very real sense, preparations for the summit started not months ago, but five years ago, when, with the help of Congress, we began strengthening our economy, restoring our national will, and rebuilding our defenses and alliances. America is once again strong, and our strength has given us the ability to speak with confidence and see that no true opportunity to advance freedom and peace is lost. We must not now abandon policies that work. I need your continued support to keep America strong.

That is the history behind the Geneva summit, and that is the context in which it occurred. And may I add that we were especially eager that our meetings give a push to important talks already underway on reducing nuclear weapons. On this subject it would be foolish not to go the extra mile or, in this case, the extra four thousand miles. We discussed the great issues of our time. I made clear before the first meeting that no question would be swept aside, no issue buried, just because either side found it uncomfortable or inconvenient. I brought these questions to the summit and put them before Mr. Gorbachev.

We discussed nuclear arms and how to reduce them. I explained our proposals for equitable, verifiable, and deep reductions. I outlined my conviction that our proposals would make not just for a world that feels safer, but one that really is safer. I am pleased to report tonight that General Secretary Gorbachev and I did make a measure of progress here. We have a long way to go, but we're still heading in the right direction. We moved arms control forward from where we were last January, when the Soviets returned to the table. We are both instructing our negotiators to hasten their vital work. The world is waiting for results.

Specifically, we agreed in Geneva that each side should move to cut offensive nuclear arms by 50 percent in appropriate categories. In our joint statement we called for early progress on this, turning the talks toward our chief goal—offensive reductions. We called for an interim accord on intermediate-range nuclear forces, leading, I hope, to the complete elimination of this class of missiles—and all of this with tough verification. We also made progress in combating, together, the spread of nuclear weapons, an arms control area in which we've cooperated effectively over the years.

We are also opening a dialogue on combating the spread and use of chemical weapons, while moving to ban them altogether. Other arms control dialogues—in Vienna on conventional forces and in Stockholm on lessening the chances for surprise attack in Europe—also received a boost. And finally, we agreed to begin work on risk reduction centers, a decision that should give special satisfaction to Senators Nunn and Warner, who so ably promoted this idea.

I described our Strategic Defense Initiative, our research effort, that envisions the possibility of defensive systems which could ultimately protect all nations against the danger of nuclear war. This discussion produced a very direct exchange of views. Mr. Gorbachev insisted that we might use a strategic defense system to put offensive weapons into space and establish nuclear superiority. I made it clear that SDI has nothing to do with offensive weapons; that, instead, we are investigating nonnuclear defense systems that would only threaten offensive missiles, not people. If our research succeeds, it will bring much closer the safer, more stable world that we seek. Nations could defend themselves against missile attack and mankind, at long last, escape the prison of mutual terror. And this is my dream.

So, I welcomed the chance to tell Mr. Gorbachev that we are a nation that defends, rather than attacks; that our alliances are defensive, not offensive. We don't seek nuclear superiority. We do not seek a first-strike advantage over the Soviet Union. Indeed, one of my fundamental arms control objectives is to get rid of first-strike weapons altogether. This is why we've proposed a 50 percent reduction in the most threatening nuclear weapons, especially those that could carry out a first strike.

I went further in expressing our peaceful intentions. I described our proposal in the Geneva negotiations for a reciprocal program of open laboratories in strategic defense research. We're offering to permit Soviet experts to see firsthand that SDI does not involve offensive weapons. American scientists would be allowed to visit comparable facilities of the Soviet strategic defense program, which, in fact, has involved much more than research for many years. Finally, I reassured Mr. Gorbachev on another point. I promised that if our research reveals that a defense against nuclear missiles is possible, we would sit down with our allies and the Soviet Union to see how together we could replace all strategic ballistic missiles with such a defense, which threatens no one.

We discussed threats to the peace in several regions of the world. I explained my proposals for a peace process to stop the wars in Afghanistan, Nicaragua, Ethiopia, Angola, and Cambodia—those places where insurgencies that speak for the people are pitted against regimes which obviously do not represent the will or the approval of the people. I tried to be very clear about where our sympathies lie; I believe I succeeded. We discussed human rights. We Americans believe that history teaches no clearer lesson than this: Those countries which respect the rights of their own people tend, inevitably, to respect the rights of their neighbors. Human rights, therefore, is not an abstract moral issue; it is a peace issue. Finally, we discussed the barriers to communication between our societies, and I elaborated on my proposals for real people-to-people contacts on a wide scale. Americans should know the people of the Soviet Union—their hopes and fears and the facts of their lives. And citizens of the Soviet Union need to know of America's deep desire for peace and our unwavering attachment to freedom.

As you can see, our talks were wide-ranging. And let me at this point tell you what we agreed upon and what we didn't. We remain far apart on a number of issues, as had to be expected. However, we reached agreement on a number of matters, and as I mentioned, we agreed to continue meeting, and this is important and very good. There's always room for movement, action, and progress when people are talking to each other instead of about each other.

We've concluded a new agreement designed to bring the best of America's artists and academics to the Soviet Union. The exhibits that will be included in this exchange are one of the most effective ways for the average Soviet citizen to learn about our way of life. This agreement will also expand the opportunities for Americans to experience the Soviet people's rich cultural heritage, because their artists and academics will be coming here. We've also decided to go forward with a number of people-to-people initiatives that will go beyond greater contact, not only between the political leaders of our two countries but our respective students, teachers, and others as well. We have emphasized youth exchanges. And this will help break down stereotypes, build friendships, and, frankly, provide an alternative to propaganda.

We've agreed to establish a new Soviet consulate in New York and a new American consulate in Kiev. And this will bring a permanent U.S. presence to the Ukraine for the first time in decades. And we have also, together with the government of Japan, concluded a Pacific air safety agreement with the Soviet Union. This is designed to set up cooperative measures to improve civil air safety in that region of the Pacific. What happened before must never to be allowed to happen there again. And as a potential way of dealing with the energy needs of the world of the future, we have also advocated international cooperation to explore the feasibility of developing fusion energy.

All of these steps are part of a long-term effort to build a more stable relationship with the Soviet Union. No one ever said it could be easy, but we've come a long way. As for Soviet expansionism in a number of regions of the world—while there is little chance of immediate change, we will continue to support the heroic efforts of those who fight for freedom. But we have also agreed to continue, and to intensify, our meetings with the Soviets on this and other regional conflicts and to work toward political solutions.

We know the limits as well as the promise of summit meetings. This is, after all, the eleventh summit of the postwar era and still the differences endure. But we believe continued meetings between the leaders of the United States and the Soviet Union can help bridge those differences. The fact is, every new day begins with possibilities; it's up to us to fill it with the things that move us toward progress and peace. Hope, therefore, is a realistic attitude and despair an uninteresting little vice.

And so, was our journey worthwhile? Well, thirty years ago, when Ike, President Eisenhower, had just returned from a summit in Geneva, he said, "The wide gulf that separates so far East and West is wide and deep." Well, today, three decades later, that is still true. But, yes, this meeting was worthwhile for both sides. A new realism spawned the summit. The summit itself was a good start, and now our byword must be "steady as we go." I am, as you are, impatient for results. But goodwill and good hopes do not always yield lasting results, and quick fixes don't fix big problems. Just as we must avoid illusions on our side, so we must dispel them on the Soviet side. I have made it clear to Mr. Gorbachev that we must reduce the mistrust and suspicions between us if we are to do such things as reduce arms, and this will take deeds, not words alone. And I believe he is in agreement.

Where do we go from here? Well, our desire for improved relations is strong. We're ready and eager for step-by-step progress. We know that peace is not just the absence of war. We don't want a phony peace or a frail peace. We didn't go in pursuit of some kind of illusory détente. We can't be satisfied with cosmetic improvements that won't stand the test of time. We want real peace.

As I flew back this evening, I had many thoughts. In just a few days families across America will gather to celebrate Thanksgiving. And again, [just] as our forefathers . . . voyaged to America, we traveled to Geneva with peace as our goal and freedom as our guide. For there can be no greater good than the quest for peace and no finer purpose than the preservation of freedom. It is 350 years since the first Thanksgiving, when Pilgrims and Indians huddled together on the edge of an unknown continent. And now here we are gathered together on the edge of an unknown future, but, like our forefathers, really not so much afraid, but full of hope and trusting in God, as ever.

Thank you for allowing me to talk to you this evening, and God bless you all.

"Tear Down This Wall!"

There is some disagreement among former Reagan staffers about how the most famous line from his second trip to West Berlin came into being. But two facts are not in dispute: First, several top Reagan advisers wanted that line cut—they did not want the president to call on the Soviets to tear down the Berlin Wall in his June 12, 1987, speech at the Brandenburg Gate. And second, Reagan himself wanted the line kept in. Biographer Steven F. Hayward notes that Reagan would go on to repeat the call to tear down the wall fourteen times during the remaining year and a half of his presidency. In 1989, less than a year after Reagan left office, the wall fell. And in 1990, as the formal reunion of West and East Germany was being finalized, Reagan returned to Berlin as a private citizen and himself took a hammer and chisel to one of the wall's remaining fragments.

Our gathering today is being broadcast throughout Western Europe and North America. I understand that it is being seen and heard as well in the East. To those listening throughout Eastern Europe, I extend my warmest greetings and the goodwill of the American people. To those listening in East Berlin, a special word: Although I cannot be with you, I address my remarks to you just as surely as to those standing here before me. For I join you, as I join your fellow countrymen in the West, in this firm, this unalterable belief: *Es gibt nur ein Berlin.* [There is only one Berlin.]

Behind me stands a wall that encircles the free sectors of this city, part of a vast system of barriers that divides the entire continent of Europe. From the Baltic, south, those barriers cut across Germany in a gash of barbed wire, concrete, dog runs, and guard towers. Farther south, there may be no visible, no obvious wall. But there remain armed guards and checkpoints all the same—still a restriction on the right to travel, still an instrument to impose upon ordinary men and women the will of a totalitarian state. Yet it is here in Berlin where the wall emerges most clearly; here, cutting across your city, where the news photo and the television screen have imprinted this brutal division of a continent upon the mind of the world. Standing before the Brandenburg Gate, every man is a German, separated from his fellow men. Every man is a Berliner, forced to look upon a scar.

[West German] President [Richard] von Weizsäcker has said, "The German question is open as long as the Brandenburg Gate is closed." Today I say, as long as this gate is closed, as long as this scar of a wall is permitted to stand, it is not the German question alone that remains open, but the question of freedom for all mankind.

Yet I do not come here to lament. For I find in Berlin a message of hope, even in the shadow of this wall, a message of triumph. . . .

In the 1950s, [Soviet premier Nikita] Khrushchev predicted, "We will bury you." But in the West today, we see a free world that has achieved a level of prosperity and well-being unprecedented in all human history. In the Communist world, we see failure, technological backwardness, declining standards of health, even want of the most basic kind: too little food. Even today, the Soviet Union still cannot feed itself. After these four decades, then, there stands before the entire world one great and inescapable conclusion: Freedom leads to prosperity. Freedom replaces the ancient hatreds among the nations with comity and peace. Freedom is the victor.

And now the Soviets themselves may, in a limited way, be coming to understand the importance of freedom. We hear much from Moscow about a new policy of reform and openness. Some political prisoners have been released. Certain foreign news broadcasts are no longer being jammed. Some economic enterprises have been permitted to operate with greater freedom from state control. Are these the beginnings of profound changes in the Soviet state? Or are they token gestures, intended to raise false hopes in the West, or to strengthen the Soviet system without changing it? We welcome change and openness; for we believe that freedom and security go together, that the advance of human liberty can only strengthen the cause of world peace.

There is one sign the Soviets can make that would be unmistakable, that would advance dramatically the cause of freedom and peace.

General Secretary Gorbachev, if you seek peace, if you seek prosperity for the Soviet Union and Eastern Europe, if you seek liberalization: Come here to this gate!

Mr. Gorbachev, open this gate!

Mr. Gorbachev, tear down this wall!

I understand the fear of war and the pain of division that afflict this continent—and I pledge to you my country's efforts to help overcome these burdens. To be sure, we in the West must resist Soviet expansion.

So we must maintain defenses of unassailable strength. Yet we seek peace; so we must strive to reduce arms on both sides. . . .

In Europe, only one nation and those it controls refuse to join the community of freedom. Yet in this age of redoubled economic growth, of information and innovation, the Soviet Union faces a choice: It must make fundamental changes, or it will become obsolete. Today thus represents a moment of hope. We in the West stand ready to cooperate with the East to promote true openness, to break down barriers that separate people, to create a safer, freer world.

And surely there is no better place than Berlin, the meeting place of East and West, to make a start. Free people of Berlin: Today, as in the past, the United States stands for the strict observance and full implementation of all parts of the Four Power Agreement of 1971. Let us use this occasion, the 750th anniversary of this city, to usher in a new era, to seek a still fuller, richer life for the Berlin of the future. Together, let us maintain and develop the ties between the Federal Republic and the Western sectors of Berlin, which is permitted by the 1971 agreement.

And I invite Mr. Gorbachev: Let us work to bring the Eastern and Western parts of the city closer together, so that all the inhabitants of all Berlin can enjoy the benefits that come with life in one of the great cities of the world. . . .

In these four decades, as I have said, you Berliners have built a great city. You've done so in spite of threats—the Soviet attempts to impose the East mark, the blockade. Today the city thrives in spite of the challenges implicit in the very presence of this wall. What keeps you here? Certainly there's a great deal to be said for your fortitude, for your defiant courage. But I believe there's something deeper, something that involves Berlin's whole look and feel and way of life—not mere sentiment. No one could live long in Berlin without being completely disabused of illusions. Something instead, that has seen the difficulties of life in Berlin but chose to accept them, that continues to build this good and proud city in contrast to a surrounding totalitarian presence that refuses to release human energies or aspirations. Something that speaks with a powerful voice of affirmation, that says yes to this city, yes to the future, yes to freedom. In a word, I would submit that what keeps you in Berlin is love—love both profound and abiding.

Perhaps this gets to the root of the matter, to the most fundamental distinction of all between East and West. The totalitarian world produces backwardness because it does such violence to the spirit, thwarting the human impulse to create, to enjoy, to worship. The totalitarian world finds even symbols of love and of worship an affront. Years ago, before the East Germans began rebuilding their churches, they erected a secular structure: the television tower at Alexanderplatz. Virtually ever since, the authorities have been working to correct what they view as the tower's one major flaw, treating the glass sphere at the top with paints and chemicals of every kind. Yet even today when the sun strikes that sphere—that sphere that towers over all Berlin—the light makes the sign of the cross. There in Berlin, like the city itself, symbols of love, symbols of worship, cannot be suppressed.

As I looked out a moment ago from the Reichstag, that embodiment of German unity, I noticed words crudely spray-painted upon the wall, perhaps by a young Berliner: "This wall will fall. Beliefs become reality." Yes, across Europe, this wall will fall. For it cannot withstand faith; it cannot withstand truth. The wall cannot withstand freedom.

6

HUMAN DIGNITY AND
CIVIL RIGHTS

*President Reagan's belief in the importance of political and economic free-
dom and his judgments about the Soviet regime were inseparable from his
belief in the dignity and uniqueness of each individual and the sacredness of
human life.*

Abortion and the Conscience
of the Nation

President Reagan frequently spoke out against abortion and ad-
dressed pro-life audiences, but his most in-depth discussion of the
subject appeared in print. Drafted for the president by the White
House policy and writing staff, this essay was first published in the
summer 1983 issue of the Human Life Review.

The tenth anniversary of the Supreme Court decision in *Roe v. Wade* is a good time for us to pause and reflect. Our nationwide policy of abortion-on-demand through all nine months of pregnancy was neither voted for by our people nor enacted by our legislators—not a single state had such unrestricted abortion before the Supreme Court decreed it to be national policy in 1973. But the consequences of this judicial decision are now obvious: Since 1973, more than fifteen million unborn children have had their lives snuffed out by legalized abortions. That is over ten times the number of Americans lost in all our nation's wars.

Make no mistake, abortion-on-demand is not a right granted by the Constitution. No serious scholar, including one disposed to agree with the court's result, has argued that the framers of the Constitution intended to create such a right. Shortly after the *Roe v. Wade* decision, Professor John Hart Ely, now dean of Stanford Law School, wrote that the opinion "is not constitutional law and gives almost no sense of an obligation to try to be." Nowhere do the plain words of the Constitution even hint at a "right" so sweeping as to permit abortion up to the time the child is ready to be born. Yet that is what the court ruled.

As an act of "raw judicial power" (to use Justice White's biting phrase), the decision by the seven-man majority in *Roe v. Wade* has so far been made to stick. But the court's decision has by no means settled the debate. Instead, *Roe v. Wade* has become a continuing prod to the conscience of the nation.

Abortion concerns not just the unborn child; it concerns every one of us. The English poet John Donne wrote, "Any man's death diminishes me, because I am involved in mankind; and therefore never send to know for whom the bell tolls; it tolls for thee."

We cannot diminish the value of one category of human life—the unborn—without diminishing the value of all human life. We saw tragic proof of this truism last year when the Indiana courts allowed the starvation death of "Baby Doe" in Bloomington because the child had Down's syndrome.

Many of our fellow citizens grieve over the loss of life that has followed *Roe v. Wade*. Margaret Heckler, soon after being nominated to head the largest department of our government, Health and Human Services, told an audience that she believed abortion to be the greatest moral crisis facing our country today. And the revered Mother Teresa, who works in the streets of Calcutta ministering to dying people in her world-famous mission of mercy, has said that "the greatest misery of our time is the generalized abortion of children."

Over the first two years of my administration I have closely followed and assisted efforts in Congress to reverse the tide of abortion— efforts of congressmen, senators, and citizens responding to an urgent moral crisis. Regrettably, I have also seen the massive efforts of those who, under the banner of "freedom of choice," have so far blocked every effort to reverse nationwide abortion-on-demand.

Despite the formidable obstacles before us, we must not lose heart. This is not the first time our country has been divided by a Supreme Court decision that denied the value of certain human lives. The *Dred*

Scott decision of 1857 was not overturned in a day, or a year, or even a decade. At first, only a minority of Americans recognized and deplored the moral crisis brought about by denying the full humanity of our black brothers and sisters; but that minority persisted in their vision and finally prevailed. They did it by appealing to the hearts and minds of their countrymen, to the truth of human dignity under God. From their example, we know that respect for the sacred value of human life is too deeply engrained in the hearts of our people to remain forever suppressed. But the great majority of the American people have not yet made their voices heard, and we cannot expect them to—any more than the public voice arose against slavery—*until* the issue is clearly framed and presented.

What, then, is the real issue? I have often said that when we talk about abortion, we are talking about two lives—the life of the mother and the life of the unborn child. Why else do we call a pregnant woman a mother? I have also said that anyone who doesn't feel sure whether we are talking about a second human life should clearly give life the benefit of the doubt. If you don't know whether a body is alive or dead, you would never bury it. I think this consideration itself should be enough for all of us to insist on protecting the unborn.

The case against abortion does not rest here, however, for medical practice confirms at every step the correctness of these moral sensibilities. Modern medicine treats the unborn child as a patient. Medical pioneers have made great breakthroughs in treating the unborn—for genetic problems, vitamin deficiencies, irregular heart rhythms, and other medical conditions. Who can forget George Will's moving account of the little boy who underwent brain surgery six times during the nine weeks before he was born? Who is the *patient* if not that tiny unborn human being, who can feel pain when he or she is approached by doctors who come to kill rather than to cure?

The real question today is not when human life begins, but, *What is the value of human life?* The abortionist who reassembles the arms and legs of a tiny baby to make sure all its parts have been torn from its mother's body can hardly doubt whether it is a human being. The real question for him and for all of us is whether that tiny human life has a God-given right to be protected by the law—the same right we have.

What more dramatic confirmation could we have of the real issue than the Baby Doe case in Bloomington, Indiana? The death of that tiny infant tore at the hearts of all Americans because the child was undeniably a live human being—one lying helpless before the eyes of the doctors and the eyes of the nation. The real issue for the courts was *not* whether Baby Doe was a human being. The real issue was whether to protect the life of a human being who had Down's syndrome, who would probably be mentally handicapped, but who needed a routine surgical procedure to unblock his esophagus and allow him to eat. A doctor testified to the presiding judge that, even with his physical problem corrected, Baby Doe would have a "nonexistent" possibility for "a minimally adequate quality of life"—in other words, that retardation was the equivalent of a crime deserving the death penalty. The judge let Baby Doe starve and die, and the Indiana Supreme Court sanctioned his decision.

Federal law does not allow federally assisted hospitals to decide that Down's syndrome infants are not worth treating, much less to decide to starve them to death. Accordingly, I have directed the Departments of Justice and HHS to apply civil rights regulations to protect handicapped newborns. All hospitals receiving federal funds must post notices which will clearly state that failure to feed handicapped babies is prohibited by federal law. The basic issue is whether to value and protect the lives of the handicapped, whether to recognize the sanctity of human life. This is the same basic issue that underlies the question of abortion.

The 1981 Senate hearings on the beginning of human life brought out the basic issue more clearly than ever before. The many medical and scientific witnesses who testified disagreed on many things, but not on the *scientific* evidence that the unborn child is alive, is a distinct individual, or is a member of the human species. They did disagree over the *value* question, whether to give value to a human life at its early and most vulnerable stages of existence.

Regrettably, we live at a time when some persons do not value all human life. They want to pick and choose which individuals have value. Some have said that only those individuals with "consciousness of self" are human beings. One such writer has followed this deadly logic and concluded that "shocking as it may seem, a newly born infant is not a human being."

A Nobel Prize–winning scientist has suggested that if a handicapped child "were not declared fully human until three days after birth, then all parents could be allowed the choice." In other words, "quality control" to see if newly born human beings are up to snuff.

Obviously, some influential people want to deny that every human life has intrinsic, sacred worth. They insist that a member of the human race must have certain qualities before they accord him or her status as a "human being."

Events have borne out the editorial in a California medical journal which explained three years before *Roe v. Wade* that the social acceptance of abortion is a "defiance of the long-held Western ethic of intrinsic and equal value for every human life regardless of its stage, condition, or status."

Every legislator, every doctor, and every citizen needs to recognize that the real issue is whether to affirm and protect the sanctity of all human life, or to embrace a social ethic where some human lives are valued and others are not. As a nation, we must choose between the "sanctity of life" ethic and the "quality of life" ethic.

I have no trouble identifying the answer our nation has always given to this basic question, and the answer that I hope and pray it will give in the future. America was founded by men and women who shared a vision of the value of each and every individual. They stated this vision clearly from the very start in the Declaration of Independence, using words that every schoolboy and schoolgirl can recite:

> *We hold these truths to be self-evident, that all men are created equal, that they are endowed by their Creator with certain unalienable Rights, that among these are Life, Liberty, and the pursuit of Happiness.*

We fought a terrible war to guarantee that one category of mankind— black people in America—could not be denied the inalienable rights with which their Creator endowed them. The great champion of the sanctity of all human life in that day, Abraham Lincoln, gave us his assessment of the Declaration's purpose. Speaking of the framers of that noble document, he said:

> *This was their majestic interpretation of the economy of the Universe. This was their lofty, and wise, and noble understanding of the justice of the Creator to His creatures. Yes, gentlemen, to all His creatures, to the whole great family of man. In their enlightened belief, nothing stamped with the divine image and likeness was sent into the world to be trodden on. . . . They grasped not only the whole race of man then living, but they reached forward and seized upon the farthest posterity. They erected a beacon to guide their children and their children's children, and the countless myriads who should inhabit the earth in other ages.*

He warned also of the danger we would face if we closed our eyes to the value of life in any category of human beings:

I should like to know, if taking this old Declaration of Independence, which declares that all men are equal upon principle, and making exceptions to it, where will it stop? If one man says it does not mean a Negro, why not another say it does not mean some other man?

When Congressman John A. Bingham of Ohio drafted the Fourteenth Amendment to guarantee the rights of life, liberty, and property to all human beings, he explained that *all* are "entitled to the protection of American law, because its divine spirit of equality declares that all men are created equal." He said the rights guaranteed by the amendment would therefore apply to "any human being." Justice William Brennan, writing in another case decided only the year before *Roe v. Wade,* referred to our society as one that "strongly affirms the sanctity of life."

Another William Brennan—not the justice—has reminded us of the terrible consequences that can follow when a nation rejects the "sanctity of life" ethic:

The cultural environment for a human holocaust is present whenever any society can be misled into defining individuals as less than human and therefore devoid of value and respect.

As a nation today, we have *not* rejected the sanctity of human life. The American people have not had an opportunity to express their view on the sanctity of human life in the unborn. I am convinced that Americans do not want to play God with the value of human life. It is not for us to decide who is worthy to live and who is not. Even the Supreme Court's opinion in *Roe v. Wade* did not explicitly reject the traditional American idea of intrinsic worth and value in all human life; it simply dodged this issue.

The Congress has before it several measures that would enable our people to reaffirm the sanctity of human life, even the smallest and the youngest and the most defenseless. The Human Life Bill expressly recognizes the unborn as human beings and accordingly protects them as persons under our Constitution. This bill, first introduced by Senator Jesse Helms, provided the vehicle for the Senate hearings in 1981 which contributed so much to our understanding of the real issue of abortion.

The Respect Human Life Act, just introduced in the Ninety-Eighth Congress, states in its first section that the policy of the United States is "to protect innocent life, both before and after birth." This bill, sponsored by Congressman Henry Hyde and Senator Roger Jepsen, prohibits the federal government from performing abortions or assisting those who do so, except to save the life of the mother. It also addresses the pressing issue of infanticide, which, as we have seen, flows inevitably from permissive abortion as another step in the denial of the inviolability of innocent human life.

I have endorsed each of these measures, as well as the more difficult route of constitutional amendment, and I will give these initiatives my full support. Each of them, in different ways, attempts to reverse the tragic policy of abortion-on-demand imposed by the Supreme Court ten years ago. Each of them is a decisive way to affirm the sanctity of human life.

We must all educate ourselves to the reality of the horrors taking place. Doctors today know that unborn children can feel a touch within the womb and that they respond to pain. But how many Americans are aware that abortion techniques are allowed today, in all fifty states, that burn the skin of a baby with a salt solution, in an agonizing death that can last for hours?

Another example: Two years ago, the *Philadelphia Inquirer* ran a Sunday special supplement on "The Dreaded Complication." The "dreaded complication" referred to in the article—the complication feared by doctors who perform abortions—is the survival of the child despite all the painful attacks during the abortion procedure. Some unborn children *do* survive the late-term abortions the Supreme Court has made legal. Is there any question that these victims of abortion deserve our attention and protection? Is there any question that those who *don't* survive were living human beings before they were killed?

Late-term abortions, especially when the baby survives but is then killed by starvation, neglect, or suffocation, show once again the link between abortion and infanticide. The time to stop both is now. As my administration acts to stop infanticide, we will be fully aware of the real issue that underlies the death of babies before and soon after birth.

Our society has, fortunately, become sensitive to the rights and special needs of the handicapped, but I am shocked that physical or mental handicaps of newborns are still used to justify their extinction. This administration has a surgeon general, Dr. C. Everett Koop, who has done perhaps more than any other American for handicapped children, by pioneering surgical techniques to help them, by speaking out on the value of their lives, and by working with them in the context of loving families. You will not find his former patients advocating the so-called "quality of life" ethic.

I know that when the true issue of infanticide is placed before the American people, with all the facts openly aired, we will have no trouble deciding that a mentally or physically handicapped baby has the same intrinsic worth and right to life as the rest of us. As the New Jersey Supreme Court said two decades ago, in a decision upholding the sanctity of human life, "a child need not be perfect to have a worthwhile life."

Whether we are talking about pain suffered by unborn children, or about late-term abortions, or about infanticide, we inevitably focus on the humanity of the unborn child. Each of these issues is a potential rallying point for the "sanctity of life" ethic. Once we as a nation rally around any one of these issues to affirm the sanctity of life, we will see the importance of affirming this principle across the board.

Malcolm Muggeridge, the English writer, goes right to the heart of the matter: "Either life is always and in all circumstances sacred, or intrinsically of no account; it is inconceivable that it should be in some cases the one, and in some the other." The sanctity of innocent human life is a principle that Congress should proclaim at every opportunity.

It is possible that the Supreme Court itself may overturn its abortion rulings. We need only recall that in *Brown v. Board of Education* the court reversed its own earlier "separate but equal" decision. I believe if the Supreme Court took another look at *Roe v. Wade*, and considered the real issue between the "sanctity of life" ethic and the "quality of life" ethic, it would change its mind once again.

As we continue to work to overturn *Roe v. Wade*, we must also continue to lay the groundwork for a society in which abortion is not the accepted answer to unwanted pregnancy. Pro-life people have already taken heroic steps, often at great personal sacrifice, to provide for unwed mothers. I recently spoke about a young pregnant woman named Victoria, who said, "In this society we save whales, we save timber wolves and bald eagles and Coke bottles. Yet, everyone wanted me to throw away my baby." She has been helped by Sav-A-Life, a group in Dallas, which provides a way for unwed mothers to preserve the human life within them when they might otherwise be tempted to resort to abortion. I think also of House of His Creation in Coatesville, Pennsylvania, where a loving couple has taken in almost two hundred young women in the past ten years. They have seen, as a fact of life, that the girls are *not* better off having abortions than saving their babies. I am also reminded of the remarkable Rossow family of Ellington,

Connecticut, who have opened their hearts and their home to nine handicapped adopted and foster children.

The Adolescent Family Life Program, adopted by Congress at the request of Senator Jeremiah Denton, has opened new opportunities for unwed mothers to give their children life. We should not rest until our entire society echoes the tone of John Powell in the dedication of his book, *Abortion: The Silent Holocaust,* a dedication to every woman carrying an unwanted child: "Please believe that you are not alone. There are many of us that truly love you, who want to stand at your side, and help in any way we can." And we can echo the always-practical woman of faith, Mother Teresa, when she says, "If you don't want the little child, that unborn child, give him to me." We have so many families in America seeking to adopt children that the slogan "every child a wanted child" is now the emptiest of all reasons to tolerate abortion.

I have often said we need to join in prayer to bring protection to the unborn. Prayer and action are needed to uphold the sanctity of human life. I believe it will not be possible to accomplish our work, the work of saving lives, "without being a soul of prayer." The famous British member of Parliament, William Wilberforce, prayed with his small group of influential friends, the "Clapham Sect," for decades to see an end to slavery in the British empire. Wilberforce led that struggle in Parliament, unflaggingly, because he believed in the sanctity of human life. He saw the fulfillment of his impossible dream when Parliament outlawed slavery just before his death.

Let his faith and perseverance be our guide. We will never recognize the true value of our own lives until we affirm the value in the life of others, a value of which Malcolm Muggeridge says, "However low it flickers or fiercely burns, it is still a Divine flame which no man dare presume to put out, be his motives ever so humane and enlightened."

Abraham Lincoln recognized that we could not survive as a free land when some men could decide that others were not fit to be free and should therefore be slaves. Likewise, we cannot survive as a free nation when some men decide that others are not fit to live and should be abandoned to abortion or infanticide. My administration is dedicated to the preservation of America as a free land, and there is no cause more important for preserving that freedom than affirming the transcendent right to life of all human beings, the right without which no other rights have any meaning.

"Dr. King Had Awakened Something Strong and True"

When asked in January 1983 about the possibility of creating a federal holiday to mark the birthday of Martin Luther King Jr., President Reagan said that he believed the day "should be nationally recognized" but not formally made a federal holiday, "a day that closes down industry, and the government closes down and so forth." In the following months, however, as it became clear that there was bipartisan support in Congress for the creation of such a holiday, the president changed his mind. In the presence of Coretta Scott King and other members of the King family, he signed the bill creating the holiday in a Rose Garden ceremony on the morning of November 2, 1983.

Mrs. King, members of the King family, distinguished members of the Congress, ladies and gentlemen, honored guests, I'm very pleased to welcome you to the White House, the home that belongs to all of us, the American people.

When I was thinking of the contributions to our country of the man that we're honoring today, a passage attributed to the American poet John Greenleaf Whittier comes to mind. "Each crisis brings its word and deed." In America, in the fifties and sixties, one of the important crises we faced was racial discrimination. The man whose words and deeds in that crisis stirred our nation to the very depths of its soul was Dr. Martin Luther King Jr.

Martin Luther King was born in 1929 in an America where, because of the color of their skin, nearly one in ten lived lives that were separate and unequal. Most black Americans were taught in segregated schools. Across the country, too many could find only poor jobs, toiling for low wages. They were refused entry into hotels and restaurants, made to use separate facilities. In a nation that proclaimed liberty and justice for all, too many black Americans were living with neither.

In one city, a rule required all blacks to sit in the rear of public buses. But in 1955, when a brave woman named Rosa Parks was told to move to the back of the bus, she said, "No." A young minister in a local Baptist church, Martin Luther King, then organized a boycott of the bus company—a boycott that stunned the country. Within six months the courts had ruled the segregation of public transportation unconstitutional.

Dr. King had awakened something strong and true, a sense that true justice must be color-blind, and that among white and black Americans, as he put it, "their destiny is tied up with our destiny, and their freedom is inextricably bound to our freedom; we cannot walk alone."

In the years after the bus boycott, Dr. King made equality of rights his life's work. Across the country, he organized boycotts, rallies, and marches. Often he was beaten, imprisoned, but he never stopped teaching nonviolence. "Work with the faith," he told his followers, "that unearned suffering is redemptive." In 1964 Dr. King became the youngest man in history to win the Nobel Peace Prize.

Dr. King's work brought him to this city often. And in one swelter-ing August day in 1963, he addressed a quarter of a million people at the Lincoln Memorial. If American history grows from two centuries to twenty, his words that day will never be forgotten. "I have a dream that one day on the red hills of Georgia, the sons of former slaves and the sons of former slave owners will be able to sit down together at the table of brotherhood."

In 1968 Martin Luther King was gunned down by a brutal assassin, his life cut short at the age of thirty-nine. But those thirty-nine short years had changed America forever. The Civil Rights Act of 1964 had guaranteed all Americans equal use of public accommodations, equal access to programs financed by federal funds, and the right to compete for employment on the sole basis of individual merit. The Voting Rights Act of 1965 had made certain that from then on black Americans would get to vote. But most important, there was not just a change of law; there was a change of heart. The conscience of America had been touched. Across the land, people had begun to treat each other not as blacks and whites, but as fellow Americans.

And since Dr. King's death, his father, the Reverend Martin Luther King Sr., and his wife, Coretta King, have eloquently and forcefully carried on his work. Also his family have joined in that cause.

Now our nation has decided to honor Dr. Martin Luther King Jr. by setting aside a day each year to remember him and the just cause he stood for. We've made historic strides since Rosa Parks refused to go to the back of the bus. As a democratic people, we can take pride in the knowledge that we Americans recognized a grave injustice and took ac-tion to correct it. And we should remember that in far too many coun-tries, people like Dr. King never have the opportunity to speak out at all.

But traces of bigotry still mar America. So, each year on Martin Luther King Day, let us not only recall Dr. King, but rededicate our-selves to the Commandments he believed in and sought to live every day: Thou shall love thy God with all thy heart, and thou shall love thy neighbor as thyself. And I just have to believe that all of us—if all of us, young and old, Republicans and Democrats, do all we can to live up to those Commandments, then we will see the day when Dr. King's dream comes true, and in his words, "all of God's children will be able to sing with new meaning, '. . . land where my fathers died, land of the pilgrim's pride, from every mountainside, let freedom ring.'"

Thank you, God bless you, and I will sign it.

"Equal Treatment and Equality Before the Law"

In his weekly radio address for June 15, 1985—made from Camp David, Maryland—President Reagan explained his opposition to quotas in the name of civil rights.

In less than three weeks we'll be celebrating the greatest blow ever struck for the cause of freedom—the Declaration of Independence. "We hold these truths to be self-evident," our Founding Fathers proclaimed, "that all men are created equal, that they are endowed by their Creator with certain unalienable Rights."

That declaration inspired our nation to reach new heights of human freedom, but its promise wasn't complete until we abolished the shame of slavery from our land and, in the lifetime of many of us, wrote the civil rights statutes that outlawed discrimination by race, religion, gender, or national origin.

Discrimination is still not yet a thing of the past, unfortunately; and for the last four and a half years, this administration has acted vigorously to defend and extend every American's fundamental right to equal treatment.

The Justice Department has worked energetically to end discrimination in employment, voting, housing—in all the areas covered by law. Our record on enforcing minority voting rights is at the top of the list. And we've increased to an all-time high the number of criminal civil rights cases filed. We have a proud record on civil rights.

The principle that guides us and the principle embodied in the law is one of nondiscrimination. I'm sure that you have all seen the statue representing justice that presides in many of our courtrooms—the woman with the blindfold covering her eyes. Her eyes are covered because true justice should never depend on whether you're rich or poor, or black or white, or if you're Hispanic or Asian, or if your ancestors came from Italy, Poland, Latvia, or any other country, including Ireland, where some of my family's from.

Equal treatment and equality before the law—these are the foundations on which a just and free society is built. But there are some today who, in the name of equality, would have us practice discrimination. They have turned our civil rights laws on their head, claiming they mean exactly the opposite of what they say. These people tell us that the government should enforce discrimination in favor of some groups through hiring quotas, under which people get or lose particular jobs or promotions solely because of their race or sex. Some bluntly assert that our civil rights laws only apply to special groups and were never intended to protect every American.

Well, they couldn't be more wrong. When the Civil Rights Act of 1964 was being debated in the Congress, Senator Hubert Humphrey, one of its leading advocates, said he'd start eating the pages of the act if it contained any language which provides that an employer will have to hire on the basis of percentage or quota. But I think if Senator Humphrey saw how some people today are interpreting that act, he'd get a severe case of indigestion.

The truth is, quotas deny jobs to many who would have gotten them otherwise, but who weren't born a specified race or sex. That's discrimination pure and simple and is exactly what the civil rights laws were designed to stop. Quotas also cast a shadow on the real achievements of minorities, which makes quotas a double tragedy.

In 1980 and 1984 I ran for president and told you I was opposed to quotas. In response to your mandate, our administration has worked to return the civil rights laws to their original meaning—to prevent discrimination against any and all Americans. . . .

Twenty-two years ago Martin Luther King proclaimed his dream of a society rid of discrimination and prejudice, a society where people would be judged on the content of their character, not by the color of their skin. That's the vision our entire administration is committed to—a society that keeps faith with the promise of our Declaration of Independence, a proud society in which all men and women truly are created free and equal under God.

Until next week, thanks for listening, and God bless you.

7

PATRIOTISM, CITIZENSHIP, AND THE AMERICAN CHARACTER

President Reagan believed in the fundamental decency of the American people: "The heart of America is strong; it's good and true. The cynics were wrong; America never was a sick society."

And to be an American, Reagan believed, meant embracing the ideal of freedom. He often paraphrased a letter he said he received: "You can leave here and move to Japan, but you can't become Japanese. You can move to France; you can't become a Frenchman or a Frenchwoman; Greece and not become a Greek; Turkey—all of these. But anybody, anyplace, from any corner in the world, can come to live in America and become an American. And I guess that we're the only place where that is true, and that's what we're all about. You know, it's the magic and the mystery and the majesty of freedom. It's your heritage, and wherever you go, be proud of it."

"All People Who Long for Freedom Are Our Fellow Countrymen"

This brief address was recorded for television broadcast by the U.S. International Communication Agency on New Year's Day in 1982.

A former president of the United States once said, "The chief ideal of the American people is idealism. . . . America is a nation of idealists." Well, that's as true today as when President Calvin Coolidge spoke those words back in 1925.

Americans remain dedicated to those concepts of liberty that have provided our people with freedom and abundance. Furthermore, we're a nation composed of people who have come here from every corner of the world, people of all races and creeds who have learned to live together in peace and prosperity. Perhaps you know someone or have relatives who now live here. Well, they're every bit as American as those who came here two centuries ago seeking freedom. In a very real sense all people who long for freedom are our fellow countrymen. That love of freedom is what brought us or our ancestors to this land.

Because of this special American character, our hearts go out to those who suffer oppression. Last year we saw the workers of Poland struggle to edge their country closer to freedom—and instead, they were given bloodshed and oppression. We saw the courageous people of Afghanistan battle against tremendous odds trying to cast off foreign domination.

During my lifetime, I have seen the rise of Fascism and Communism. Both philosophies glorify the arbitrary power of the state. These ideologies held, at first, a certain fascination for some intellectuals. But both theories fail. Both deny those God-given liberties that are the inalienable right of each person on this planet; indeed they deny the existence of God. Because of this fundamental flaw, Fascism has already been destroyed, and the bankruptcy of Communism has been laid bare for all to see—a system that is efficient in producing machines of war but cannot feed its people.

Americans begin this new year with a renewed commitment to our ideals and with confidence that the peace will be maintained and that freedom for all men will ultimately prevail. So, wherever you are, America sends to you a New Year's wish of goodwill. To all who yearn to breathe free, who long for a better life, we think of you; we pray for you; we're with you always.

"There's Got to Be a Pony in Here Somewhere"

President Reagan often told versions of this joke about optimism. He made this particular one in his remarks to the Reagan Administration Executive Forum on January 20, 1982.

This is an exciting time to be alive, an exciting time to be in Washington, a time of both challenge and reaffirmation. Each of us has been put here for a purpose. We must redress past errors, errors that have already cost the people we serve far too much in economic stagnation, joblessness, crippling taxes, and inflation. It isn't going to be easy; nothing really worth achieving ever is. But this is an optimistic nation, and I am optimistic. If I wasn't I'd never have left the ranch to come here in the first place. [*Laughter*]

Now, you know there's a simple definition for an optimist and a pessimist. An optimist asks, "Will you please pass the cream?" A pessimist says, "Is there any milk in that pitcher?" [*Laughter*]

But there's a story that maybe some of you know, and I just can't resist at this point telling it, because it has to do with the definition of "optimism." A man had two sons, and he was very disturbed about them. One was a pessimist beyond recall, and the other one was an optimist beyond reason. He talked to a child psychiatrist, who made a suggestion.

He said, "I think we can fix that." He said, "We'll get a room and we'll fill it with the most wonderful toys any boy ever had. And," he said, "we'll put the pessimist in, and when he finds out they're for him, he'll get over being a pessimist."

His father said, "What will you do about the optimist?"

"Well," he said, "I have a friend who's got a racing stable and they clean out the stalls every morning. And," he said, "I can get quite an amount of *that substance*." [*Laughter*] And he said, "We'll put that in another room, and when the optimist who's seen his brother get all those toys is then shown into that room and that's there, he'll get over being an optimist."

Well, they did, and they waited about five minutes. And then they opened the door, and the pessimist was sitting there crying as if his heart would break. He said, "I know somebody's going to come in and take these away from me." [*Laughter*]

Then they went down to the other room and they opened the door and there was the kid happy as a clam, throwing that stuff over his shoulders as fast as he could. And they said, "What are you doing?" And he says, "There's got to be a pony in here somewhere." [*Laughter*]

But I'm confident that if we all do our best today and in the months ahead, we can turn things around. There is a pony in here. [*Laughter*]

"Only in Our Melting Pot"

At the Republican National Convention in Dallas on August 23, 1984, President Reagan for the second time accepted his party's nomination for the presidency. The patriotic images with which he concluded his convention speech depict an America with a diversity of backgrounds but united in the love of freedom.

Holding the Olympic Games here in the United States began defining the promise of this season. [*Chants of "USA! USA! USA!"*] All through the spring and summer, we marveled at the journey of the Olympic torch as it made its passage east to west. Over nine thousand miles, by some four thousand runners, that flame crossed a portrait of our nation.

From our Gotham City, New York, to the Cradle of Liberty, Boston, across the Appalachian springtime, to the City of the Big Shoulders, Chicago. Moving south toward Atlanta, over to St. Louis, past its Gateway Arch, across wheat fields, into the stark beauty of the Southwest, and then up into the still, snowcapped Rockies. And, after circling the greening Northwest, it came down to California, across the Golden Gate, and finally into Los Angeles. And all along the way, that torch became a celebration of America. And we all became participants in the celebration.

Each new story was typical of this land of ours. There was Ansel Stubbs, a youngster of ninety-nine, who passed the torch in Kansas to four-year-old Katie Johnson. In Pineville, Kentucky, it came at one a.m., so hundreds of people lined the streets with candles. At Tupelo, Mississippi, at seven a.m. on a Sunday morning, a robed church choir sang "God Bless America" as the torch went by.

That torch went through the Cumberland Gap, past the Martin Luther King Jr. Memorial, down the Santa Fe Trail, and alongside Billy the Kid's grave.

In Richardson, Texas, it was carried by a fourteen-year-old boy in a special wheelchair. In West Virginia the runner came across a line of deaf children and let each one pass the torch for a few feet, and at the end these youngsters' hands talked excitedly in their sign language. Crowds spontaneously began singing "America the Beautiful" or "The Battle Hymn of the Republic."

And then, in San Francisco a Vietnamese immigrant, his little son held on his shoulders, dodged photographers and policemen to cheer a nineteen-year-old black man pushing an eighty-eight-year-old white woman in a wheelchair as she carried the torch.

My friends, that's America. [*Chants of "USA! USA! USA!"*]

We cheered in Los Angeles as the flame was carried in and the giant Olympic torch burst into a billowing fire in front of the teams, the youth of 140 nations assembled on the floor of the coliseum. And in that moment, maybe you were struck as I was with the uniqueness of what was taking place before a hundred thousand people in the stadium, most of them citizens of our country, and over a billion worldwide watching on television. There were athletes representing 140 countries here to compete in the one country in all the world whose people carry the bloodlines of all those 140 countries and more. Only in the United States is there such a rich mixture of races, creeds, and nationalities—only in our melting pot.

And that brings to mind another torch, the one that greeted so many of our parents and grandparents. Just this past Fourth of July, the torch atop the Statue of Liberty was hoisted down for replacement. We can be forgiven for thinking that maybe it was just worn out from lighting the way to freedom for seventeen million new Americans. So, now we'll put up a new one.

The poet called Miss Liberty's torch the "lamp beside the golden door." Well, that was the entrance to America, and it still is. And now you really know why we're here tonight.

The glistening hope of that lamp is still ours. Every promise, every opportunity, is still golden in this land. And through that golden door our children can walk into tomorrow with the knowledge that no one can be denied the promise that is America.

Her heart is full; her door is still golden, her future bright. She has arms big enough to comfort and strong enough to support, for the strength in her arms is the strength of her people. She will carry on in the eighties unafraid, unashamed, and unsurpassed.

In this springtime of hope, some lights seem eternal; America's is.

Thank you, God bless you, and God bless America.

"We Stand as a Beacon"

President Reagan often talked about America's inspiring example to the world, although never more eloquently than in these remarks to a patriotic festival in Decatur, Alabama, on Independence Day in 1984. As he did on hundreds of other occasions going back at least to 1969, Reagan paraphrased the speech that Puritan leader John Winthrop gave in April 1630 to those joining him on a voyage from England to Massachusetts Bay: "For we must consider that we shall be as a city upon a hill. The eyes of all people are upon us."

But I'm so happy to be here tonight. I don't get to the South often enough to suit me. Come to think of it, I don't get to California as much as I'd like either. [*Laughter*] But I always feel a special affinity for this part of the country and the people in it.

And even now in these modern times when people who aren't from the South talk about it, they tend to dwell on the physical beauty of the Old South and wax poetic about moonlight on the magnolias. Well, of course the South is lovely, and that is true; but there are those—and I'm one—who feel a special affection for its people. I respect the values that took root here and the pride that's part of the southern character. I'm drawn to your good sense and decent traditions, your fidelity to God, and your faithfulness to your region. And I know that you love our country and are very protective toward it.

I mean no slight to the other parts of the country—to my heritage, which was up in the heartland there in the Middle West, or now my home in the West. But I have been struck when, now and then, on news for some reason or other—on the TV news—there will be an occasion where the commentator is talking to one of our men in uniform, and I've often been struck by how often the young man in uniform, when he replies, you hear the lilting cadence of Charleston or Memphis or Winston-Salem or Decatur. The South was the home of patriots in 1776, when a southerner drew up our Declaration of Independence. And it's the home of patriots today, 208 years later.

We're here tonight at a great celebration, a birthday party for the nation. And we come together to honor those who invented this country and who saw to it that it would always be a place of high ideals. And we celebrate those who, in each generation, have protected those ideals and advanced the cause of democracy. . . .

But the cause of democracy, that's a subject of high seriousness when, on a night like this, it's hard to be somber and full of deep thoughts, it's hard not to be happy. We have so much to be thankful for. . . .

I want to talk to you about something, if I could, that I've been thinking about a great deal lately. You know, when you work in the Oval Office, a lot of problems cross your desk. We're repeatedly reminded that there's a lot to do, so many causes to . . . care about, and carry forward in our country and in the world. But I think what's impressed me most and what's given me a very deep feeling over the last three and a half years is how very lucky we are. We are truly blessed to live in this time and this place.

Now, I say that because there are so many people that get more attention than they deserve. They run around and survey the modern landscape and see the problems of mankind, and they say, "Oh, it's such a troubled world." We hear people say that this is a terrible century and that we live in an increasingly totalitarian age, that freedom is dead or an illusion to begin with and man is just a powerless victim of historical forces, and that history is something beyond our control, something we can't affect. Well, the counsel of these sour souls would seem to be that mankind has had it and we might as well just give up. Well, let me tell you, they aren't talking about the American people I know.

This is a wonderful time to be alive. And we're so lucky because as a people, we still have the opportunity to be patriots, and as a nation, we still stand for something. . . .

We stand for freedom in the world. We see the gulags and the prisons, those places where man is not free to do work of his choosing and profit from his labor, places where the freedom to worship God has been extinguished and where souls have withered. But we're blessed by God with the right to say of our country: This is where freedom is. This is the land of limitless possibilities.

And you don't have to travel too far in the world to realize that we stand as a beacon, that America is today what it was two centuries ago, a place that dreamers dream of, that it is what Winthrop said standing on the deck of the tiny *Arabella* off the Massachusetts coast, with a little group of pilgrims gathered around him, and he said, "We shall be as a shining city for all the world upon the hill."

It isn't so of other places and other systems. Can you think of a time when you heard of a West Berliner jumping over the wall to get into

East Berlin? Can you think of a time when someone took a homemade balloon—hot-air balloon—and tried to float from free Western Europe into Czechoslovakia? Or when someone took a leaky fishing trawler on a death-defying journey so they could enjoy the freedom of Havana, Cuba? Can you think of a time when any family, thirsting for opportunity, left a democracy to live in a country that was not free?

The truth is that the totalitarian world is a tired place held down by the gravity of its own devising. And America is a rocket pushing upward to the stars. Other countries see our entrepreneurial spirit and seek to emulate it. More and more, the world is reawakening to the fact that freedom is better than tyranny, that democracy is better than the iron fist of dictators, that freedom is the one condition in which man can flourish. And man was meant to flourish, was meant to be free. And that is why we were created. That's why it's been said that democracy is just a political reading of the Bible.

The world has flirted with systems other than democracy, and for a while, some of them were in vogue. There were those who said our problems are intractable, and we need huge government to tell us what to do. For a while, the doctrine of Marx and Lenin seemed something new and revolutionary. And some among us said, "Well, that's an idea. We should look at it." Well, all for a while. Times have changed. Man has moved on, and more and more we can see that the tide of the future is a freedom tide.

Man still thirsts for freedom. And wherever the persecuted fight for freedom, our souls and our spirits are with them. We're with the trade unionist in Kraków, Poland, marching behind a crucifix. We're with the Afghan rebel fighting the tanks with an undying ancestral will. We're with the people of Central America, who struggle each day for liberty.

And in spite of decades of troubles and sometimes self-doubt, look across the world for the persecuted and punished, for those who yearn to be free, for those who fight for the right to worship, to speak freely, to write what they want, to enjoy the freedom God meant us to have. For all those people, America's not just a word; it is a hope, a torch shedding light to all the hopeless of the world.

You know, throughout the world the persecuted hear the word "America," and in that sound they can hear the sunrise, hear the rivers push, hear the cold, swift air at the top of the peak. Yes, you can hear freedom. It was so 208 years ago, and it's so today.

My friends, we're so lucky: We've been granted the right to stand for something. So much of our greatness is behind us, but so much of our greatness is still before us, out there waiting for us to take advantage of it. It is, in truth, a wonderful time to be alive. And those young people that I mentioned first, with those present in our country who have been trying to frighten them into believing that maybe there isn't a future for them, don't any of us who are grown up let them believe that for one moment. They're going to see things we've never seen, they're going to have advantages we've never had.

I thank you. God bless you, and may He continue to bless the nation that has showered this land with love for more than two centuries. Thank you all. God bless you all.

"A Light unto the Nations of All the World"

In 1982, President Reagan asked Lee Iacocca, the CEO of Chrysler, to lead a nationwide fundraising campaign to pay for the conservation and restoration of the Statue of Liberty. That process of cleaning, repair, and upgrades began in 1984, and included replacing the old copper-and-glass "flame" inside the statue's torch with a new,

*gold-plated one. On the night of July 3, 1986, after President Reagan
delivered these remarks, the new flame was lit for the first time.*

Thank you. And Lee Iacocca, thank you on behalf of all of America.
President and Madame Mitterrand, my fellow Americans:

The ironworkers from New York and New Jersey who came here to
begin restoration work were at first puzzled and a bit put off to see foreign
workers, craftsmen from France, arrive. Jean Wiart, the leader of the
French workers, said his countrymen understood. After all, he asked,
how would Frenchmen feel if Americans showed up to help restore the
Eiffel Tower? But as they came to know each other—these Frenchmen
and Americans—affections grew; and so, too, did perspectives.

The Americans were reminded that Miss Liberty, like the many
millions she's welcomed to these shores, is of foreign birth, the gift of
workers, farmers, and shopkeepers and children who donated hundreds
of thousands of francs to send her here. They were the ordinary people
of France. This statue came from their pockets and from their hearts.
The French workers, too, made discoveries. Monsieur Wiart, for example, normally lives in a 150-year-old cottage in a small French town, but
for the last year he's been riding the subway through Brooklyn. "A
study in contrasts," he said—contrasts indeed. But he has also told the
newspapers that he and his countrymen learned something else at Liberty Island. For the first time, they worked in proximity with Americans
of Jewish, black, Italian, Irish, Russian, Polish, and Indian backgrounds. "Fascinating," he said, "to see different ethnic and national
types work and live so well together." Well, it's how we like to think of
America. And it's good to know that Miss Liberty is still giving life to
the dream of a new world where old antagonisms could be cast aside
and people of every nation could live together as one.

It's especially fitting that this lesson should be relived and relearned here by Americans and Frenchmen. President Mitterrand, the French and American people have forged a special friendship over the course of two centuries. Yes, in the 1700s, France was the midwife of our liberty. In two world wars, America stood with France as she fought for her life and for civilization. And today, Mr. President, with infinite gentleness, your countrymen tend the final resting places, marked now by rows of white crosses and stars, of more than sixty thousand Americans who remain on French soil, a reminder since the days of Lafayette of our mutual struggles and sacrifices for freedom. So, tonight, as we celebrate the friendship of our two nations, we also pray: May it ever be so. God bless America, and *vive la France!*

And yet, my fellow Americans, it is not only the friendship of two peoples but the friendship of all peoples that brings us here tonight. We celebrate something more than the restoration of this statue's physical grandeur. Another worker here, Scott Aronsen, a marble restorer, has put it well: "I grew up in Brooklyn and never went to the Statue of Liberty. But when I first walked in there to work, I thought about my grandfathers coming through here." And which of us does not think of other grandfathers and grandmothers, from so many places around the globe, for whom this statue was the first glimpse of America?

"She was silhouetted very clear," one of them wrote about standing on deck as their ship entered New York Harbor. "We passed her very slowly. Of course we had to look up. She was beautiful."

Another talked of how all the passengers rushed to one side of the boat for a fast look at their new home and at her. "Everybody was crying. The whole boat bent toward her. She was beautiful with the early morning light."

To millions returning home, especially from foreign wars, she was also special. A young World War I captain of artillery described how, on a troopship returning from France, even the most hard-bitten veteran had trouble blinking back the tears. "I've never seen anything that looked so good," that doughboy Harry Truman wrote to his fiancée, Bess, back in Independence, Missouri, "as the Liberty Lady in New York Harbor."

And that is why tonight we celebrate this mother of exiles who lifts her light beside the golden door. Many of us have seen the picture of another worker here, a tool belt around his waist, balanced on a narrow metal rod of scaffolding, leaning over to place a kiss on the forehead of Miss Liberty. Tony Soraci, the grandson of immigrant Italians, said it was something he was proud to do, "something to tell my grandchildren."

Robert Kearney feels the same way. At work on the statue after a serious illness, he gave ten thousand dollars' worth of commemorative pins to those who visited here. Part of the reason, he says, was an earlier construction job over in Hoboken and his friend named Blackie. They could see the harbor from the building they were working on, and every morning Blackie would look over the water, give a salute, and say, "That's my gal!"

Well, the truth is, she's everybody's gal. We sometimes forget that even those who came here first to settle the new land were also strangers. I've spoken before of the tiny *Arabella*, a ship at anchor just off the Massachusetts coast. A little group of Puritans huddled on the deck. And then John Winthrop, who would later become the first governor of Massachusetts, reminded his fellow Puritans there on that tiny deck that they must keep faith with their God, that the eyes of all the world were upon them, and that they must not forsake the mission that God had sent them on, and they must be a light unto the nations of all the world—a shining city upon a hill.

Call it mysticism if you will, I have always believed there was some divine providence that placed this great land here between the two great oceans, to be found by a special kind of people from every corner of the world, who had a special love for freedom and a special courage that enabled them to leave their own land, leave their friends and their countrymen, and come to this new and strange land to build a new world of peace and freedom and hope. Lincoln spoke about hope as he left the hometown he would never see again to take up the duties of the presidency and bring America through a terrible civil war. At each stop on his long train ride to Washington, the news grew worse: The nation was dividing; his own life was in peril. On he pushed, undaunted. In Philadelphia he spoke in Independence Hall, where eighty-five years earlier the Declaration of Independence had been signed. He noted that much more had been achieved there than just independence from Great Britain. It was, he said, "hope to the world, future for all time."

Well, that is the common thread that binds us to those Quakers [Puritans] on the tiny deck of the *Arabella*, to the beleaguered farmers and landowners signing the Declaration in Philadelphia in that hot Philadelphia hall, to Lincoln on a train ready to guide his people through the conflagration, to all the millions crowded in the steerage who passed this lady and wept at the sight of her, and those who've worked here in the scaffolding with their hands and with their love—Jean Wiart, Scott Aronsen, Tony Soraci, Robert Kearney, and so many others.

We're bound together because, like them, we too dare to hope— hope that our children will always find here the land of liberty in a land that is free. We dare to hope too that we'll understand our work can never be truly done until every man, woman, and child shares in our gift, in our hope, and stands with us in the light of liberty—the light that, tonight, will shortly cast its glow upon her, as it has upon us for two centuries, keeping faith with a dream of long ago and guiding millions still to a future of peace and freedom.

And now we will unveil that gallant lady. Thank you, and God bless you all.

8

THE FOUNDING

In 1976 the bicentennial of the Declaration of Independence was celebrated with pomp and circumstance, hoopla and kitsch. One thing that was absent: presidential rhetoric worthy of the occasion. President Gerald Ford's bicentennial speeches were entirely forgettable.

The 1980s brought other important patriotic anniversaries, however, and President Reagan relished the opportunities he had to talk about the Founders and what we can learn from their example.

"The World Turned Upside Down"

On the afternoon of October 19, 1981, the bicentennial of the British surrender at Yorktown, Virginia, that ended the last major military campaign of the American Revolution, President Reagan gave these remarks from a reviewing stand overlooking the battlefield. The quotation from Thomas Paine's Common Sense *with which the president ends this address—"We have it within our power to begin the world over again"—is profoundly unconservative but was a particular favorite line of Reagan's.*

Mr. President [of France, François Mitterrand], Mrs. Mitterrand, Lord Chancellor [Right Honorable Lord Hailsham, lord chancellor of the United Kingdom], Governor John Dalton—and I thank you very much for that most gracious introduction—members of the Congress, members of the Cabinet, distinguished guests, and my fellow citizens:

I open with something of an announcement before my remarks. Since today is a day to celebrate freedom, I feel it only appropriate that I exercise one of the more pleasant powers of the presidency. After consultation with Governor Dalton and with his approval, by the power vested in me as president of the United States, I hereby grant amnesty to the corps of cadets of the Virginia Military Institute under the terms and conditions to be specified by the superintendent. [*Laughter*]

And now, this field, this ceremony, and this day hold a special meaning for people the world over, whether free in their lives or only in their dreams. Not long after the Battle of Yorktown, Lafayette wrote home to France. "Here," he said, "humanity has won its battle, liberty now has a country."

It was an extraordinary moment in history. The Continental Army, as you've been told, had marched more than four hundred miles from the Hudson River in New York to the tidewaters of Virginia. They surprised and stranded Lord Cornwallis on the tip of this peninsula. When Admiral de Grasse and his French fleet blockaded the Chesapeake, the trap was sprung. There could be no rescue by land or by sea.

Nearly eight thousand British soldiers had swept from Charleston to Richmond to this spot between the York and the James Rivers, with far more victories than defeats. But as they were encircled and besieged by the Continentals, as they withstood day after day of grueling bombardment, they must have known in their hearts they were fighting for a cause they could not win.

Their enemies were a band of colonists with bandaged feet and muskets that couldn't be counted on to fire, but the British were thousands of miles from home and the Americans were fighting where they lived. Those rebels may not have had fancy uniforms or even adequate resources, but they had a passion for liberty burning in their hearts.

In a masterly execution of a textbook siege, General Washington and his grab-bag army defeated the finest troops King George could field.

The morning of the surrender must have been very much like this one today. The first real chill of autumn was in the air. The trees were turning brilliant with the hues of red and gold and brown. The sky was bright and clear. Quiet had finally returned to this lovely countryside. How strange the silence must have seemed after the thundering violence of war.

And then the silence was broken by a muffled beat of British drums, covered with black handkerchiefs, as the Redcoats marched to surrender. The pageantry was spectacular. The French in their spotless white uniforms lined one side of the road. The ragged Continentals were brown and dreary on the other side. But the journals of those who were present mention that the Americans stood every bit as straight and equally as proud as any army could. They had, on that day, a military bearing that was not to be outdone by their comrades in white and blue nor by King George's men in their brilliant red.

As the British marched between the allied armies to the field of surrender, tears streamed down many of their faces. Their musicians played a tune popular in England at the time, yes, "The World Turned Upside Down." And that's just what the colonists had done.

But those Americans were not professional soldiers at all. They had fought for freedom from Quebec to Saratoga, from Camden and Cowpens to Germantown, Valley Forge, and Monmouth—towns and countrysides once so anonymous that King George complained he could neither pronounce them nor find them on the map.

By Yorktown, they were veterans, but they were still not soldiers. They were farmers, backwoodsmen, tradesmen, clerks, and laborers—common men from all walks of life, anxious to return to their families and the building of a nation. On that day in 1781 a philosophy found a people, and the world would never be the same.

We who have traveled here today—and I'm told we number more than sixty thousand—did not come just to admire the strategies, battlements, and trenches of a siege. We did not come to idealize human suffering.

The wounds of this battle have long since healed. Our nations have matured, and bonds of friendship now exist between one-time enemies. The same has been true of other wars since, which makes you wonder if after all the hatred, all the pain, and all the sacrifice, we find ourselves able to be friends and allies, why couldn't we find ourselves able to be friends without first going to war?

We have come to this field to celebrate the triumph of an idea—that freedom will eventually triumph over tyranny. It is and always will be a warning to those who would usurp the rights of others: Time will find them beaten. The beacon of freedom shines here for all who will see, inspiring free men and captives alike, and no wall, no curtain, nor totalitarian state can shut it out.

The commemoration of this battle marks the end of the revolution and the beginning of a new world era. The promise made on July 4 was kept on October 19. The dream described in that Pennsylvania hall was fulfilled on this Virginia field. Through courage, the support of our allies, and by the gracious hand of God, a revolution was won, a people were set free, and the world witnessed the most exciting adventure in the history of nations: the beginning of the United States of America.

But we didn't win this battle or this war by ourselves. From your country, Mr. President, came men and ships and goods. Generals Rochambeau and Lafayette and Admirals de Grasse and de Barras were among those without whose help this battle and this war could never have been won. France was first to our side, first to recognize our independence, and steadfast in friendship ever since. We are bonded in spirit and, in fact, by freedom. "Entre vous, entre nous, à la vie, à la mort," Rochambeau said: "Between you, between us, through life, or death."

And others came to our aid—Poles, Spaniards, Scots, Canadians, Swedes, Germans, Dutch, Irish, and still more.

Our revolution was won by and for all who cherish the timeless and universal rights of man. This battle was a vindication of ideas that had been forming for centuries in the Western mind.

From the Mediterranean had come the philosophies of Greece and the laws of Rome. England contributed representative government, and the French and the Poles shared their dreams of equality and liberty. On our own frontier, we learned dependence on family and neighbors, and in our revolution free men were taught reliance on other free men.

We of the West have lived the central truths, the values around which we now must rally—human dignity, individual rights, and representative democracy. Our nations share the foundation of common law, separation of powers, and limited government. We must unite behind our own common cause of freedom.

There are those in the world today, as there always have been, who recognize human rights as only selective favors to be doled out by the state. They preach revolution against tyranny, but they intend to replace it with the tyranny of totalitarianism.

Once again, today, thousands of free men and women have gathered on this battlefield in testimony to their beliefs. Let the struggle that took place here remind us all: The freedom we enjoy today has not always existed and carries no guarantees. In our search for an everlasting peace, let all of us resolve to remain so sure of our strength that the victory for mankind we won here is never threatened.

Will we meet the challenge, will we meet the challenge Joseph Warren put forth to Americans two hundred years ago? Will we act worthy of ourselves?

Each generation before us has struggled and sacrificed for freedom. Can we do any less?

The men and boys who fought on this field somehow understood that government must be close to people and responsive to them; that if all men are free to prosper, all will benefit.

Today in our country those concepts are threatened by government's bloated size and the distortion of its true functions. Our people are struggling under a punishing tax burden many times heavier than that which ignited our first rebellion. Regulations that inhibit our growth and prosperity would be incomprehensible to the colonists who revolted because of the Stamp Act.

Our Founding Fathers devised a system of government unique in all the world—a federation of sovereign states, with as much law and decision-making authority as possible kept at the local level. This concept of federalism has been the secret of America's success and will be a priority again as we restore the balance between the federal, state, and local levels that was intended in the Constitution.

But of equal concern to me is the uncertainty some seem to have about the need for a strong American defense. Now, that is a proper task for the national government. Military inferiority does not avoid a conflict; it only invites one and then ensures defeat. We have been trusted with freedom. We have been trusted with freedom and must ensure it for our children and for their children. We're rebuilding our defenses so that our sons and daughters never need to be sent to war.

Where are the voices of courage and vision that inspired us in the past? Are we ever to hear those voices again? Yes. Thomas Paine, a voice of patriotism, said, "Those who expect to reap the blessings of freedom must . . . undergo the fatigue of supporting it." We always have, and we always will. That's just part of being an American.

Our Declaration of Independence has been copied by emerging nations around the globe, its themes adopted in places many of us have never heard of.

Here in this land, for the first time, it was decided that man is born with certain God-given rights. We the people declared that government is created by the people for their own convenience. Government has no power except those voluntarily granted to it by we the people.

There have been revolutions before and since ours, revolutions that simply exchanged one set of rulers for another. Ours was a philosophical revolution that changed the very concept of government.

John Adams wrote home from Philadelphia shortly before signing the Declaration of Independence, and he said, "I am well aware of the Toil and Blood and Treasure, that it will cost Us to maintain this Declaration, and support and defend these States. Yet through all the Gloom, I can see the Rays of ravishing Light and Glory. I can see that the End is more than worth all the Means—and that Posterity will triumph."

It is that vision we recall today. We have economic problems at home, and we live in a troubled and violent world. But there is a moral fiber running through our people that makes us more than strong enough to face the tests ahead. We can look at our past with pride, and our future can be whatever we make it. We can remember that saying Thomas Paine said, "We have it within our power to begin the world over again." We only have to act worthy of ourselves.

And as has been said already today, God bless America.

"The Architecture of Democratic Government"

On September 17, 1987, the two hundredth anniversary of the adjournment of the Constitutional Convention, President Reagan gave this address in front of Independence Hall in Philadelphia, the site of the convention. Former chief justice Warren Burger, whom the president mentions at the beginning of his remarks, was the chairman of the Commission on the Bicentennial of the United States Constitution.

Thank you all very much. With so many distinguished guests, I hope you'll excuse me if I single out just one. He has devoted a lifetime of service to his country, and occupied one of the highest offices in our land. And recently he stepped down to lead the nation in our bicentennial celebrations. Well, by a happy coincidence, this day that marks the two hundredth anniversary of the signing of our Constitution also happens to be his birthday. Today, Chief Justice Warren Burger is eighty years old. [*Applause*] And Warren, we of the younger generation salute you. [*Laughter*] Congratulations!

As we stand here today before Independence Hall, we can easily imagine that day, September 17, 1787, when the delegates rose from their chairs and arranged themselves according to the geography of their states, beginning with New Hampshire and moving south to Georgia. They had labored for four months through the terrible heat of the Philadelphia summer, but they knew as they moved forward to sign their names to that new document that in many ways their work had just begun. This new Constitution, this new plan of government, faced a skeptical, even hostile reception in much of the country.

To look back on that time, at the difficulties faced and surmounted, can only give us perspective on the present. Each generation, every age, I imagine, is prone to think itself beset by unusual and particularly threatening difficulties, to look back on the past as a golden age when issues were not so complex and politics not so divisive, when problems did not seem so intractable.

Sometimes we're tempted to think of the birth of our country as one such golden age, a time characterized primarily by harmony and cooperation. In fact, the Constitution and our government were born in crisis. The years leading up to our Constitutional Convention were some of the most difficult our nation ever endured. This young nation, threatened on every side by hostile powers, was on the verge of economic collapse. In some states inflation raged out of control; debt was crushing. In Massachusetts, ruinously high taxes provided—or provoked—an uprising of poor farmers led by a former Revolutionary War captain, Daniel Shays.

Trade disputes between the states were bitter and sometimes violent, threatening not only the economy but even the peace. No one thought him guilty of exaggeration when Edmund Randolph described the perilous state of the confederacy. "Look at the public countenance," he said, "from New Hampshire to Georgia! Are we not on the eve of war, which is only prevented by the hopes from this Convention?" Yes, but these hopes were matched in many others by equally strong suspicions. Wasn't this convention just designed to steal from the states their sovereignty, to usurp their freedoms so recently fought for? Patrick Henry, the famous orator of the revolution, thought so. He refused to attend the convention, saying, with his usual talent for understatement, that he "smelt a rat."

The Articles of Confederation, all could see, were not strong enough to hold this new nation together. But there was no general agreement on how a stronger federal government should be constituted—or, indeed, whether one should be constituted at all. There were strong secessionist feelings in many parts of the country. In Boston, some were calling for a separate nation of New England. Others felt the thirteen states should divide into three independent nations. And it came as a shock to George Washington, recently traveling in New England, to find that sentiment in favor of returning to a monarchy still ran strong in that region.

No, it wasn't the absence of problems that won the day in 1787. It wasn't the absence of division and difficulty; it was the presence of something higher—the vision of democratic government founded upon those self-evident truths that still resounded in Independence Hall. It was that ideal, proclaimed so proudly in this hall a decade earlier, that enabled them to rise above politics and self-interest, to transcend their differences and together create this document, this Constitution that would profoundly and forever alter not just these United States but the world. In a very real sense, it was then, in 1787, that the revolution truly began. For it was with the writing of our Constitution, setting down the architecture of democratic government, that the noble sentiments and brave rhetoric of 1776 took on substance, that the hopes and dreams of the revolutionists could become a living, enduring reality.

All men are created equal and endowed by their Creator with certain unalienable rights—until that moment some might have said that was just a high-blown sentiment, the dreams of a few philosophers and their hotheaded followers. But could one really construct a government, run a country, with such idealistic notions? But once those ideals took root in living, functioning institutions, once those notions became a nation—well, then, as I said, the revolution could really begin, not just in America but around the world, a revolution to free man from tyranny of every sort and secure his freedom the only way possible in this world, through the checks and balances and institutions of limited, democratic government.

Checks and balances, limited government—the genius of our constitutional system is its recognition that no one branch of government alone could be relied on to preserve our freedoms. The great safeguard of our liberty is the totality of the constitutional system, with no one part getting the upper hand. And that's why the judiciary must be independent. And that's why it also must exercise restraint.

If our Constitution has endured, through times perilous as well as prosperous, it has not been simply as a plan of government, no matter how ingenious or inspired that might be. This document that we honor today has always been something more to us, filled with a deeper feeling than one of simple admiration—a feeling, one might say, more of reverence. One scholar described our Constitution as a kind of covenant. It is a covenant we've made not only with ourselves but with all of mankind. As John Quincy Adams promised, "Whenever the standard of freedom and independence has been or shall be unfurled, there will be America's heart, her benedictions and her prayers." It's a human covenant; yes, and beyond that, a covenant with the Supreme Being to whom our Founding Fathers did constantly appeal for assistance.

It is an oath of allegiance to that in man that is truly universal, that core of being that exists before and beyond distinctions of class, race, or national origin. It is a dedication of faith to the humanity we all share, that part of each man and woman that most closely touches on the divine. And it was perhaps from that divine source that the men who came together in this hall two hundred years ago drew the inspiration and strength to face the crisis of their great hopes and overcome their many divisions. After all, both Madison and Washington were to refer to the outcome of the Constitutional Convention as a miracle; and miracles, of course, have only one origin.

"No people," said George Washington in his inaugural address, "can be bound to acknowledge and adore the Invisible Hand which conducts the affairs of men more than those of the United States. Every step by which they have advanced to the character of an independent nation seems to have been distinguished by some providential agency." No doubt he was thinking of the great and good fortune of this young land: the abundant and fertile continent given us, far from the warring powers of Europe; the successful struggle against the greatest proof— or power—of that day, England; the happy outcome of the Constitutional Convention and the debate over ratification. But he knew, too, as he also said, that there is an "indissoluble union" between duty and advantage, and that the guiding hand of providence did not create this new nation of America for ourselves alone, but for a higher cause: the preservation and extension of the sacred fire of human liberty. This is America's solemn duty.

During the summer of 1787, as the delegates clashed and debated, Washington left the heat of Philadelphia with his trout fishing companion, Gouverneur Morris of Pennsylvania, made a pilgrimage to Valley Forge. Ten years before, his Continental Army had been camped there through the winter. Food was low, medical supplies nonexistent, his soldiers had to go "half in rags in the killing cold, their torn feet leaving bloodstains as they walked shoeless on the icy ground." Gouverneur Morris reported that the general was silent throughout the trip. He did not confide his emotions as he surveyed the scene of past hardship.

One can imagine that his conversation was with someone else—that it took more the form of prayer for this new nation, that such sacrifices be not in vain, that the hope and promise that survived such a terrible winter of suffering not be allowed to wither now that it was summer. One imagines that he also did what we do today in this gathering and celebration, what will always be America's foremost duty—to constantly renew that covenant with humanity, with a world yearning to breathe free; to complete the work begun two hundred years ago, that grand, noble work that is America's particular calling—the triumph of human freedom, the triumph of human freedom under God.

On George Washington

In February 1982, President Reagan issued a proclamation calling upon Americans to commemorate the 250th anniversary of the birth of George Washington "by reflecting on the character and accomplishments of this great man" and "rededicat[ing] ourselves to the fulfillment of his ideals and his faith in the people and resources of the United States." The fortieth president also published this written statement about the first president.

In celebrating the 250th birthday of George Washington, we commemorate the birth of a man whose unsurpassed contributions to our nation place him first in the hearts of all patriotic Americans. From our earliest struggle for independence, his easy, erect, and noble manner combined with his valor and dedication to duty earned him the esteem of his countrymen and gave his life the tenor of greatness.

He served without pay as commander of the Continental Army, endured the privations of Valley Forge, and secured our independence with a great victory at Yorktown. His daring and unshakable belief in this nation's destiny carried us through the darkest hours of that protracted conflict to nationhood. Without the faith and vision of General Washington, our democratic experiment might well have expired at an early age.

As president he unified the hearts and minds of his fellow citizens and inaugurated principles of state that continue to serve us today. His character and magnanimity of spirit permitted him to reconcile and harmonize contending factions and establish the chief executive as the president of all the people, not the servant of any single group. His judgment and self-command were instrumental in bringing respect and honor to our national government from the beginning.

But, most important, George Washington was a leader among men who believed that "honor, justice, and humanity" called upon them to be the trustees of liberty for posterity. He spoke to every generation of Americans when he said that "the preservation of the sacred fire of liberty and the destiny of the Republican model of Government, are justly considered as deeply, perhaps as finally staked, on the experiment entrusted to the hands of the American people."

Through ages yet to come, George Washington will be remembered with reverence in the hearts of free people everywhere. His life, his deeds, and his spirit are the noble expression of the hopes and dreams of all who seek the liberty essential to human dignity and progress.

On Thomas Jefferson

On December 16, 1988, in the closing weeks of his second term, President Reagan visited the University of Virginia. Although the chief purpose of his visit was to deliver an address on foreign policy, he began his remarks with this extended discussion about the university's founder.

Here at UVA, we are surrounded with memories of Thomas Jefferson. One of my staff mentioned that Thomas Jefferson's favorite recreation was horseback riding, and I said he was a wise man. [*Laughter*] And another member of the staff said that Thomas Jefferson thought the White House was a noble edifice, and I said he was a man of refined taste. [*Laughter*] And a third member noted that, after retiring as president, Thomas Jefferson, in his seventies, didn't sit back and rest, but founded the University of Virginia; and I said: There's always an overachiever who makes it hard for the rest of us.

But no speaker can come to these grounds or see the Lawn without appreciating the symmetry not just of the architecture but of the mind that created it. The man to whom that mind belonged is known to you as Mr. Jefferson. And I think the familiarity of that term is justified; his influence here is everywhere. And yet, while those of you at UVA are fortunate to have before you physical reminders of the power of your founder's intellect and imagination, it should be remembered that all you do here, indeed, all of higher education in America, bears signs, too, of his transforming genius. The pursuit of science, the study of the great works, the value of free inquiry, in short, the very idea of living the life of the mind—yes, these formative and abiding principles of higher education in America had their first and firmest advocate, and their greatest embodiment, in a tall, fair-headed, friendly man who watched this university take form from the mountainside where he lived, the university whose founding he called a crowning achievement to a long and well-spent life.

Well, you're not alone in feeling his presence. Presidents know about this, too. You've heard many times that during the first year of his presidency, John F. Kennedy said to a group of Nobel laureates in the State Dining Room of the White House that there had not been such a collection of talent in that place since Jefferson dined there alone. [*Laughter*] And directly down the lawn, across the Ellipse from the White House, are those ordered, classic lines of the Jefferson Memorial and the eyes of the nineteen-foot statue that gaze directly into the White House, a reminder to any of us who might occupy that mansion of the quality of mind and generosity of heart that once abided there and [has been] so rarely seen there again.

But it's not just students and presidents; it is every American— indeed, every human life ever touched by the daring idea of self-government—that Mr. Jefferson has influenced. Yes, Mr. Jefferson was obliged to admit all previous attempts at popular government had proven themselves failures. But he believed that here on this continent, as one of his commentators put it, "here was virgin soil, an abundance of land, no degrading poverty, a brave and intelligent people which had just vindicated its title to independence after a long struggle with the mightiest of European powers."

Well, here was another chance, an opportunity for enlightened government, government based on the principles of reason and tolerance, government that left to the people the fruits of their labor and the pursuit of their own definition of happiness in the form of commerce or education or religion. And so, it's no wonder he asked that his epitaph read simply, "Here was born [buried] Thomas Jefferson, Author of the Declaration of [American] Independence, of the Statute of Virginia for religious freedom, and Father of the University of Virginia."

Well, as that epitaph shows, for all his learning and bookishness, Mr. Jefferson was a practical man, a man who made things, things like a university, a state government, a national government. In founding and sustaining these institutions, he wanted them to be based on the same symmetry, the same balance of mind and faith in human creativity evidenced in the Lawn. He had known personal tragedy. He knew how disorderly a place the world could be. Indeed, as a leader of a rebellion, he was himself an architect, if you will, of disorder. But he also believed that man had received from God a precious gift of enlightenment—the gift of reason, a gift that could extract from the chaos of life meaning, truth, order.

Just as we see in his architecture, the balancing of circular with linear, of rotunda with pillar, we see in his works of government the same disposition toward balance, toward symmetry and harmony. He knew successful self-government meant bringing together disparate interests and concerns, balancing, for example, on the one hand the legitimate duties of government—the maintenance of domestic order and protection from foreign menace—with government's tendency to preempt its citizens' rights, take the fruits of their labors, and reduce them ultimately to servitude. So he knew that governing meant balance, harmony. And he knew from personal experience the danger posed to such harmony by the voices of unreason, special privilege, partisanship, or intolerance.

And I do mean personal experience. You see, despite all of George Washington's warnings about the divisiveness of the partisan spirit, Federalists and Republicans were constantly at each other in those days. The Federalists of the Northeast had held power for a long time and were not anxious to relinquish it. Years later, a New York congress-man honored the good old days when, as he put it, "a Federalist could knock a Republican down in the streets of New York and not be ques-tioned about it." The Federalists referred to Mr. Jefferson as—and here I quote—"a mean-spirited, low-lived fellow, raised wholly on hotcake made of coarse-ground Southern corn, bacon, and hominy, with an occasional fricasseed bullfrog." [*Laughter*] Well, by the way—was the 1800 equivalent of what I believe is known here at UVA as a Gus Burger. [*Laughter*] And an editorial in the Federalist *Connecticut Courant* also announced that as soon as Mr. Jefferson was elected, "Murder, robbery, rape, and adultery and incest will be openly taught and practiced." [*Laughter*]

Well, that was politics in 1800. So, you see, not all that much has changed. [*Laughter*] Actually, I've taken a moment for these brief re-flections on Thomas Jefferson and his time precisely because there are such clear parallels to our own. We too have seen a new populism in America, not at all unlike that of Jefferson's time. We've seen the growth of a Jefferson-like populism that rejects the burden placed on the people by excessive regulation and taxation; that rejects the notion that judgeships should be used to further privately held beliefs not yet approved by the people; and finally, rejects, too, the notion that foreign policy must reflect only the rarefied concerns of Washington rather than the common sense of a people who can frequently see far more plainly dangers to their freedom and to our national well-being.

9

FAITH AND FAMILY

*"Only those who don't know us believe that America is a materialistic land,"
Reagan said in 1987. "But the true America is not supermarkets filled with
meats, milk, and goods of all descriptions. It is not highways filled with cars.
No, true America is a land of faith and family. You can find it in our
churches, synagogues, and mosques—in our homes and schools."*

*Reagan referred hundreds of times to the "basic values" of faith and fam-
ily. Religious faith, he believed, provided the moral foundation for American
greatness. And the love of family, he said, is "the engine that gives our country life. It is the reason that we produce. . . . It's the power of the family that
holds the nation together, that gives America her conscience, and that serves
as the cradle of our country's soul."*

"The Twin Beacons of Faith
and Freedom"

Although President Reagan's Oval Office address on the evening of December 23, 1981, focused mostly on the recent crackdown in Poland, he opened with these remarks about Christmas.

At this special time of year, we all renew our sense of wonder in recalling the story of the first Christmas in Bethlehem, nearly two thousand years ago.

Some celebrate Christmas as the birthday of a great and good philosopher and teacher. Others of us believe in the divinity of the child born in Bethlehem, that he was and is the promised Prince of Peace. Yes, we've questioned why he who could perform miracles chose to come among us as a helpless babe, but maybe that was his first miracle, his first great lesson that we should learn to care for one another.

Tonight, in millions of American homes, the glow of the Christmas tree is a reflection of the love Jesus taught us. Like the shepherds and wise men of that first Christmas, we Americans have always tried to follow a higher light, a star, if you will. At lonely campfire vigils along the frontier, in the darkest days of the Great Depression, through war and peace, the twin beacons of faith and freedom have brightened the American sky. At times our footsteps may have faltered, but trusting in God's help, we've never lost our way.

Just across the way from the White House stand the two great emblems of the holiday season: a menorah, symbolizing the Jewish festival of Hanukkah, and the National Christmas Tree, a beautiful towering blue spruce from Pennsylvania. Like the National Christmas Tree, our country is a living, growing thing planted in rich American soil. Only our devoted care can bring it to full flower. So, let this holiday season be for us a time of rededication.

"Let Us Go Forth from Here and Rekindle the Fire of Our Faith"

Every year of his presidency, Ronald Reagan spoke at the National Prayer Breakfast in Washington, DC. In his remarks before the gathering on February 4, 1982, he called for a restoration of "our spirit of neighbor caring for neighbor."

I also believe this blessed land was set apart in a very special way, a country created by men and women who came here not in search of gold, but in search of God. They would be free people, living under the law with faith in their Maker and their future.

Sometimes, it seems we've strayed from that noble beginning, from our conviction that standards of right and wrong do exist and must be lived up to. God, the source of our knowledge, has been expelled from the classroom. He gives us His greatest blessing, life, and yet many would condone the taking of innocent life. We expect Him to protect us in a crisis, but turn away from Him too often in our day-to-day living. I wonder if He isn't waiting for us to wake up.

There is . . . in the American heart a spirit of love, of caring, and a willingness to work together. If we remember the parable of the Good Samaritan, he crossed the road, knelt down, and bound up the wounds of the beaten traveler, the Pilgrim, and then carried him into the nearest town. He didn't just hurry on by into town and then look up a caseworker and tell him there was a fellow back out on the road that looked like he might need help.

Isn't it time for us to get personally involved, for our churches and synagogues to restore our spirit of neighbor caring for neighbor? But talking to this particular gathering, I realize I'm preaching to the choir. If all of you worked for the federal government, you would be classified as essential. We need you now more than ever to remind us that we should be doing God's work on earth. We'll never find every answer, solve every problem, or heal every wound, but we can do a lot if we walk together down that one path that we know provides real hope.

You know, in one of the conflicts that was going on throughout the past year when views were held deeply on both sides of the debate, I recall talking to one senator who came into my office. We both deeply believed what it was we were espousing, but we were on opposite sides. And when we finished talking, as he rose he said, "I'm going out of here and do some praying." And I said, "Well, if you get a busy signal, it's me there ahead of you." [*Laughter*]

We have God's promise that what we give will be given back many times over, so let us go forth from here and rekindle the fire of our faith. Let our wisdom be vindicated by our deeds.

We are told in 2 Timothy that when our work is done, we can say, "We have fought the good fight. We have finished the race. We have kept the faith." This is an evidence of it.

I hope that on down through the centuries not only is this great land preserved but this great tradition is preserved and that all over the land there will always be this one day in the year when we remind ourselves of what our real task is.

God bless you. Thank you.

"One Voice That Spoke the Truth in God's Name"

President Reagan's remarks at the National Prayer Breakfast on January 31, 1985, began by recounting the origins of the annual gathering. He concluded by repeating a story he told at the previous year's prayer breakfast: the tale of Saint Telemachus. Reagan's rendering of the story varies somewhat from the historical record (which is itself scanty), but taken as a parable of courage and Christian witness, it is quite affecting.

Thank you, ladies and gentlemen. It's very good to be here again. I look forward to this meeting every year more than any other. And I want to personally welcome our guests from other countries to Washington, our capital. We're happy to have you here with us.

I would like to say something more about this National Prayer Breakfast and how it came about. We've already heard some of the history from representatives of the two houses. But I think some of the story may be unknown, even to a few of our hosts from the Congress here today. Back in 1942, at the height of World War II, a handful of senators and congressmen discussed how they might be of personal and spiritual support to one another. If they could gather now and then to pray together, they might discover an added resource, which would be of sustaining value. And so, very informally, they began to meet.

In time, in both the House and Senate groups, some informal rules evolved. The members would meet in the spirit of peace and in the spirit of Christ, but they need not be Christians. All members would be welcome, regardless of their political or religious affiliation. Sincere seekers, as well as the deeply devoted, all on a common journey to understand the place of faith in their lives and to discover how to love God and one's fellow man.

They wouldn't publicize the meetings, nor would they use them for any kind of political gain. The meetings would be off-the-record. No one would repeat what was said. And, above all, the members could talk about any personal problem on which they needed guidance, any sadness for which they needed prayers.

Well, the two groups met quietly and with no fanfare for ten years. And then President Eisenhower, as we've been told, came into the story. In 1952, when he was running for president, one of his most important strategists. . . . was a fine man, a senator named Frank Carlson. . . . One night, out on the campaign trail, Eisenhower confided to Senator Carlson that during the war, when he was commanding the Allied forces in Europe, he had had a spiritual experience. He had felt the hand of God guiding him and felt the presence of God. And he spoke of how his friends had provided real spiritual strength in the days before D-Day. Senator Carlson said he understood, that he himself was getting spiritual strength from members of a little prayer group in the Senate.

A few months later, just a few days after he was sworn in as president, Eisenhower invited Frank Carlson over to the White House. He said, "Frank, this is the loneliest house I've ever been in. What can I do?" And Carlson said, "I think this may be a good time for you to come and meet with our prayer group." And Eisenhower did. In 1953 he attended the first combined prayer breakfast. And presidents have been coming here for help ever since. And here I am.

The prayer meetings in the House and Senate are not widely known by the public. Members of the media know, but they have, with great understanding and dignity, generally kept it quiet. I've had my moments with the press, but I commend them this day, for the way they've worked to maintain the integrity of this movement.

Some wonderful things have come out of this fellowship. A number of public figures have changed as human beings, changed in ways I'd like to talk about, but it might reveal too much about the membership. Fellowships have begun to spring up throughout the Capitol. They exist now in all three branches of the government, and they have spread throughout the capitals of the world, to parliaments and congresses far away.

Since we met last year, members of the fellowship throughout the world have begun meeting with each other. Members of our Congress have met with leaders and officials from other countries, approaching them and speaking to them, not on a political level, but a spiritual level.

I wish I could say more about it, but it's working precisely because it is private. In some of the most troubled parts of the world, political figures who are old enemies are meeting with each other in a spirit of peace and brotherhood. And some who've been involved in such meetings are here today.

There are many wars in the world and much strife, but these meetings build relationships, which build trust, and trust brings hope and courage.

I think we often forget in the daily rush of events the importance in all human dealings of the spiritual dimension. There are such diversities in the world, such terrible and passionate divisions between men, but prayer and fellowship among the great universe of God's believers are the beginning of understanding and reconciliation. They remind us of the great, overarching things that really unite us.

In this job of mine, you meet with so many people, deal with so many of the problems of man, you can't help being moved by the quiet, unknown heroism of all kinds of people—the prime minister of another country who makes the bravest of brave decisions that's right, but may not be too popular with his constituency; or the fellow from Indiana who writes to me about some problems he's been having and what he did to solve them.

You see the heroism and the goodness of man and know in a special way that we are all God's children. The clerk and the king and the Communist were made in His image. We all have souls, and we all have the same problems. I'm convinced, more than ever, that man finds liberation only when he binds himself to God and commits himself to his fellow man.

Will you forgive me if I repeat a story that I told here last year? It's a story that goes back to the fourth [fifth] century.

There was an Asian monk living in a little remote village, tending his garden, spending much of his time in prayer. And then one day, he thought he heard the voice of God telling him to go to Rome.

Well, he obeyed the Lord's command, and he set out on foot. And many weary weeks later, he arrived in the capital city of the Roman Empire at the time of a great festival that was going on in Rome.

And the little monk followed the crowd that was surging down the streets into the Colosseum. He saw the gladiators come forth, stand before the emperor, and say, "We who are about to die salute you."

And, then, he realized these men were going to fight to the death for the entertainment of the crowd. And he cried out, "In the name of Christ, stop!"

And as the games began, he fought his way down through the crowd, climbed over the wall, and dropped to the floor of the arena. And when the crowd saw this tiny figure making his way out to the gladiators, saying, "In the name of Christ, stop," they thought it was part of the entertainment. And they began laughing.

But when they realized it wasn't, then their laughter turned to anger. And as he was pleading with the gladiators to stop, one of them plunged a sword into his body, and he fell to the sand of the arena, and as he was dying, his last words were, "In the name of Christ, stop."

Then a strange thing began to happen. The gladiator stood looking at the tiny figure lying there in the sand. A hush fell over the Colosseum.

Way up in the upper tiers, a man stood and made his way to the exit. Others began to follow. In dead silence, everyone left the Colosseum.

And that was the last battle to the death between gladiators in the Roman Colosseum. Never again in the great stadium did men kill each other for the entertainment of the crowd. And all because of one tiny voice that could hardly be heard above the tumult. One voice that spoke the truth in God's name.

I believe we witness here this morning that that voice is alive today. May it continue to rise above the tumult and be heard.

Thank you so much. And God bless you.

"The Relentless Drive to Eliminate God from Our Schools Can and Should Be Stopped"

"Prayer," said President Reagan, "is today as powerful a force in our nation as it has ever been. We as a nation should never forget this source of strength." He backed an amendment to the Constitution that would protect the right to nonmandatory prayer in schools, and made these remarks to supporters of the amendment at a September 25, 1982, candle-lighting ceremony at the White House.

We want to welcome each of you to the White House. We gather together to draw attention to an issue that is as vital to the future of this country as any that we face. No one should doubt that economic and technological progress will have very little impact unless the spirit of our people remains strong.

Calvin Coolidge, a president whom I greatly admire, once said, "The government of a country never gets ahead of the religion of a country." Fostering the faith and character of our people is one of the great trusts of responsible leadership. I deeply believe that if those in government offer a good example, and if the people preserve the freedom which is their birthright as Americans, no one need fear the future.

Unfortunately, in the last two decades we've experienced an onslaught of such twisted logic that if Alice were visiting America, she might think she'd never left Wonderland. [*Laughter*] We're told that it somehow violates the rights of others to permit students in school who desire to pray to do so. Clearly this infringes on the freedom of those who choose to pray—a freedom taken for granted since the time of our Founding Fathers.

This would be bad enough, but the purge of God from our schools went much farther. In one case, a federal court ruled against the right of children to voluntarily say grace before lunch in the school cafeteria. In another situation a group of children, again on their own initiative and with their parents' approval, wanted to begin the school day with a minute of prayer and meditation, and they, too, were prohibited from doing so. Students have even been prevented from having voluntary prayer groups on school property after class hours just on their own.

Now, no one is suggesting that others should be forced into any religious activity, but to prevent those who believe in God from expressing their faith is an outrage. And the relentless drive to eliminate God from our schools can and should be stopped.

This issue has brought people of goodwill and every faith together to make the situation right. We believe that permitting voluntary prayer in public schools is within the finest traditions of this country and consistent with the principles of American liberty. Neither the constitutional amendment that I've endorsed nor the legislative remedies offered by others permits anyone to be coerced into religious activity.

Instead, these measures are designed to protect the rights of those who choose to pray as well as those who choose not to. . . .

And today I'd like to take this opportunity to urge the Senate to move directly on the constitutional amendment now awaiting action. But Senate action is not enough. The leadership in the House has the proposed constitutional amendment bottled up and has, thus far, failed to hold the appropriate hearings. Some suggest we should keep religion out of politics. Well, the opposite is also true. Those in politics should keep their hands off of the religious freedom of our people, and especially our children.

Earlier I quoted Calvin Coolidge. He had some other words I'd like to share with you. "It would be difficult for me to conceive," President Coolidge said, "of anyone being able to administer the duties of a great office like the Presidency without a belief in the guidance of Divine Providence. Unless the President is sustained by an abiding faith in the divine power, I cannot understand how he would have the courage to attempt to meet the various problems that constantly pour in upon him from all parts of the earth."

Well, after twenty months I can attest to the truth of those words. Faith in God is a vital guidepost, a source of inspiration, and a pillar of strength in times of trial. In recognition of this, the Congress and the Supreme Court begin each day with a prayer, and that's why we provide chaplains for the armed forces. We can and must respect the rights of those who are nonbelievers, but we must not cut ourselves off from this indispensable source of strength and guidance.

I think it'd be a tragedy for us to deny our children what the rest of us, in and out of government, find so valuable. If the president of the United States can pray with others in the Oval Office—and I have on a number of occasions—then let's make certain that our children have the same right as they go about preparing for their futures and for the future of this country.

"The Greatest Message Ever Written"

President Reagan gave these remarks at the Washington Hilton on the morning of February 3, 1983, before proclaiming 1983 the "Year of the Bible."

You know, on the way over, I remembered something that happened a long time ago when teachers could talk about things like religion in the classroom. And a very lovely teacher was talking to her class of young boys, and she asked, "How many of you would like to go to heaven?" And all the hands instantly shot into the air at once, except one, and she was astounded. And she said, "Charlie, you mean you don't want to go to heaven?" He said, "Sure, I want to go to heaven, but not with that bunch." [*Laughter*]

Maybe there's a little bit of Charlie in each of us. [*Laughter*] But somehow I don't think that wanting to go to heaven, but only on our terms, and certainly not with that other bunch, is quite what God had in mind. The prayer that I sometimes think we don't often use enough—and one that I learned a few years ago and only after I had gotten into the business that I'm in—is one of asking forgiveness for the resentment and the bitterness that we sometimes feel towards someone, whether it's in business dealings or in government or whatever we're doing, and forgetting that we are brothers and sisters and that each of them is loved equally by God as much as we feel that He loves us.

I'm so thankful that there will always be one day in the year when people all over our land can sit down as neighbors and friends and remind ourselves of what our real task is. This task was spelled out in the Old and the New Testament. Jesus was asked, "Master, which is the great commandment in the law?" And He replied, "Thou shalt love the Lord thy God with all thy heart, and with all thy soul, and with all thy mind. This is the first and great commandment. The second is like unto it, thou shalt love thy neighbour as thyself. On these two commandments hang all the law and the prophets."

Can we resolve to reach [teach], learn, and try to heed the greatest message ever written—God's word and the Holy Bible? Inside its pages lie all the answers to all the problems that man has ever known.

Now, I am assuming a new position; but I should warn our friends in the loyal opposition, this new job won't require me to leave the White House. With the greatest enthusiasm, I have agreed to serve as honorary chairman for the Year of the Bible.

When we think how many people in the world are imprisoned or tortured, harassed for even possessing a Bible or trying to read one— something that maybe we should realize now—and take advantage of what we can do so easily. In its lessons and the great wealth of its words, we find comfort, strength, wisdom, and hope. And when we find ourselves feeling a little like Charlie, we might remember something that Abraham Lincoln said over a hundred years ago: "We have forgotten the gracious hand that preserved us in peace, and multiplied and enriched and strengthened us; and we have vainly imagined, in the deceitfulness of our hearts, that all these blessings were produced by some superior wisdom and virtue of our own. . . . We have become too proud to pray to the God that made us!" Well, isn't it time for us to say, "We're not too proud to pray"?

We face great challenges in this country, but we've faced great challenges before and conquered them. What carried us through was a willingness to seek power and protection from One much greater than ourselves, to turn back to Him and to trust in His mercy. Without His help, America will not go forward.

I have a very special old Bible. And alongside a verse in the Second

Book of Chronicles there are some words, handwritten, very faded by now. And, believe me, the person who wrote those words was an authority. Her name was Nelle Wilson Reagan. She was my mother. And she wrote about that verse, "A most wonderful verse for the healing of the nations."

Now, the verse that she'd marked reads, "If my people, which are called by my name, shall humble themselves, and pray, and seek my face, and turn from their wicked ways; then will I hear from heaven . . . and will heal their land."

I know that at times all of us—I do—feel that perhaps in our prayers we ask for too much. And then there are those other times when we feel that something isn't important enough to bother God with it. Maybe we should let Him decide those things.

The war correspondent Marguerite Higgins, who received the Pulitzer Prize for international reporting because of her coverage of the Korean War, among all her writings had an account one day of the Fifth Company of Marines who were part of an eight-thousand-man force that was in combat with a hundred thousand of the enemy. And she described an incident that took place early, just after dawn on a very cold morning. It was forty-two degrees below zero. And the weary Marines, half frozen, stood by their dirty, mud-covered trucks, eating their breakfast from tin cans.

She saw one huge Marine was eating cold beans with a trench knife. His clothes were frozen stiff as a board; his face was covered with a heavy beard and crusted with mud. And one of the little group of war correspondents who were on hand went up to him and said, "If I were God and could grant you anything you wished, what would you most like?" And the Marine stood there for a moment, looking down at that cold tin of beans, and then he raised his head and said, "Give me tomorrow."

"Government Is Not Supposed to Wage War Against God and Religion"

On the evening of October 13, 1983, before taking questions from a group of women leaders of Christian religious organizations gathered in the Old Executive Office Building (part of the White House complex), President Reagan offered these remarks.

Many groups come to visit here, but I believe yours is the first leadership group of Christian women to be welcomed to the White House in a long, long time, and I'm glad to be the one that's doing the greeting. I won't speculate why this hasn't been done before. I only know that as long as I'm president, your group and others who stand up for our Judeo-Christian values will be welcome here, because you belong here.

I can't say strongly enough what a tremendous force for good you are. As life-bearers, carrying on traditions of family in the home, but also in our schools, the corporate world, in the workplace, you're teachers of cooperation, tolerance, compassion, and responsibility. No greater truth shines through than the one you live by every day: that preserving America must begin with faith in the God who has blessed our land. And we don't have the answers; He does.

Isaiah reminded us that "the Lord opens His gates and keeps in peace the nation that trusts in Him." I hope you won't mind my saying I think I know you all very well. Nelle Reagan, my mother, God rest her soul, had an unshakable faith in God's goodness. And while I may not have realized it in my youth, I know now that she planted that faith very deeply in me. She made the most difficult Christian message seem very easy. And, like you, she knew you could never repay one bad deed with another. Her way was forgiveness and goodness, and both began with love.

For some time now I believe that America has been hungering for a return to spiritual values that some of us fear we've tended to forget—things like faith, families, family values, the bedrock of our nation. Thanks to the creation of new networks of faith by so many of you and your families, we're seeing more clearly again. We're remembering that freedom carries responsibilities. And we're not set free so that we can become slaves to sin. . . .

And I hope that we will also recognize the true meaning of the first amendment. Its words were meant to guarantee freedom of religion to everyone. But I believe the first amendment has been twisted to the point that freedom of religion is in danger of becoming freedom from religion. But keep the faith. This year the Supreme Court took two big steps toward common sense. [*Laughter*] It said that the first amendment does not prevent legislators in the Nebraska State Assembly from hiring a chaplain to open their sessions with prayer. And it said the Constitution does not prevent the state of Minnesota from giving a tax break to parents who choose private or religious schooling for their children. In both cases the court decided in favor of what our Justice Department recommended in friend-of-the-court briefs.

Now we're making another recommendation. We believe the city of Pawtucket, Rhode Island, and for that matter, any city in America, has the right to include the Nativity scene as part of its annual Christmas performance.

Government is not supposed to wage war against God and religion, not in the United States of America. I want to see the Congress act on our constitutional amendment permitting voluntary prayer in America's schoolrooms. And here you can be our greatest help. Tell the millions of our friends to send a message of thunder from the grassroots, fill the halls of Congress with calls, with letters and telegrams—not postcards. I understand they don't take postcards as seriously as they take letters. [*Laughter*] And tell them, "The people have waited too long; we want action." . . .

Finally, let me just say a few words about another part of freedom that is under siege: the sanctity of human life. Either the law protects human beings, or it doesn't. When we're dealing with a handicapped child—say, a mentally retarded baby girl who needs medical care to survive—is she not entitled to the protection of the law? Will she be denied her chance for love and life because someone decides she's too weak to warrant our help, or because someone has taken it upon themselves to decide the quality of her life doesn't justify keeping her alive? Is that not God's decision to make? And isn't it our duty to serve even the least of these, for in so doing, we serve Him?

Our administration has tried to make sure the handicapped receive the respect of the law for the dignity of their lives. And the same holds true, I believe deeply, for the unborn. It may not help me in some polls to say this publicly, but until and unless it can be proven that the unborn child is not a living human being—and I don't think it can be proven— then we must protect the right of the unborn to life, liberty, and the pursuit of happiness.

Now, I've been talking longer than I intended, because I had a little something else to suggest here. But hardly a day goes by that I'm not told—sometimes in letters and sometimes by people that I meet and perfect strangers—and they tell me that they're praying for me. Well, thanks to Nelle Reagan, I believe in intercessionary prayer. And I know that those prayers are giving me a strength that I otherwise would not possess.

I believe in the goodness of our people. And yet, I wonder if we shouldn't be reminded of the promise in Second Chronicles: "If my people which are called by my name shall humble themselves and pray, and seek my face, and turn from their wicked ways, then I will hear from heaven and will forgive their sin and heal their land."

"The Same Goals of Peace, Freedom, and Humanity"

Six weeks after the March 30, 1981, assassination attempt on President Reagan's life in Washington, Pope John Paul II in Vatican City was also shot by a would-be assassin. The two leaders—both today remembered for helping to defeat Soviet Communism—met for the first time on June 7, 1982, the first time any U.S. president met alone with a pope.

Your Holiness, Your Eminences, Your Excellencies, members of the clergy, and ladies and gentlemen:

On behalf of myself and for all Americans, I want to express profound appreciation to you, Your Holiness, and to all of those from the Holy City who made it possible for us to meet in Vatican City.

This is truly a city of peace, love, and charity, where the highest to the humblest among us seek to follow in the footsteps of the fishermen. As you know, Your Holiness, this is my first visit to Europe as president. And I would like to think of it as a pilgrimage for peace, a journey aimed at strengthening the forces for peace in the free West by offering new opportunities for realistic negotiations with those who may not share the values of freedom and the spirit we cherish.

This is no easy task, but I leave this audience with a renewed sense of hope and dedication. Hope—because one cannot meet a man like

Your Holiness without feeling that a world that can produce such courage and vision out of adversity and oppression is capable, with God's help, of building a better future. Dedication—because one cannot enter this citadel of faith, the fountainhead of so many of the values we in the free West hold dear, without coming away resolved to do all in one's power to live up to them.

Certain common experiences we've shared in our different walks of life, Your Holiness, and the warm correspondence we've carried on, also, gave our meeting a special meaning for me. I hope that others will follow. Let me add that all Americans remember with great warmth your historic visit to our shores in 1979. We all hope that you'll be back again with your timeless message. Ours is a nation grounded on faith, faith in man's ability through God-given freedom to live in tolerance and peace and faith that a Supreme Being guides our daily striving in this world. Our national motto, "In God We Trust," reflects that faith.

Many of our earliest settlers came to America seeking a refuge where they could worship God unhindered, so our dedication to individual freedom is wedded to religious freedom as well. Liberty has never meant license to Americans. We treasure it precisely because it protects the human and spiritual values that we hold most dear: the right to worship as we choose, the right to elect democratic leaders, the right to choose the type of education we want for our children, and freedom from fear, want, and oppression. These are God-given freedoms, not the contrivances of man.

We also believe in helping one another through our churches and charitable institutions or simply as one friend, one good Samaritan, to another. The Ten Commandments and the Golden Rule are as much a part of our living heritage as the Constitution we take such pride in. And we have tried—not always successfully, but always in good conscience—to extend those same principles to our role in the world.

We know that God has blessed America with the freedom and

abundance many of our less fortunate brothers and sisters around the world have been denied. Since the end of World War II, we have done our best to provide assistance to them, assistance amounting to billions of dollars' worth of food, medicine, and materials. And we'll continue to do so in the years ahead. Americans have always believed that in the words of the Scripture, "Unto whomsoever much is given, of him shall be much required."

To us, in a troubled world, the Holy See and your pastorate represent one of the world's greatest moral and spiritual forces. We admire your active efforts to foster peace and promote justice, freedom, and compassion in a world that is still stalked by the forces of evil. As a people and as a government, we seek to pursue the same goals of peace, freedom, and humanity along political and economic lines that the Church pursues in its spiritual role. So, we deeply value your counsel and support and express our solidarity with you.

Your Holiness, one of the areas of our mutual concern is Latin America. We want to work closely with the Church in that area to help promote peace, social justice, and reform, and to prevent the spread of repression and godless tyranny. We also share your concern in seeking peace and justice in troubled areas of the Middle East, such as Lebanon.

Another special area of mutual concern is the martyred nation of Poland—your own homeland. Through centuries of adversity, Poland has been a brave bastion of faith and freedom in the hearts of her courageous people, if not in those who rule her.

We seek a process of reconciliation and reform that will lead to a new dawn of hope for the people of Poland, and we'll continue to call for an end to martial law, for the freeing of all political prisoners, and to resume dialogue among the Polish government, the Church, and the Solidarity movement which speaks for the vast majority of Poles. While denying financial assistance to the oppressive Polish regime, America will continue to provide the Polish people with as much food and commodity support as possible through church and private organizations.

Today, Your Holiness, marks the beginning of the United Nations Special Session on Disarmament. We pledge to do everything possible in these discussions, as in our individual initiatives for peace and arms reduction, to help bring a real, lasting peace throughout the world. To us, this is nothing less than a sacred trust.

Dante has written that "the infinite goodness has such wide arms that it takes whatever turns to it." We ask your prayers, Holy Father, that God will guide us in our efforts for peace on this journey and in the years ahead and that the wide arms of faith and forgiveness can someday embrace a world at peace, with justice and compassion for all mankind.

"The Nucleus of Civilization"

President Reagan used the occasion of his weekly radio address on December 26, 1986, to talk about the importance of the family unit.

The holiday season is a time of gift giving and merrymaking; a time when millions help churches, synagogues, and organizations like the Salvation Army and Toys for Tots provide for the less fortunate among us; a time when huge turkey dinners are cooked, parents find themselves staying up late wrapping toys, and children's eyes are filled with more and more excitement every day—a time, indeed, when all the world seems taken up with plans and celebrations and family.

That last word, "family," is one that I'd like to consider for a moment. To be sure, family is very much on our minds during the holidays, as children and grandchildren, parents and grandparents, gather to share the happiness of the season. We know how good it feels to be with our families—how it warms and comforts us, how it gives us strength and joy.

But I wonder whether we always give our families all the appreciation they deserve. Consider, for example, that the philosopher-historians Will and Ariel Durant called the family "the nucleus of civilization." They understood that all those aspects of civilized life that we most deeply cherish—freedom, the rule of law, economic prosperity and opportunity—that all these depend upon the strength and integrity of the family. If you think about it, you'll see that it's in the family that we must all learn the fundamental lesson of life—right and wrong, respect for others, self-discipline, the importance of knowledge, and, yes, a sense of our own self-worth. All of our lives, it's the love of our families that sustains us when times are hard. And it is perhaps above all to provide for our children that we work and save.

Some have suggested that in today's world, the family has somehow become less important. Well, I can't help thinking just the opposite: that when so much around us is whispering the little lie that we should live only for the moment and for ourselves, it's more important than ever for our families to affirm an older and more lasting set of values. Yet, for all that, in recent decades the American family has come under virtual attack. It has lost authority to government rule writers. It has seen its central role in the education of young people narrowed and distorted. And it's been forced to turn over to big government far too many of its own resources in the form of taxation.

Even so, the family today remains the fundamental unit of American life. But statistics show that it has lost ground, and I don't believe there's much doubt that the American family could be, and should be, much, much stronger. Just last month, I received a report on this from my Working Group on the Family, providing recommendations for giving the family new strength. Our administration will be giving these recommendations serious consideration in the days ahead. But for now we might all do well to keep our families in mind, to make certain that we don't take them for granted. For perhaps at no other time of the year are we able to enjoy our families so thoroughly or see so clearly their importance to ourselves and our country.

And let us remember that in the midst of all the happy bustle of the season there is a certain quietness, a certain calm: the calm of one still night long ago and of a family—father, mother, and newborn child. Listen for a moment to the words of the Scriptures:

"And there were in the same country shepherds abiding in the field, keeping watch over their flock by night. And, lo, the angel of the Lord came upon them, and the glory of the Lord shone round about them. And they were sore afraid. And the angel said unto them, 'Fear not, for behold, I bring you good tidings of great joy, which shall be to all people. For unto you is born this day in the city of David a Savior, which is Christ the Lord. And this shall be a sign unto you. Ye shall find the babe wrapped in swaddling clothes, lying in a manger.' And suddenly there was with the angel a multitude of the heavenly host praising God and saying, 'Glory to God in the highest, and on earth peace, good will toward men.'"

Now, some revere Christ as just a great prophet. Others worship Him as the Son of God. But to all, this season in which we mark His birth is indeed a time of glad tidings. So, in the midst of our celebrations, let us remember that one holy family in a manger on that still night in Bethlehem so long ago and give renewed thanks for the blessings of our own families. And, yes, let us pray for "peace on earth, good will toward men."

Until next week, thanks for listening, God bless, and from the Reagan family to your family, Merry Christmas!

10

TRIBUTES AND TRAGEDIES

Presidents have often participated in our national moments of grieving and remembrance. President Reagan understood the power and possibility of oratory and images on such occasions, but he also knew their limitations: Few such speeches, he remarked during a Memorial Day address, "have become part of our national heritage—not because of the inadequacy of the speakers, but because of the inadequacy of words." But by virtue of his temperament, political philosophy, and rhetorical style, President Reagan was able to deliver several speeches of mourning and commemoration that can help us to better understand our past and ourselves.

"For Truth to Prevail We Must Have the Courage to Proclaim It"

President Reagan was greeted by Elie Wiesel as he arrived to deliver this address to the American Gathering of Jewish Holocaust Survivors on the evening of April 11, 1983, in Landover, Maryland, a suburb of Washington, DC.

Tonight we stand together to give thanks to America for providing freedom and liberty and, for many here tonight, a second home and a second life.

The opportunity to join with you this evening as a representative of the people of the United States will be for me a cherished memory. I am proud to accept your thanks on behalf of our fellow Americans and also to express our gratitude to you for choosing America, for being the good citizens that you are, and for reminding us of how important it is to remain true to our ideals as individuals and as a nation.

We are here, first and foremost, to remember. These are the days of remembrance, Yom HaShoah. Ours is the only nation other than Israel that marks this time with an official national observance. For the last two years I've had the privilege of participating personally in the Days of Remembrance commemoration, as President Carter did before me. May we take a moment to pause and contemplate, perhaps in silent prayer, the magnitude of this occasion, the millions of lives, the courage and dignity, the malevolence and hatred, and what it all means to our lives and the decisions that we make more than a generation later.

Would you please join me and stand in a tribute to those who are not with us for a moment of silence. [*At this point, the audience stood for a moment of silent prayer.*] Amen.

In the early days of our country, our first president, George Washington, visited a Hebrew congregation in Newport, Rhode Island. In response to their address, he wrote them a now rather famous letter reflecting on the meaning of America's newly won freedom. He wrote, "All possess alike liberty of conscience and immunities of citizenship. For happily the Government of the United States, which gives to bigotry no sanction, to persecution no assistance, requires only that they who live under its protection should demean themselves as good citizens."

Well, certainly our country doesn't have a spotless record, but our fundamental beliefs, the ones that inspired Washington when he penned that letter, are sound. Our whole way of life is based on a compact between good and decent people, a voluntary agreement to live here together in freedom, respecting the rights of others and expecting that our rights in return will be respected.

But the freedom we enjoy carries with it a tremendous responsibility. You, the survivors of the Holocaust, remind us of that. Good and decent people must not close their eyes to evil, must not ignore the suffering of the innocent, and must never remain silent and inactive in times of moral crisis.

A generation ago, the American people felt like many others in the Western World—that they could simply ignore the expanding power of a totalitarian ideology. Looking back now, we must admit that the warning signs were there, that the world refused to see. The words and ideology of the Nazis were rationalized, explained away as if they had no meaning. Violations of religious freedom, the attacks on Jewish property, the censorship, the heavy taxes imposed on those who wished to emigrate, even the first concentration camps—all this ignored, as was the incredible expansion of Germany's war machine.

A few brave voices tried to warn of the danger. Winston Churchill was driven into the political wilderness for speaking the unpleasant truth. There were also those who in their sincere desire for peace were all too ready to give totalitarians every benefit of the doubt and all too quick to label Churchill a warmonger. Well, time has proven that those who gloss over the brutality of tyrants are no friends of peace or freedom.

Tonight, let us pledge that we will never shut our eyes, never refuse to acknowledge the truth, no matter how unpleasant. If nothing else, the painful memory we share should strengthen our resolve to do this. Our Founding Fathers believed in certain self-evident truths, but for truth to prevail we must have the courage to proclaim it.

Last week we reaffirmed our belief in the most meaningful truths of our Judeo-Christian heritage—Passover and Easter. These two religious observances link our faiths and celebrate the liberation of the body and soul. The rites of Passover remind us of the freeing of our common ancestors from the yoke of Pharaoh's bondage and their exodus to freedom. And today, you bear witness to a modern-day exodus from the darkness of unspeakable horror to the light and refuge of safe havens—the two most important being America and what soon became the State of Israel.

As a man whose heart is with you and as president of a people you are now so much a part of, I promise you that the security of your safe haven here and in Israel will never be compromised. Our most sacred task now is ensuring that the memory of this greatest of human tragedies, the Holocaust, never fades; that its lessons are not forgotten.

Although so much has been written and said, words somehow are never enough. If a young person, the son or daughter of a neighbor or friend, should die or suffer a terrible illness, we feel the sorrow and share the pain. But how can we share the agony of a million young people suffering unspeakable deaths? It's almost too great a burden for the human soul. Indeed, its very enormity may make it seem unreal. Simon Wiesenthal has said, "When a hundred people die, it's a catastrophe. When a million people die, it's just a statistic."

We must see to it that the immeasurable pain of the Holocaust is not dehumanized, that it is not examined clinically and dispassionately, that its significance is not lost on this generation or any future generation. Though it is now a dry scar, we cannot let the bleeding wound be forgotten. Only when it is personalized will it be real enough to play a role in the decisions we make. Those victims who cannot be with us today do a vital service to mankind by being remembered. But we must be their vessel of remembrance. This reunion is part of our duty to them. . . .

Imparting the message of the Holocaust, using it to reinforce the moral fiber of our society, is much more than a Jewish responsibility. It rests upon all of us who, not immobilized by cynicism and negativism, believe that mankind is capable of greater goodness. For just as the genocide of the Holocaust debased civilization, the outcome of the struggle against those who ran the camps and committed the atrocities gives us hope that the brighter side of the human spirit will, in the end, triumph.

During the dark days when terror reigned on the continent of Europe, there were quiet heroes, men and women whose moral fiber held firm. Some of those are called "righteous gentiles." At this solemn time, we remember them also.

Alexander Roslan and his wife, for example, now live in Clearwater, Florida. But during the war, they lived in Poland, and they hid three Jewish children in their home for more than four years. They knew the terrible risk they were taking. Once, when German soldiers searched their home, the Roslans kept serving wine and whiskey until the troops were so drunk they forgot what they were looking for. Later, Roslan's own son was in the hospital with scarlet fever. The boy hid half of the medicine under his pillow so he could give it to the Jewish children his family were hiding, because they, too, had scarlet fever.

There are many such stories. The picturesque town of Assisi, Italy, sheltered and protected three hundred Jews. Father Rufino Niccacci organized the effort, hiding people in his monastery and in the homes of parishioners. A slip of the tongue by a single informant could have condemned the entire village to the camps, yet they did not yield.

And, of course, there was Raoul Wallenberg, one of the moral giants of our time, whose courage saved thousands. He could have remained in his native Sweden, safe from the conflagration that engulfed the continent. He chose to follow his conscience. Yes, we remember him, too.

I would affirm, as president of the United States and, if you would permit me, in the names of the survivors, that if those who took him from Budapest would win our trust, let them start by giving us an accounting of Raoul Wallenberg. Wallenberg and others who displayed such bravery did not consider themselves heroes. I understand that some of them, when asked about why they risked so much, often for complete strangers, replied, "It was the right thing to do." And that was that. It was just their way.

That kind of moral character, unfortunately, was the exception and not the rule. But for that very reason, it's a consciousness we must foster.

Earlier, I described our country as a compact between good and decent people. I believe this, because it is the love of freedom, not nationalistic rituals and symbols, that unites us. And because of this, we are also bound in spirit to all those who yearn to be free and to live without fear. We are the keepers of the flame of liberty.

I understand that in Hebrew, the word for "engraved" is charut. It is very similar to the word for "freedom," cheyrut. Tonight, we recognize that for freedom to survive and prosper it must be engraved in our character, so that when confronted with fundamental choices we will do what is right—because that is our way.

Looking around this room tonight I realize that although we come from many lands, we share a wealth of common experiences. Many of us remember the time before the Second World War. How we and our friends reacted to certain events has not faded from our memory. There are also in this room many young people, sons and daughters, maybe even a few grandchildren. Perhaps some of the younger ones can't understand why we're making so much of a fuss. Perhaps some of them think we're too absorbed by the heartaches of the past and should move on.

Well, what we do tonight is not for us; it's for them. We who are old enough to remember must make certain those who take our place understand. So, if a youngster should ask you why you're here, just tell that young person, "Because I love God, because I love my country, because I love you—*Zachor*" [remember].

I can't close without remembering something else. Some years ago, I was sent on a mission to Denmark. And while there, I heard stories of the war. And I heard how the order had gone out for the Danish people, under the Nazi occupation, to identify the Jews among them. And the next day, every Dane appeared on the street wearing a Star of David.

Thank you all, and God bless you.

"These Are the Boys of Pointe du Hoc"

This speech, the first of two that President Reagan delivered on June 6, 1984—the fortieth anniversary of the D-Day invasion of Normandy—is among his finest. These remarks were delivered at the site of the U.S. Ranger Monument at Pointe du Hoc, the high cliff between the two major beach landing zones for U.S. troops on D-Day (code-named Utah and Omaha). Veterans of the invasion sat assembled near him as he spoke.

We're here to mark that day in history when the Allied armies joined in battle to reclaim this continent to liberty. For four long years, much of Europe had been under a terrible shadow. Free nations had fallen, Jews cried out in the camps, millions cried out for liberation. Europe was enslaved, and the world prayed for its rescue. Here in Normandy the rescue began. Here the Allies stood and fought against tyranny in a giant undertaking unparalleled in human history.

We stand on a lonely, windswept point on the northern shore of France. The air is soft, but forty years ago at this moment, the air was dense with smoke and the cries of men, and the air was filled with the crack of rifle fire and the roar of cannon. At dawn, on the morning of the sixth of June, 1944, 225 Rangers jumped off the British landing craft and ran to the bottom of these cliffs. Their mission was one of the most difficult and daring of the invasion: to climb these sheer and desolate cliffs and take out the enemy guns. The Allies had been told that some of the mightiest of these guns were here and they would be trained on the beaches to stop the Allied advance.

The Rangers looked up and saw the enemy soldiers—the edge of the cliffs shooting down at them with machine guns and throwing grenades. And the American Rangers began to climb. They shot rope ladders over the face of these cliffs and began to pull themselves up. When one Ranger fell, another would take his place. When one rope was cut, a Ranger would grab another and begin his climb again. They climbed, shot back, and held their footing. Soon, one by one, the Rangers pulled themselves over the top, and in seizing the firm land at the top of these cliffs, they began to seize back the continent of Europe. Two hundred and twenty-five came here. After two days of fighting, only ninety could still bear arms.

Behind me is a memorial that symbolizes the Ranger daggers that were thrust into the top of these cliffs. And before me are the men who put them there.

These are the boys of Pointe du Hoc. These are the men who took the cliffs. These are the champions who helped free a continent. These are the heroes who helped end a war.

Gentlemen, I look at you and I think of the words of Stephen Spender's poem. You are men who in your "lives fought for life . . . and left the vivid air signed with your honor."

I think I know what you may be thinking right now—thinking "we were just part of a bigger effort; everyone was brave that day." Well, everyone was. Do you remember the story of Bill Millin of the Fifty-First Highlanders? Forty years ago today, British troops were pinned down near a bridge, waiting desperately for help. Suddenly, they heard the sound of bagpipes, and some thought they were dreaming. Well, they weren't. They looked up and saw Bill Millin with his bagpipes, leading the reinforcements and ignoring the smack of the bullets into the ground around him.

Lord Lovat was with him—Lord Lovat of Scotland, who calmly announced when he got to the bridge, "Sorry I'm a few minutes late," as if he'd been delayed by a traffic jam, when in truth he'd just come from the bloody fighting on Sword Beach, which he and his men had just taken.

There was the impossible valor of the Poles who threw themselves between the enemy and the rest of Europe as the invasion took hold, and the unsurpassed courage of the Canadians who had already seen the horrors of war on this coast. They knew what awaited them there, but they would not be deterred. And once they hit Juno Beach, they never looked back.

All of these men were part of a roll call of honor with names that spoke of a pride as bright as the colors they bore: the Royal Winnipeg Rifles, Poland's Twenty-Fourth Lancers, the Royal Scots Fusiliers, the Screaming Eagles, the Yeomen of England's armored divisions, the forces of Free France, the Coast Guard's "Matchbox Fleet," and you, the American Rangers.

Forty summers have passed since the battle that you fought here. You were young the day you took these cliffs; some of you were hardly more than boys, with the deepest joys of life before you. Yet, you risked everything here. Why? Why did you do it? What impelled you to put aside the instinct for self-preservation and risk your lives to take these cliffs? What inspired all the men of the armies that met here? We look at you, and somehow we know the answer. It was faith and belief; it was loyalty and love.

The men of Normandy had faith that what they were doing was right, faith that they fought for all humanity, faith that a just God would grant them mercy on this beachhead or on the next. It was the deep knowledge—and pray God we have not lost it—that there is a profound, moral difference between the use of force for liberation and the use of force for conquest. You were here to liberate, not to conquer, and so you and those others did not doubt your cause. And you were right not to doubt.

You all knew that some things are worth dying for. One's country is worth dying for, and democracy is worth dying for, because it's the most deeply honorable form of government ever devised by man. All of you loved liberty. All of you were willing to fight tyranny, and you knew the people of your countries were behind you.

The Americans who fought here that morning knew word of the invasion was spreading through the darkness back home. They fought— or felt in their hearts, though they couldn't know in fact, that in Georgia they were filling the churches at four a.m., in Kansas they were kneeling on their porches and praying, and in Philadelphia they were ringing the Liberty Bell.

Something else helped the men of D-Day: their rock-hard belief that Providence would have a great hand in the events that would unfold here; that God was an ally in this great cause. And so, the night before the invasion, when Colonel Wolverton asked his parachute troops to kneel with him in prayer, he told them: Do not bow your heads, but look up so you can see God and ask His blessing in what we're about to do. Also that night, General Matthew Ridgway on his cot, listening in the darkness for the promise God made to Joshua: "I will not fail thee nor forsake thee."

These are the things that impelled them; these are the things that shaped the unity of the Allies.

When the war was over, there were lives to be rebuilt and governments to be returned to the people. There were nations to be reborn. Above all, there was a new peace to be assured. These were huge and daunting tasks. But the Allies summoned strength from the faith, belief, loyalty, and love of those who fell here. They rebuilt a new Europe together.

There was first a great reconciliation among those who had been enemies, all of whom had suffered so greatly. The United States did its part, creating the Marshall Plan to help rebuild our allies and our former enemies. The Marshall Plan led to the Atlantic Alliance—a great alliance that serves to this day as our shield for freedom, for prosperity, and for peace.

In spite of our great efforts and successes, not all that followed the end of the war was happy or planned. Some liberated countries were lost. The great sadness of this loss echoes down to our own time in the streets of Warsaw, Prague, and East Berlin. Soviet troops that came to the center of this continent did not leave when peace came. They're still there, uninvited, unwanted, unyielding, almost forty years after the war. Because of this, allied forces still stand on this continent. Today, as forty years ago, our armies are here for only one purpose—to protect and defend democracy. The only territories we hold are memorials like this one and graveyards where our heroes rest.

We in America have learned bitter lessons from two world wars: It is better to be here ready to protect the peace, than to take blind shelter across the sea, rushing to respond only after freedom is lost. We've learned that isolationism never was and never will be an acceptable response to tyrannical governments with an expansionist intent.

But we try always to be prepared for peace; prepared to deter aggression; prepared to negotiate the reduction of arms; and, yes, prepared to reach out again in the spirit of reconciliation. In truth, there is no reconciliation we would welcome more than a reconciliation with the Soviet Union, so, together, we can lessen the risks of war, now and forever.

It's fitting to remember here the great losses also suffered by the Russian people during World War II: Twenty million perished, a terrible price that testifies to all the world the necessity of ending war. I tell you from my heart that we in the United States do not want war. We want to wipe from the face of the earth the terrible weapons that man now has in his hands. And I tell you, we are ready to seize that beachhead. We look for some sign from the Soviet Union that they are willing to move forward, that they share our desire and love for peace, and that they will give up the ways of conquest. There must be a changing there that will allow us to turn our hope into action.

We will pray forever that someday that changing will come. But for now, particularly today, it is good and fitting to renew our commitment to each other, to our freedom, and to the alliance that protects it.

We are bound today by what bound us forty years ago, the same loyalties, traditions, and beliefs. We're bound by reality. The strength of America's allies is vital to the United States, and the American security guarantee is essential to the continued freedom of Europe's democracies. We were with you then; we are with you now. Your hopes are our hopes, and your destiny is our destiny.

Here, in this place where the West held together, let us make a vow to our dead. Let us show them by our actions that we understand what they died for. Let our actions say to them the words for which Matthew Ridgway listened: "I will not fail thee nor forsake thee."

Strengthened by their courage, heartened by their value [valor], and borne by their memory, let us continue to stand for the ideals for which they lived and died.

Thank you very much, and God bless you all.

"Stainless Patriotism"

Although President Reagan did not speak at the 1982 dedication of the Vietnam Veterans Memorial in Washington, DC, he did visit the black granite wall on his own in May 1983. ("It's quite a place—a very impressive & moving experience," he wrote in his diary.) On Veterans Day in 1984, he spoke at the dedication ceremony for a new statue of three soldiers being added to the memorial.

Ladies and gentlemen, honored guests, my remarks today will be brief because so much has been said over the years and said so well about the loyalty and the valor of those who served us in Vietnam. It's occurred to me that only one very important thing has been left unsaid, and I will try to speak of it today.

It's almost ten years now since U.S. military involvement in Vietnam came to a close. Two years ago, our government dedicated the memorial bearing the names of those who died or are still missing. Every day, the families and friends of those brave men and women come to the wall and search out a name and touch it.

The memorial reflects as a mirror reflects, so that when you find the name you're searching for you find it in your own reflection. And as you touch it, from certain angles, you're touching, too, the reflection of the Washington Monument or the chair in which great Abe Lincoln sits.

Those who fought in Vietnam are part of us, part of our history. They reflected the best in us. No number of wreaths, no amount of music and memorializing, will ever do them justice, but it is good for us that we honor them and their sacrifice. And it's good that we do it in the reflected glow of the enduring symbols of our republic.

The fighting men depicted in the statue we dedicate today, the three young American servicemen, are individual only in terms of their battle dress; all are as one, with eyes fixed upon the memorial bearing the names of their brothers-in-arms. On their youthful faces, faces too young to have experienced war, we see expressions of loneliness and profound love and a fierce determination never to forget.

The men of Vietnam answered the call of their country. Some of them died in the arms of many of you here today, asking you to look after a newly born child or care for a loved one. They died uncomplaining. The tears staining their mud-caked faces were not for self-pity but for the sorrow they knew the news of their death would cause their families and friends.

As you knelt alongside his litter and held him one last time, you heard his silent message—he asked you not to forget.

Today we pay homage not only to those who gave their lives but to their comrades present today and all across the country. You didn't forget. You kept the faith. You walked from the litter, wiped away your tears, and returned to the battle. You fought on, sustained by one another and deaf to the voices of those who didn't comprehend. You performed with a steadfastness and valor that veterans of other wars salute, and you are forever in the ranks of that special number of Americans in every generation that the nation records as true patriots.

Also among the service men and women honored here today is a unique group of Americans whose fate is still unknown to our nation and to their families. Nearly 2,500 of the names on this memorial are still missing in Southeast Asia, and some may still be serving. Their names are distinguished by a cross rather than the diamond; thus, this memorial is a symbol of both past and current sacrifice.

The war in Vietnam threatened to tear our society apart, and the political and philosophical disagreements that animated each side continue to some extent.

It's been said that these memorials reflect a hunger for healing. Well, I do not know if perfect healing ever occurs, but I know that sometimes when a bone is broken, if it's knit together well, it will in the end be stronger than if it had not been broken. I believe that in the decade since Vietnam the healing has begun, and I hope that before my days as commander in chief are over the process will be completed.

There were great moral and philosophical disagreements about the rightness of the war, and we cannot forget them because there is no wisdom to be gained in forgetting. But we can forgive each other and ourselves for those things that we now recognize may have been wrong, and I think it's time we did.

There's been much rethinking by those who did not serve and those who did. There's been much rethinking by those who held strong views on the war and by those who did not know which view was right. There's been rethinking on all sides, and this is good. And it's time we moved on in unity and with resolve—with the resolve to always stand for freedom, as those who fought did, and to always try to protect and preserve the peace.

And we must in unity work to account for those still missing and aid those returned who still suffer from the pain and memory of Vietnam. We must, as a society, take guidance from the fighting men memorialized by this statue. The three servicemen are watchful, ready, and challenged, but they are also standing forever together.

And let me say to the Vietnam veterans gathered here today: When you returned home, you brought solace to the loved ones of those who fell, but little solace was given to you. Some of your countrymen were unable to distinguish between our native distaste for war and the stainless patriotism of those who suffered its scars. But there's been a rethinking there, too. And now we can say to you, and say as a nation: Thank you for your courage. Thank you for being patient with your countrymen. Thank you. Thank you for continuing to stand with us together.

The men and women of Vietnam fought for freedom in a place where liberty was in danger. They put their lives in danger to help a people in a land far away from their own. Many sacrificed their lives in the name of duty, honor, and country. All were patriots who lit the world with their fidelity and courage.

They were both our children and our heroes. We will never, ever forget them. We will never forget their devotion and their sacrifice. They stand before us, marching into time and into shared memory, forever. May God bless their souls.

And now I shall sign the document by which this memorial has been gratefully received by our government.

And now it belongs to all of us, just as those men who have come back belong to all of us. Thank you.

"Horror Cannot Outlast Hope"

During his trip to Europe coinciding with the fortieth anniversary of V-E Day, President Reagan and West German chancellor Helmut Kohl on May 5, 1985, visited the site of the Bergen-Belsen concentration camp. Tens of thousands of inmates died in the camp before it was liberated in 1945. The president delivered this speech after he laid a wreath at a memorial in the camp.

Chancellor Kohl and honored guests:

This painful walk into the past has done much more than remind us of the war that consumed the European continent. What we have seen makes unforgettably clear that no one of the rest of us can fully understand the enormity of the feelings carried by the victims of these camps. The survivors carry a memory beyond anything that we can comprehend. The awful evil started by one man, an evil that victimized all the world with its destruction, was uniquely destructive of the millions forced into the grim abyss of these camps.

Here lie people—Jews—whose death was inflicted for no reason other than their very existence. Their pain was borne only because of who they were and because of the God in their prayers. Alongside them lay many Christians—Catholics and Protestants.

For year after year, until that man and his evil were destroyed, hell yawned forth its awful contents. People were brought here for no other purpose but to suffer and die—to go unfed when hungry, uncared for when sick, tortured when the whim struck, and left to have misery consume them when all there was around them was misery.

I'm sure we all share similar first thoughts, and that is: What of the youngsters who died at this dark stalag [prison camp]? All was gone for them forever—not to feel again the warmth of life's sunshine and promise, not the laughter and the splendid ache of growing up, nor the consoling embrace of a family. Try to think of being young and never having a day without searing emotional and physical pain—desolate, unrelieved pain.

Today, we've been grimly reminded why the commandant of this camp was named "the Beast of Belsen." Above all, we're struck by the horror of it all—the monstrous, incomprehensible horror. And that's what we've seen but is what we can never understand as the victims did.

Nor with all our compassion can we feel what the survivors feel to this day and what they will feel as long as they live. What we've felt and are expressing with words cannot convey the suffering that they endured. That is why history will forever brand what happened as the Holocaust.

Here, death ruled, but we've learned something as well. Because of what happened, we found that death cannot rule forever, and that's why we're here today. We're here because humanity refuses to accept that freedom of the spirit of man can ever be extinguished. We're here to commemorate that life triumphed over the tragedy and the death of the Holocaust—overcame the suffering, the sickness, the testing, and, yes, the gassings. We're here today to confirm that the horror cannot outlast hope, and that even from the worst of all things, the best may come forth. Therefore, even out of this overwhelming sadness, there must be some purpose, and there is. It comes to us through the transforming love of God.

We learn from the Talmud that "it was only through suffering that the children of Israel obtained three priceless and coveted gifts: The Torah, the Land of Israel, and the World to Come." Yes, out of this sickness—as crushing and cruel as it was—there was hope for the world as well as for the world to come. Out of the ashes—hope; and from all the pain—promise.

So much of this is symbolized today by the fact that most of the leadership of free Germany is represented here today. Chancellor Kohl, you and your countrymen have made real the renewal that had to happen. Your nation and the German people have been strong and resolute in your willingness to confront and condemn the acts of a hated regime of the past. This reflects the courage of your people and their devotion to freedom and justice since the war. Think how far we've come from that time when despair made these tragic victims wonder if anything could survive.

As we flew here from Hanover, low over the greening farms and the emerging springtime of the lovely German countryside, I reflected, and there must have been a time when the prisoners at Bergen-Belsen and those of every other camp must have felt the springtime was gone forever from their lives. Surely we can understand that when we see what is around us—all these children of God under bleak and lifeless mounds, the plainness of which does not even hint at the unspeakable acts that created them. Here they lie, never to hope, never to pray, never to love, never to heal, never to laugh, never to cry.

And too many of them knew that this was their fate, but that was not the end. Through it all was their faith and a spirit that moved their faith.

Nothing illustrates this better than the story of a young girl who died here at Bergen-Belsen. For more than two years Anne Frank and her family had hidden from the Nazis in a confined annex in Holland, where she kept a remarkably profound diary. Betrayed by an informant, Anne and her family were sent by freight car first to Auschwitz and finally here to Bergen-Belsen.

Just three weeks before her capture, young Anne wrote these words: "It's really a wonder that I haven't dropped all my ideals because they seem so absurd and impossible to carry out. Yet I keep them because in spite of everything I still believe that people are good at heart. I simply can't build up my hopes on a foundation consisting of confusion, misery, and death. I see the world gradually being turned into a wilderness. I hear the ever approaching thunder which will destroy us too; I can feel the suffering of millions and yet, if I looked up into the heavens I think that it will all come right, that this cruelty too will end and that peace and tranquility will return again." Eight months later, this sparkling young life ended here at Bergen-Belsen. Somewhere here lies Anne Frank.

Everywhere here are memories—pulling us, touching us, making us understand that they can never be erased. Such memories take us where God intended His children to go—toward learning, toward healing, and, above all, toward redemption. They beckon us through the endless stretches of our heart to the knowing commitment that the life of each individual can change the world and make it better.

We're all witnesses; we share the glistening hope that rests in every human soul. Hope leads us, if we're prepared to trust it, toward what our President Lincoln called the better angels of our nature. And then, rising above all this cruelty, out of this tragic and nightmarish time, beyond the anguish, the pain, and the suffering for all time, we can and must pledge: Never again.

"Mourn the Human Wreckage of Totalitarianism"

One of the biggest diplomatic and cultural controversies of the Reagan presidency involved a planned visit to a military cemetery in Bitburg, West Germany, on May 5, 1985. The announced visit was controversial for several reasons, but especially because buried among the dead in the cemetery were members of Hitler's elite Waffen-SS. An uproar in the press and a campaign intended to pressure Reagan into skipping the cemetery only caused him to dig in. ("Well I'm not going to cancel anything no matter how much the bastards scream," he wrote in his diary. "I think it is morally right to go and I'm going.") After giving the "Horror Cannot Outlast Hope" speech at the Bergen-Belsen concentration camp, the president flew with Kohl to Bitburg, visited the cemetery, and then gave the following remarks at the Bitburg Air Base before an audience of German and American military personnel.

Thank you very much. I have just come from the cemetery where German war dead lay at rest. No one could visit there without deep and conflicting emotions. I felt great sadness that history could be filled with such waste, destruction, and evil, but my heart was also lifted by the knowledge that from the ashes has come hope and that from the terrors of the past we have built forty years of peace, freedom, and reconciliation among our nations.

This visit has stirred many emotions in the American and German people, too. I've received many letters since first deciding to come to Bitburg cemetery; some supportive, others deeply concerned and questioning, and others opposed. Some old wounds have been reopened, and this I regret very much because this should be a time of healing.

To the veterans and families of American servicemen who still carry the scars and feel the painful losses of that war, our gesture of reconciliation with the German people today in no way minimizes our love and honor for those who fought and died for our country. They gave their lives to rescue freedom in its darkest hour. The alliance of democratic nations that guards the freedom of millions in Europe and America today stands as living testimony that their noble sacrifice was not in vain.

No, their sacrifice was not in vain. I have to tell you that nothing will ever fill me with greater hope than the sight of two former war heroes who met today at the Bitburg ceremony; each among the bravest of the brave; each an enemy of the other forty years ago; each a witness to the horrors of war. But today they came together, American and German, General Matthew B. Ridgway and General Johannes Steinhoff, reconciled and united for freedom. They reached over the graves to one another like brothers and grasped their hands in peace.

To the survivors of the Holocaust: Your terrible suffering has made you ever vigilant against evil. Many of you are worried that reconciliation means forgetting. Well, I promise you, we will never forget. I have just come this morning from Bergen-Belsen, where the horror of that terrible crime, the Holocaust, was forever burned upon my memory.

No, we will never forget, and we say with the victims of that Holocaust: Never again.

The war against one man's totalitarian dictatorship was not like other wars. The evil war of Nazism turned all values upside down. Nevertheless, we can mourn the German war dead today as human beings crushed by a vicious ideology.

There are over two thousand buried in Bitburg cemetery. Among them are forty-eight members of the SS—the crimes of the SS must rank among the most heinous in human history—but others buried there were simply soldiers in the German Army. How many were fanatical followers of a dictator and willfully carried out his cruel orders? And how many were conscripts, forced into service during the death throes of the Nazi war machine? We do not know. Many, however, we know from the dates on their tombstones, were only teenagers at the time. There is one boy buried there who died a week before his sixteenth birthday.

There were thousands of such soldiers to whom Nazism meant no more than a brutal end to a short life. We do not believe in collective guilt. Only God can look into the human heart, and all these men have now met their supreme judge, and they have been judged by Him as we shall all be judged.

Our duty today is to mourn the human wreckage of totalitarianism, and today in Bitburg cemetery we commemorated the potential good in humanity that was consumed back then, forty years ago. Perhaps if that fifteen-year-old soldier had lived, he would have joined his fellow countrymen in building this new democratic Federal Republic of Germany, devoted to human dignity and the defense of freedom that we celebrate today. Or perhaps his children or his grandchildren might be among you here today at the Bitburg Air Base, where new generations of Germans and Americans join together in friendship and common cause, dedicating their lives to preserving peace and guarding the security of the free world.

Too often in the past each war only planted the seeds of the next. We celebrate today the reconciliation between our two nations that has liberated us from that cycle of destruction. Look at what together we've accomplished. We who were enemies are now friends; we who were bitter adversaries are now the strongest of allies.

In the place of fear we've sown trust, and out of the ruins of war has blossomed an enduring peace. Tens of thousands of Americans have served in this town over the years. As the mayor of Bitburg has said, in that time there have been some six thousand marriages between Germans and Americans, and many thousands of children have come from these unions. This is the real symbol of our future together, a future to be filled with hope, friendship, and freedom.

The hope that we see now could sometimes even be glimpsed in the darkest days of the war. I'm thinking of one special story—that of a mother and her young son living alone in a modest cottage in the middle of the woods. And one night as the Battle of the Bulge exploded not far away, and around them, three young American soldiers arrived at their door—they were standing there in the snow, lost behind enemy lines. All were frostbitten; one was badly wounded. Even though sheltering the enemy was punishable by death, she took them in and made them a supper with some of her last food. Then, they heard another knock at the door. And this time four German soldiers stood there. The woman was afraid, but she quickly said with a firm voice, "There will be no shooting here." She made all the soldiers lay down their weapons, and they all joined in the makeshift meal. Heinz and Willi, it turned out, were only sixteen; the corporal was the oldest at twenty-three. Their natural suspicion dissolved in the warmth and the comfort of the cottage. One of the Germans, a former medical student, tended the wounded American.

But now, listen to the rest of the story through the eyes of one who was there, now a grown man, but that young lad that had been her son.

He said, "The Mother said grace. I noticed that there were tears in her eyes as she said the old, familiar words, 'Komm, Herr Jesus. Be our guest.' And as I looked around the table, I saw tears, too, in the eyes of the battle-weary soldiers, boys again, some from America, some from Germany, all far from home."

That night—as the storm of war tossed the world—they had their own private armistice. And the next morning, the German corporal showed the Americans how to get back behind their own lines. And they all shook hands and went their separate ways. That happened to be Christmas Day, forty years ago.

Those boys reconciled briefly in the midst of war. Surely we allies in peacetime should honor the reconciliation of the last forty years.

To the people of Bitburg, our hosts and the hosts of our servicemen, like that generous woman forty years ago, you make us feel very welcome. Vielen dank. [Many thanks.]

And to the men and women of Bitburg Air Base, I just want to say that we know that even with such wonderful hosts, your job is not an easy one. You serve around the clock far from home, always ready to defend freedom. We're grateful, and we're very proud of you.

Four decades ago we waged a great war to lift the darkness of evil from the world, to let men and women in this country and in every country live in the sunshine of liberty. Our victory was great, and the Federal Republic, Italy, and Japan are now in the community of free nations. But the struggle for freedom is not complete, for today much of the world is still cast in totalitarian darkness.

Twenty-two years ago President John F. Kennedy went to the Berlin Wall and proclaimed that he, too, was a Berliner. Well, today freedom-loving people around the world must say: I am a Berliner. I am a Jew in a world still threatened by anti-Semitism. I am an Afghan, and I am a prisoner of the gulag. I am a refugee in a crowded boat foundering off the coast of Vietnam. I am a Laotian, a Cambodian, a Cuban, and a

Miskito Indian in Nicaragua. I, too, am a potential victim of totalitarianism.

The one lesson of World War II, the one lesson of Nazism, is that freedom must always be stronger than totalitarianism and that good must always be stronger than evil. The moral measure of our two nations will be found in the resolve we show to preserve liberty, to protect life, and to honor and cherish all God's children.

That is why the free, democratic Federal Republic of Germany is such a profound and hopeful testament to the human spirit. We cannot undo the crimes and wars of yesterday nor call . . . the millions back to life, but we can give meaning to the past by learning its lessons and making a better future. We can let our pain drive us to greater efforts to heal humanity's suffering.

Today I've traveled 220 miles from Bergen-Belsen, and, I feel, forty years in time. With the lessons of the past firmly in our minds, we've turned a new, brighter page in history.

One of the many who wrote me about this visit was a young woman who had recently been bas mitzvahed. She urged me to lay the wreath at Bitburg cemetery in honor of the future of Germany. And that is what we've done.

On this fortieth anniversary of World War II, we mark the day when the hate, the evil, and the obscenities ended, and we commemorate the rekindling of the democratic spirit in Germany.

There's much to make us hopeful on this historic anniversary. One of the symbols of . . . hope, a little while ago, when we heard a German band playing the American national anthem and an American band playing the German national anthem. While much of the world still huddles in the darkness of oppression, we can see a new dawn of freedom sweeping the globe. And we can see in the new democracies of Latin America, in the new economic freedoms and prosperity in Asia, in the slow movement toward peace in the Middle East, and in the strengthening alliance of democratic nations in Europe and America that the light from that dawn is growing stronger.

Together, let us gather in that light and walk out of the shadow. Let us live in peace.

Thank you, and God bless you all.

"The Future Doesn't Belong to the Fainthearted"

At 11:38 a.m. on January 28, 1986, the space shuttle Challenger *blew up seventy-three seconds after takeoff. The short speech about the tragedy that President Reagan delivered at five p.m. from the Oval Office is among the best and most powerful of his presidency, and—especially remarkable considering how quickly the speech was prepared—it ranks among the most memorable examples of presidential rhetoric in history.*

Ladies and gentlemen, I'd planned to speak to you tonight to report on the state of the Union, but the events of earlier today have led me to change those plans. Today is a day for mourning and remembering. Nancy and I are pained to the core by the tragedy of the shuttle *Challenger*. We know we share this pain with all of the people of our country. This is truly a national loss.

Nineteen years ago, almost to the day, we lost three astronauts in a terrible accident on the ground. But we've never lost an astronaut in flight; we've never had a tragedy like this. And perhaps we've forgotten the courage it took for the crew of the shuttle. But they, the Challenger Seven, were aware of the dangers, but overcame them and did their jobs brilliantly. We mourn seven heroes: Michael Smith, Dick Scobee, Judith Resnik, Ronald McNair, Ellison Onizuka, Gregory Jarvis, and Christa McAuliffe. We mourn their loss as a nation together.

For the families of the seven, we cannot bear, as you do, the full impact of this tragedy. But we feel the loss, and we're thinking about you so very much. Your loved ones were daring and brave, and they had that special grace, that special spirit that says, "Give me a challenge, and I'll meet it with joy." They had a hunger to explore the universe and discover its truths. They wished to serve, and they did. They served all of us. We've grown used to wonders in this century. It's hard to dazzle us. But for twenty-five years the United States space program has been doing just that. We've grown used to the idea of space, and perhaps we forget that we've only just begun. We're still pioneers. They, the members of the *Challenger* crew, were pioneers.

And I want to say something to the schoolchildren of America who were watching the live coverage of the shuttle's takeoff. I know it is hard to understand, but sometimes painful things like this happen. It's all part of the process of exploration and discovery. It's all part of taking a chance and expanding man's horizons. The future doesn't belong to the fainthearted; it belongs to the brave. The *Challenger* crew was pulling us into the future, and we'll continue to follow them.

I've always had great faith in and respect for our space program, and what happened today does nothing to diminish it. We don't hide our space program. We don't keep secrets and cover things up. We do it all up front and in public. That's the way freedom is, and we wouldn't change it for a minute. We'll continue our quest in space. There will be more shuttle flights and more shuttle crews and, yes, more volunteers, more civilians, more teachers in space. Nothing ends here; our hopes and our journeys continue. I want to add that I wish I could talk to every man and woman who works for NASA or who worked on this mission and tell them, "Your dedication and professionalism have moved and impressed us for decades. And we know of your anguish. We share it."

There's a coincidence today. On this day 390 years ago, the great explorer Sir Francis Drake died aboard ship off the coast of Panama. In his lifetime the great frontiers were the oceans, and a historian later said, "He lived by the sea, died on it, and was buried in it." Well, today we can say of the *Challenger* crew: Their dedication was, like Drake's, complete.

The crew of the space shuttle *Challenger* honored us by the manner in which they lived their lives. We will never forget them, nor the last time we saw them, this morning, as they prepared for their journey and waved goodbye and "slipped the surly bonds of earth" to "touch the face of God."

11

ENDINGS

"Nostalgia has its time and place," Reagan said early in his presidency. "But nostalgia isn't enough. The challenge is now. It's time we stopped looking backward at how we got here." Even as his presidency came to a close and he indulged in some nostalgia, he continued to look forward—to the end of Communism, to tomorrows of freedom, prosperity, and peace. "Like most Americans," he said, "I live for the future."

"The Story of an Entire People"

On December 14, 1985, the president spoke at a dinner for the Ronald Reagan Presidential Foundation, the organization that would later help build the Reagan Library and Reagan Museum, and that today operates the museum and various projects to perpetuate his memory and legacy.

But I look out here tonight and I see so many old friends. I'm gravely tempted to reminisce. I could tell a few stories that I think would interest future historians, but there isn't time for that this evening, except to say the moments that we've spent together are locked away forever in our memory and our hearts. Nancy and I want you to know that we looked forward to this dinner for a special reason: We thought this a particularly good time to extend our thanks, first, because of the season—and we wanted to share the joy of it with you—and second, through this foundation you are helping to guide future generations of Americans to a deeper appreciation of our nation's past.

Now, in that film you just saw, I mentioned how living in the White House can overwhelm you with a sense of the past—so many events, so many presidents. I know all of you share this sentiment and this attachment to history, so I think we are here for a good cause and a noble work. But I can assure you in one century or ten, scholars and students looking through these records will find an anecdote of heart or humor or a detail of warmth and wit that will not so much tell the story of one man's presidency as the story of an entire people, a good and generous people, proud of their heritage of freedom, determined that America shall be, as it was said on that tiny ship, the *Arabella*, off the

Massachusetts coast some three centuries ago, "a light unto the nations, a shining city on a hill."

"There's No Sweeter Day Than Each New One"

All told, Ronald Reagan spoke at seven Republican National Conventions (1968, 1972, 1976, 1980, 1984, 1988, and 1992). This excerpt is taken from his remarks to the 1988 convention at the New Orleans Superdome, on the evening of August 15, 1988.

When people tell me that I became president on January 20, 1981, I feel I have to correct them. You don't become president of the United States. You are given temporary custody of an institution called the presidency, which belongs to our people. Having temporary custody of this office has been for me a sacred trust and an honor beyond words or measure. That trust began with many of you in this room many conventions ago. Many's the time that I've said a prayer of thanks to all Americans who placed this trust in my hands. And tonight, please accept again our heartfelt gratitude, Nancy's and mine, for this special time that you've given in our lives.

Just a moment ago, you multiplied the honor with a moving tribute, and being only human, there's a part of me that would like to take credit for what we've achieved. But tonight, before we do anything else, let us remember that tribute really belongs to the 245 million citizens who make up the greatest—and the first—three words in our Constitution: "We the People." It is the American people who endured the great challenge of lifting us from the depths of national calamity, renewing our mighty economic strength, and leading the way to restoring our respect in the world. They are an extraordinary breed we call Americans. So, if there's any salute deserved tonight, it's to the heroes everywhere in this land who make up the doers, the dreamers, and the life-builders without which our glorious experiment in democracy would have failed.

This convention brings back so many memories to a fellow like me. I can still remember my first Republican convention: Abraham Lincoln giving a speech that—[*laughter*]—sent tingles down my spine. No, I have to confess, I wasn't actually there. The truth is, way back then, I belonged to the other party. [*Laughter*] But surely we can remember another convention. Eight years ago, we gathered in Detroit in a troubled time for our beloved country. And we gathered solemnly to share our dreams. When I look back, I wonder if we dared be so bold to take on those burdens. But in that same city of Detroit, when the twentieth century was only in its second year, another great Republican, Teddy Roosevelt, told Americans not to hold back from dangers ahead but to rejoice: "Our hearts lifted with the faith that to us and to our children it shall be given to make this Republic the mightiest among the peoples of mankind." Teddy said those, years ago. In 1980 we needed every bit of that kind of faith. . . .

This is the last Republican convention I will address as president. Maybe you'll see your way to inviting me back sometime. But like so many of us, as I said earlier, I started out in the other party. But forty years ago, I cast my last vote as a Democrat. It was a party in which Franklin Delano Roosevelt promised the return of power to the states. It was a party where Harry Truman committed a strong and resolute America to preserving freedom. FDR had run on a platform of eliminating useless boards and commissions and returning autonomy and authority to local governments and to the states. That party changed, and it will never be the same. They left me; I didn't leave them. So, it was our Republican Party that gave me a political home. When I signed up for duty, I didn't have to check my principles at the door. And I soon found out that the desire for victory did not overcome our devotion to ideals.

And what ideals those have been. Our party speaks for human freedom, for the sweep of liberties that are at the core of our existence. We do not shirk from our duties to preserve freedom, so it can unfold across the world for yearning millions. We believe that lasting peace comes only through strength and not through the goodwill of our adversaries. We have a healthy skepticism of government, checking its excesses at the same time we're willing to harness its energy when it helps improve the lives of our citizens. We have pretty strong notions that higher tax receipts are no inherent right of the federal government. We don't think that inflation and high interest rates show compassion for the poor, the young, and the elderly. We respect the values that bind us together as families and as a nation. For our children, we don't think it's wrong to have them committed to pledging each day to the "one nation, under God, indivisible, with liberty and justice for all." And we have so many requirements in their classrooms; why can't we at least have one thing that is voluntary, and that is allow our kids to repair quietly to their faith to say a prayer to start the day, as Congress does? For the unborn, quite simply, shouldn't they be able to live to become children in those classrooms?

Those are some of our principles. You in this room, and millions like you watching and listening tonight, are selfless and dedicated to a better world based on these principles. You aren't quitters. You walk not just precincts but for a cause. You stand for something—the finest warriors for free government that I have known. Nancy and I thank you for letting us be a part of your tireless determination to leave a better world for our children. And that's why we're here, isn't it? A better world?

I know I've said this before, but I believe that God put this land between the two great oceans to be found by special people from every corner of the world who had that extra love for freedom that prompted them to leave their homeland and come to this land to make it a brilliant light beam of freedom to the world. It's our gift to have visions, and I want to share that of a young boy who wrote to me shortly after I took office. In his letter he said, "I love America because you can join Cub Scouts if you want to. You have a right to worship as you please. If you have the ability, you can try to be anything you want to be. And I also like America because we have about two hundred flavors of ice cream." Well, truth through the eyes of a child: freedom of association, freedom of worship, freedom of hope and opportunity, and the pursuit of happiness—in this case, choosing among two hundred flavors of ice cream—that's America, everyone with his or her vision of the American promise. That's why we're a magnet for the world: for those who dodged bullets and gave their lives coming over the Berlin Wall and others, only a few of whom avoided death, coming in tiny boats on turbulent oceans. This land, its people, the dreams that unfold here, and the freedom to bring it all together—well, those are what make America soar, up where you can see hope billowing in those freedom winds.

When our children turn the pages of our lives, I hope they'll see that we had a vision to pass forward a nation as nearly perfect as we could, where there's decency, tolerance, generosity, honesty, courage, common sense, fairness, and piety. This is my vision, and I'm grateful to God for blessing me with a good life and a long one. But when I pack up my bags in Washington, don't expect me to be happy to hear all this talk about the twilight of my life.

Twilight? Twilight? Not in America. Here, it's a sunrise every day—fresh new opportunities, dreams to build. Twilight? That's not possible, because I confess there are times when I feel like I'm still little Dutch Reagan racing my brother down the hill to the swimming hole under the railroad bridge over the Rock River. You see, there's no sweeter day than each new one, because here in our country it means something wonderful can happen to you. And something wonderful happened to me.

We lit a prairie fire a few years back. Those flames were fed by passionate ideas and convictions, and we were determined to make them run all—burn, I should say, all across America. And what times we've had! Together we've fought for causes we love. But we can never let the fire go out or quit the fight, because the battle is never over. Our freedom must be defended over and over again—and then again.

There's still a lot of brush to clear out at the ranch, fences that need repair, and horses to ride. But I want you to know that if the fires ever dim, I'll leave my phone number and address behind just in case you need a foot soldier. Just let me know, and I'll be there, as long as words don't leave me and as long as this sweet country strives to be special during its shining moment on earth.

Twilight, you say? Listen to H. G. Wells. H. G. Wells says, "The past is but the beginning of a beginning, and all that is and has been is but the twilight of the dawn." Well, that's a new day—our sunlit new day—to keep alive the fire so that when we look back at the time of choosing, we can say that we did all that could be done—never less.

Thank you. Good night. God bless you, and God bless America.

"The Heart of a Great Nation"

President Reagan delivered this farewell address from the Oval Office on the evening of January 11, 1989.

My fellow Americans:

This is the thirty-fourth time I'll speak to you from the Oval Office and the last. We've been together eight years now, and soon it'll be time for me to go. But before I do, I wanted to share some thoughts, some of which I've been saving for a long time.

It's been the honor of my life to be your president. So many of you have written the past few weeks to say thanks, but I could say as much to you. Nancy and I are grateful for the opportunity you gave us to serve.

One of the things about the presidency is that you're always somewhat apart. You spend a lot of time going by too fast in a car someone else is driving, and seeing the people through tinted glass—the parents holding up a child, and the wave you saw too late and couldn't return. And so many times I wanted to stop and reach out from behind the glass, and connect. Well, maybe I can do a little of that tonight.

People ask how I feel about leaving. And the fact is, "parting is such sweet sorrow." The sweet part is California and the ranch and freedom. The sorrow—the goodbyes, of course, and leaving this beautiful place.

You know, down the hall and up the stairs from this office is the part of the White House where the president and his family live. There are a few favorite windows I have up there that I like to stand and look out of early in the morning. The view is over the grounds here to the Washington Monument, and then the Mall and the Jefferson Memorial. But on mornings when the humidity is low, you can see past the Jefferson to the river, the Potomac, and the Virginia shore. Someone said that's the view Lincoln had when he saw the smoke rising from the Battle of Bull Run. I see more prosaic things: the grass on the banks, the morning traffic as people make their way to work, now and then a sailboat on the river.

I've been thinking a bit at that window. I've been reflecting on what the past eight years have meant and mean. And the image that comes to mind like a refrain is a nautical one—a small story about a big ship, and a refugee, and a sailor. It was back in the early eighties, at the height of the boat people. And the sailor was hard at work on the carrier *Midway*, which was patrolling the South China Sea. The sailor, like most American servicemen, was young, smart, and fiercely observant. The crew spied on the horizon a leaky little boat. And crammed inside were refugees from Indochina hoping to get to America. The *Midway* sent a small launch to bring them to the ship and safety. As the refugees made their way through the choppy seas, one spied the sailor on deck, and stood up, and called out to him. He yelled, "Hello, American sailor. Hello, freedom man."

A small moment with a big meaning, a moment the sailor, who wrote it in a letter, couldn't get out of his mind. And, when I saw it, neither could I. Because that's what it was to be an American in the 1980s. We stood, again, for freedom. I know we always have, but in the past few years the world again—and in a way, we ourselves—rediscovered it.

It's been quite a journey this decade, and we held together through some stormy seas. And at the end, together, we are reaching our destination.

The fact is, from Grenada to the Washington and Moscow summits, from the recession of '81 to '82, to the expansion that began in late '82 and continues to this day, we've made a difference. The way I see it, there were two great triumphs, two things that I'm proudest of. One is the economic recovery, in which the people of America created—and filled—nineteen million new jobs. The other is the recovery of our morale. America is respected again in the world and looked to for leadership.

Something that happened to me a few years ago reflects some of this. It was back in 1981, and I was attending my first big economic summit, which was held that year in Canada. The meeting place rotates among the member countries. The opening meeting was a formal dinner for the heads of government of the seven industrialized nations. Now, I sat there like the new kid in school and listened, and it was all

François this and Helmut that. They dropped titles and spoke to one another on a first-name basis. Well, at one point I sort of leaned in and said, "My name's Ron." Well, in that same year, we began the actions we felt would ignite an economic comeback—cut taxes and regulation, started to cut spending. And soon the recovery began.

Two years later, another economic summit with pretty much the same cast. At the big opening meeting we all got together, and all of a sudden, just for a moment, I saw that everyone was just sitting there looking at me. And then one of them broke the silence. "Tell us about the American miracle," he said.

Well, back in 1980, when I was running for president, it was all so different. Some pundits said our programs would result in catastrophe. Our views on foreign affairs would cause war. Our plans for the economy would cause inflation to soar and bring about economic collapse. I even remember one highly respected economist saying, back in 1982, that "the engines of economic growth have shut down here, and they're likely to stay that way for years to come." Well, he and the other opinion leaders were wrong. The fact is, what they called "radical" was really "right." What they called "dangerous" was just "desperately needed."

And in all of that time I won a nickname, "The Great Communicator." But I never thought it was my style or the words I used that made a difference: It was the content. I wasn't a great communicator, but I communicated great things, and they didn't spring full bloom from my brow; they came from the heart of a great nation—from our experience, our wisdom, and our belief in the principles that have guided us for two centuries. They called it the "Reagan Revolution." Well, I'll accept that, but for me it always seemed more like the "great rediscovery," a rediscovery of our values and our common sense.

Common sense told us that when you put a big tax on something, the people will produce less of it. So, we cut the people's tax rates, and the people produced more than ever before. The economy bloomed like a plant that had been cut back and could now grow quicker and stronger. Our economic program brought about the longest peacetime expansion in our history: real family income up, the poverty rate down, entrepreneurship booming, and an explosion in research and new technology. We're exporting more than ever because American industry became more competitive, and at the same time, we summoned the national will to knock down protectionist walls abroad instead of erecting them at home.

Common sense also told us that to preserve the peace, we'd have to become strong again after years of weakness and confusion. So, we rebuilt our defenses, and this New Year we toasted the new peacefulness around the globe. Not only have the superpowers actually begun to reduce their stockpiles of nuclear weapons—and hope for even more progress is bright—but the regional conflicts that rack the globe are also beginning to cease. The Persian Gulf is no longer a war zone. The Soviets are leaving Afghanistan. The Vietnamese are preparing to pull out of Cambodia, and an American-mediated accord will soon send fifty thousand Cuban troops home from Angola.

The lesson of all this was, of course, that because we're a great nation, our challenges seem complex. It will always be this way. But as long as we remember our first principles and believe in ourselves, the future will always be ours. And something else we learned: Once you begin a great movement, there's no telling where it will end. We meant to change a nation, and instead, we changed a world.

Countries across the globe are turning to free markets and free speech and turning away from the ideologies of the past. For them, the great rediscovery of the 1980s has been that, lo and behold, the moral way of government is the practical way of government: Democracy, the profoundly good, is also the profoundly productive.

When you've got to the point when you can celebrate the anniversaries of your thirty-ninth birthday you can sit back sometimes, review your life, and see it flowing before you. For me there was a fork in the river, and it was right in the middle of my life. I never meant to go into politics. It wasn't my intention when I was young. But I was raised to believe you had to pay your way for the blessings bestowed on you. I was happy with my career in the entertainment world, but I ultimately went into politics because I wanted to protect something precious.

Ours was the first revolution in the history of mankind that truly reversed the course of government, and with three little words: "We the People." "We the People" tell the government what to do; it doesn't tell us. "We the People" are the driver; the government is the car. And we decide where it should go, and by what route, and how fast. Almost all the world's constitutions are documents in which governments tell the people what their privileges are. Our Constitution is a document in which "We the People" tell the government what it is allowed to do. "We the People" are free. This belief has been the underlying basis for everything I've tried to do these past eight years.

But back in the 1960s, when I began, it seemed to me that we'd begun reversing the order of things—that through more and more rules and regulations and confiscatory taxes, the government was taking more of our money, more of our options, and more of our freedom. I went into politics in part to put up my hand and say, "Stop." I was a citizen politician, and it seemed the right thing for a citizen to do.

I think we have stopped a lot of what needed stopping. And I hope we have once again reminded people that man is not free unless government is limited. There's a clear cause and effect here that is as neat and predictable as a law of physics: As government expands, liberty contracts.

Nothing is less free than pure Communism—and yet we have, the past few years, forged a satisfying new closeness with the Soviet Union. I've been asked if this isn't a gamble, and my answer is no because we're basing our actions not on words but deeds. The détente of the 1970s was based not on actions but promises. They'd promise to treat their own people and the people of the world better. But the gulag was still the gulag, and the state was still expansionist, and they still waged proxy wars in Africa, Asia, and Latin America.

Well, this time, so far, it's different. President Gorbachev has brought about some internal democratic reforms and begun the withdrawal from Afghanistan. He has also freed prisoners whose names I've given him every time we've met.

But life has a way of reminding you of big things through small incidents. Once, during the heady days of the Moscow summit, Nancy and I decided to break off from the entourage one afternoon to visit the shops on Arbat Street—that's a little street just off Moscow's main shopping area. Even though our visit was a surprise, every Russian there immediately recognized us and called out our names and reached for our hands. We were just about swept away by the warmth. You could almost feel the possibilities in all that joy. But within seconds, a KGB detail pushed their way toward us and began pushing and shoving the people in the crowd. It was an interesting moment. It reminded me that while the man on the street in the Soviet Union yearns for peace, the government is Communist. And those who run it are Communists, and that means we and they view such issues as freedom and human rights very differently.

We must keep up our guard, but we must also continue to work together to lessen and eliminate tension and mistrust. My view is that President Gorbachev is different from previous Soviet leaders. I think he knows some of the things wrong with his society and is trying to fix them. We wish him well. And we'll continue to work to make sure that the Soviet Union that eventually emerges from this process is a less threatening one. What it all boils down to is this: I want the new closeness to continue. And it will, as long as we make it clear that we will continue to act in a certain way as long as they continue to act in a helpful manner. If and when they don't, at first pull your punches. If they persist, pull the plug. It's still "trust but verify." It's still "play, but cut the cards." It's still "watch closely." And don't be afraid to see what you see.

I've been asked if I have any regrets. Well, I do. The deficit is one. I've been talking a great deal about that lately, but tonight isn't for arguments, and I'm going to hold my tongue. But an observation: I've had my share of victories in the Congress, but what few people noticed is that I never won anything you didn't win for me. They never saw my troops, they never saw Reagan's regiments, the American people. You won every battle with every call you made and letter you wrote demanding action. Well, action is still needed. If we're to finish the job, Reagan's regiments will have to become the Bush brigades. Soon he'll be the chief, and he'll need you every bit as much as I did.

Finally, there is a great tradition of warnings in presidential farewells, and I've got one that's been on my mind for some time. But oddly enough it starts with one of the things I'm proudest of in the past eight years: the resurgence of national pride that I called the "new patriotism." This national feeling is good, but it won't count for much, and it won't last, unless it's grounded in thoughtfulness and knowledge.

An informed patriotism is what we want. And are we doing a good enough job teaching our children what America is and what she represents in the long history of the world? Those of us who are over thirty-five or so years of age grew up in a different America. We were taught, very directly, what it means to be an American. And we absorbed, almost in the air, a love of country and an appreciation of its institutions. If you didn't get these things from your family you got them from the neighborhood, from the father down the street who fought in Korea or the family who lost someone at Anzio. Or you could get a sense of patriotism from school. And if all else failed you could get a sense of patriotism from the popular culture. The movies celebrated democratic values and implicitly reinforced the idea that America was special. TV was like that, too, through the mid-sixties.

But now, we're about to enter the nineties, and some things have changed. Younger parents aren't sure that an unambivalent appreciation of America is the right thing to teach modern children. And as for those who create the popular culture, well-grounded patriotism is no longer the style. Our spirit is back, but we haven't reinstitutionalized it. We've got to do a better job of getting across that America is freedom— freedom of speech, freedom of religion, freedom of enterprise. And freedom is special and rare. It's fragile; it needs production [protection].

So, we've got to teach history based not on what's in fashion but what's important—why the Pilgrims came here, who Jimmy Doolittle was, and what those thirty seconds over Tokyo meant. You know, four years ago on the fortieth anniversary of D-Day, I read a letter from a young woman writing to her late father, who'd fought on Omaha Beach. Her name was Lisa Zanatta Henn, and she said, "We will always remember, we will never forget what the boys of Normandy did." Well, let's help her keep her word. If we forget what we did, we won't know who we are. I'm warning of an eradication of the American memory that could result, ultimately, in an erosion of the American spirit. Let's start with some basics: more attention to American history and a greater emphasis on civic ritual.

And let me offer lesson number one about America: All great change in America begins at the dinner table. So, tomorrow night in the kitchen I hope the talking begins. And children, if your parents haven't been teaching you what it means to be an American, let 'em know and nail 'em on it. That would be a very American thing to do.

And that's about all I have to say tonight, except for one thing. The past few days when I've been at that window upstairs, I've thought a bit of the "shining city upon a hill." The phrase comes from John Winthrop, who wrote it to describe the America he imagined. What he imagined was important because he was an early Pilgrim, an early free-dom man. He journeyed here on what today we'd call a little wooden boat; and like the other Pilgrims, he was looking for a home that would be free.

I've spoken of the shining city all my political life, but I don't know if I ever quite communicated what I saw when I said it. But in my mind it was a tall, proud city built on rocks stronger than oceans, windswept, God-blessed, and teeming with people of all kinds living in harmony and peace; a city with free ports that hummed with commerce and creativity. And if there had to be city walls, the walls had doors and the doors were open to anyone with the will and the heart to get here. That's how I saw it, and see it still.

And how stands the city on this winter night? More prosperous, more secure, and happier than it was eight years ago. But more than that: After two hundred years, two centuries, she still stands strong and true on the granite ridge, and her glow has held steady no matter what storm. And she's still a beacon, still a magnet for all who must have freedom, for all the pilgrims from all the lost places who are hurtling through the darkness, toward home.

We've done our part. And as I walk off into the city streets, a final word to the men and women of the Reagan revolution, the men and women across America who for eight years did the work that brought America back. My friends: We did it. We weren't just marking time. We made a difference. We made the city stronger, we made the city freer, and we left her in good hands. All in all, not bad, not bad at all.

And so, goodbye, God bless you, and God bless the United States of America.

On January 20, 1989, George H. W. Bush was sworn in as president. Ronald Reagan, a private citizen again, flew with Nancy Reagan back home to California.

On November 4, 1991, the Ronald Reagan Presidential Library in Simi Valley, California, was dedicated in a ceremony involving all the living U.S. presidents. In his remarks at the ceremony, Reagan said, "I . . . have been described as an undying optimist, always seeing the glass half-full when some see it as half-empty. And, yes, it's true. I always see the sunny side of life. And that's not just because I've been blessed by achieving so many of my dreams. My optimism comes not just from my strong faith in God, but from my strong and enduring faith in man. . . . I've seen war and peace, feast and famine, depression and prosperity, sickness and health. I've seen the depths of suffering and the peaks of triumph. And I know in my heart that man is good; that what is right will always eventually triumph; and that there is purpose and worth to each and every life."

On November 5, 1994, he published a letter addressed to "My Fellow Americans" explaining that he had recently been diagnosed with Alzheimer's disease. "At the moment I feel just fine. I intend to live the remainder of the years God gives me on this earth doing the things I have always done. . . . In closing let me thank you, the American people, for giving me the great honor of allowing me to serve as your President. When the Lord calls me home, whenever that may be, I will leave with the greatest love for this country of ours and eternal optimism for its future. I now begin the journey that will lead me into the sunset of my life. I know that for America there will always be a bright dawn ahead."

On June 5, 2004, Ronald Wilson Reagan died in Los Angeles, aged ninety-three. He was interred at his presidential library. After her death in 2016 at the age of ninety-four, Nancy Davis Reagan was interred beside him.

EDITOR'S NOTE

The statements of Ronald Reagan collected in these pages represent his public expressions while president. The selected speeches, proclamations, toasts, articles, letters, remembrances, holiday messages, and radio addresses were crafted with the assistance of a corps of writers in the White House and in consultation with staffers and officials from elsewhere in the Reagan administration. For some of the works collected here, especially the major speeches, President Reagan was intimately involved in the process of writing and editing; many of the items also include his last-minute, off-the-cuff changes. Taken together, they exemplify the vision, rhetorical style, and public philosophy of the fortieth president.

All of these works are in the public domain, and most appear in the fifteen Reagan volumes of the Public Papers of the Presidents series published by the National Archives and Records Administration. They can also all be found in the Ronald Reagan Presidential Library and on its website (ReaganLibrary.gov).

Minor clarifications added to the items collected here are always set off in square brackets. Many of these items are excerpted from longer documents; ellipses are used to indicate internal passages that have been cut, but not passages cut from the beginnings and endings of items. Misspellings in the source material have been corrected, and minor formatting adjustments to standardize punctuation and capitalization across the items have been made to enhance readability. The text otherwise remains unaltered.

INDEX